DREAMING AMERICA

Popular Front Ideals and Aesthetics in
Children's Plays of the Federal Theatre Project

LESLIE ELAINE FROST

THE OHIO STATE UNIVERSITY PRESS | COLUMBUS

Copyright © 2013 by The Ohio State University.
All rights reserved.

Library of Congress Cataloging-in-Publication Data
Frost, Leslie Elaine.
  Dreaming America : popular front ideals and aesthetics in children's plays of the Federal Theatre Project / Leslie Elaine Frost.
      p. cm.
  Includes bibliographical references and index.
  ISBN 978-0-8142-1213-4 (cloth : alk. paper) — ISBN 0-8142-1213-1 (cloth : alk. paper) — ISBN 978-0-8142-9314-0 (cd-rom)
  1. Federal Theatre Project (U.S.) 2. American drama—20th century—History and criticism. 3. Children's plays, American—History and criticism. I. Title.
  PS351.F76 2013
  812'.5099282—dc23
                                2012032475
Paper (ISBN: 978-0-8142-5630-5)
Cover design by Janna Thompson-Chordas
Type set in Adobe Minion Pro and Poppl-Laudatio

CONTENTS

List of Illustrations v

Acknowledgments vii

INTRODUCTION   Children's Theatre of a People's Theatre   1

CHAPTER 1   Federal Theatre Project Dreams:
Raising an Educated Audience for a Permanent
American National Theatre   23

CHAPTER 2   "We Should Have Called It *Rumpelstiltskin*":
A Labor Fairy Tale Gets Real in *The Revolt of the Beavers*   43

CHAPTER 3   "I Looked Him Right Square in the Eye":
Being African American in *The Story of Little Black Sambo*   71

CHAPTER 4   "Shadows of Your Thoughts Are Marching":
Anti-Fascism and Home-front Patriotism in Federal Theatre's
A Letter to Santa Claus and Hollywood's *The Little Princess*   108

CHAPTER 5   Wishing on a Star:
Pinocchio's Journey from the Federal Stage to Disney's World   128

CONCLUSION   Death of a Dream   140

Notes   149

Works Cited   177

Index   188

ILLUSTRATIONS

FIGURE 1.	Boy Sweeper, Lincoln Cotton Mills, Evansville, Ind. Carding Machines: Floor Slippery. (See report for conditions.) Location: Evansville, Indiana	29
FIGURE 2.	A typical spinner. Mamie --------- Lancaster Cotton Mills, S.C. Location: Lancaster, South Carolina	33
FIGURE 3.	Gastonia, N.C. Boy from Loray Mill. "Been at it right smart two years." Location: Gastonia, North Carolina	39
FIGURE 4.	*The Revolt of the Beavers (New York City, New York)*: Paul, Mary, and Windy	44
FIGURE 5.	*The Revolt of the Beavers (New York City, New York)*: Paul, Professor Beaver, and Mary lean their heads together	51
FIGURE 6.	*The Revolt of the Beavers (New York City, New York)*: Professor Beaver tells a story	61
FIGURE 7.	*Little Black Sambo (Washington, DC)*	72
FIGURE 8.	*Little Black Sambo (Chicago, Ilinois)*	82
FIGURE 9.	*Little Black Sambo (Newark, New Jersey)*	96
FIGURE 10.	*Pinocchio (New York City, New York)*: Gepetto leads Pinocchio from the mouth of the Whale	130

ACKNOWLEDGMENTS

This book has been one long labor of love, and for the help I've received both personally and professionally I am deeply grateful. For my brief moment in the footlights that made my love of theatre personal, I am grateful for Samantha Cheek Swan's intercession on my behalf. When she was cast as a chorus girl in a local production of Tom Stoppard's *Rough Crossing*, and I said, "I'm writing my thesis on Tom Stoppard! I want to be a chorus girl too!" she got me an audition. My dancing and singing under the lights may not have lit up the local reviews, but it still makes me smile to remember. And it set the trajectory of my scholarship.

I am indebted to many colleagues and friends for their advice and support. This project would never have come to be without Joy Kasson's early encouragement and advice. Bob Cantwell's insights helped shape early versions of *The Revolt of the Beavers* chapter. Derek Goldman helped me to see issues of staging. Kimball King gave me scholarly opportunities to work with theatrical productions. Beverly Taylor provided key signatures and kind words. Barbara Thaden read an early chapter, and the late Freddie Jones not only encouraged me to persevere, but was a mentor who modeled how to be a gracious friend and colleague. Jim Ryan, Kelly Reames, Neil Watson, Katie Drowne, Mary Floyd-Wilson, Maude Hines, Brad Hammer, Jim Pearce, and Paul Hanson have all listened to me think through ideas and have given thoughtful, deeply meaningful support. Edee Dalke provided a writing haven. Thank you all.

I would like to thank the National Endowment for the Humanities for funding study of African American theatre. I'd like to thank Richard Flynn and the editors of the *Children's Literature Association Quarterly,* where an earlier version of Chapter 4 appeared.

I would like to thank the U.S. and Cyprus Fulbright Commissions for the opportunity to teach the Federal Theatre Project in Cyprus.

My year as a Fulbright professor in Cyprus placed me in a dynamic scholarly community where my work benefited from the rich intellectual life centered at the Association for Historical Dialogue and Research. I would like to thank the members of the Brew Crew, especially Marios Epaminondas, Yiannis Papadakis, Kyriakos Pachoulides, and Lisa Davis for their friendship and support. For our conversations about theatre and for introducing me to the writing collective of Rooftop Theatre, I would like to thank Ellada Evangelou. Thanks to Evi Haggipavlu for reading chapters while cooking fabulous meals in a home by the sea.

To two friends, I owe a particular and immeasurable debt of gratitude. Karen Emmerich read the entire manuscript and offered invaluable feedback sprinkled with generous encouragement. And Katie Rose Guest Pryal, who encouraged me over and over to do the structural revisions that brought the project into its current form, pushed neither too little nor too much, but just right. Thank you.

My parents raised three self-confident kids to adulthood. Thanks to my mother, Elaine Frost, whose strength of character and belief in us helped us to be who we are today and without whom this first book would not be. Thanks to my father, a Marine fighter pilot who taught me to have faith in the courage of my convictions. Thanks to my brothers Rob and Bert for being the bright, interesting, funny men who you are and for so often showing me how to do it right; thanks to my sisters-in-law Ladona and Dana for being amazing, wonderful women. And thanks to Alan and M. A., whose adventurous academic life inspired me.

In working with a project for a long time, one can forget the initial enthusiasm with which one begins. My students at the University of Cyprus, with their profoundly moving engagement with the Federal Theatre Project, reminded me of why I began this project. Thanks to Theodora, Rafaela, Despina, Savvas, Jasmin, Andria, Styliana, Eleni, Xanthi, Monika, and Aurelija for their amazing performances. Thanks to Andrew Power for tech support. And thank you to my English 105 fall 2012 students at UNC, whose regular expressions of support and interest in their teacher's work connected teaching and research meaningfully.

In working with various collections over time, I have the highest regard for the staff of George Mason University's Special Collections and Archives. I would particularly like to thank Leah Richardson and Yvonne Carignan.

UNC's Department of English and Comparative Literature generously funded a research trip to the Library of Congress and George Mason University's archival collections. The University Research Council generously funded publication work. Thank you.

I would also like to thank Eric Meckley for his attentive editing assistance and Paula Durbin-Westby for her indexing expertise.

The team of editors at The Ohio State University Press has been superlative. I'm very grateful to Sandy Crooms for her amazing stewardship of this project. Eugene O'Connor's expertise is also greatly appreciated. I thank Kristen Ebert-Wagner for her careful editing and her helpful correspondence.

One person has been present for every step of this long journey from project to book. I have been lucky as a scholar to have grown up under her mentorship. For her generosity and commitment to me and to this project I will be forever in awe and ever grateful. For this reason, this book is very affectionately dedicated to Linda Wagner-Martin.

INTRODUCTION

CHILDREN'S THEATRE OF A PEOPLE'S THEATRE

The 1999 film *Cradle Will Rock* celebrates the triumph of the eponymous 1937 Federal Theatre Project production over government censorship. But director Tim Robbins offers no illusion that the triumph is larger than one night's heroism in an unused theatre. Crosscuts juxtapose shots of Rockefeller's workmen swinging axes to destroy Diego Rivera's mural *Man at the Crossroads* with shots of actors on WPA relief standing up in the audience to defiantly sing Marc Blitzstein's labor opera. Both play and mural were grounded in artistic support of newly emerging labor solidarity and strength. Blitzstein's opera, under the direction of Orson Welles, allegorizes labor relations as it chronicles the efforts of Larry Foreman to unionize the corrupt steel mill of the powerful Mr. Mister. Similarly, Rivera's mural depicts labor facing a crossroads of socialism and capitalism. The contrapuntal rhythm of soaring voices and swinging axe scores a scathing indictment of capitalist power's ruthless suppression of both the American working class and leftist artistic expression.

The allegorical opposition of the people to power underscores the Popular Front political ideals and working-class affiliation of both play and film. To quibble with the film's historical inaccuracies—most obviously, Rivera's mural, with its prominent placement of Lenin's face, was destroyed by Rockefeller Center workmen two years before the advent of the Federal Theatre Project—is to miss the significance of the mural as a metaphor for the scope and vision of America's one experiment in national theatre. The Federal Theatre Project (1935–39) was dreamed as and designed to be a people's theatre for a people's century. One of four Federal One arts projects of the Works Progress (later Works Projects) Administration, it was envisioned as the national theatre that would develop a distinctly American stage growing out of native artistic traditions and attentive to regional pluralistic voices. To this end, its administration structured a federal organization of loosely confederated regional offices. Its staff documented everything: reader responses to scripts, audience and critical responses to productions, detailed production books, internal memos, letters, reports. The infrastructural groundwork was laid for a permanent American national theatre.

Project Director Hallie Flanagan dreamed that an arts project designed to put the unemployed back to work could develop into a federated national theatre responsive to pluralistic American society:

> To set up theatres which have possibilities of growing into social institutions in the communities in which they are located . . . and to lay the foundation for the development of a truly creative theatre in the United States with outstanding producing centers in each of those regions which have common interests as a result of geography, language, origins, history, tradition, custom, occupations of the people.[1]

A people's theatre! Taking Kenneth Burke's inclusive symbol of the American worker as its ideal core and its constituency, the Federal Theatre Project aimed to revolutionize art in America. For the FTP's newsletter *Federal Theatre* Flanagan reported that

> From Maine to Texas, the story is the same. From North Carolina to California, the same public recognition of our work is being bestowed. "The People's Theatre!"—we did not call it that because only the people can make the name appropriate. But where and as the people make it appropriate, we welcome it as describing what the Federal Theatre should be.[2]

This intoxicating vision of a stalwart people sustained by a correspondingly vigorous theatre would remain an ideal for which Flanagan struggled for four years. It was not to be. Although it produced more than 42,000 performances, the total audience of about 40 million for Federal Theatre productions over the course of those four years was slightly more than half the average weekly audience that flocked to see Hollywood films during the 1930s. Its difficulties were legion and its enemies numerous, including members of the Martin Dies, Jr.–led House Committee on Un-American Activities, which was established in 1938. The FTP struggled to put on plays in the midst of government investigations, political censorship and audience outrage, budget cuts, union strikes, and WPA/FTP disputes. It was shut down unceremoniously when Congress failed to renew its funding.

And yet by many measures, not least in its dramatic narrative, the Federal Theatre performed admirably as a people's theatre. At its height, the FTP employed more than 12,700 people, and over the duration of its existence it gave work to more than 30,000—in an enterprise in which all but 10 percent of costs were mandated to be labor costs. Nine of ten workers came from the relief rolls. Federal Theatre shows were cheap for many and free for "the underprivileged." The FTP produced new plays, classical plays, children's plays, African American plays, marionette shows, vaudeville shows, and caravan theatre performances in America's parks.[3] Its units produced religious theatre and foreign-language theatre. Hundreds of thousands of New York children went to the FTP circus. Companies toured the Civilian Conservation Corps camps across the country where men worked on infrastructure building relief projects. Successful urban productions toured other parts of the country, so although concentrated in the largest cities, Federal Theatre came to small towns and isolated regions. It played to churches, prisons, hospitals, and orphanages.[4]

Government theatre gave work to actors, writers, and technicians during desperate times; upon its demise, these individuals then fanned out across universities, theatres, and the movie industry. Famous and infamous names such as Orson Welles, John Houseman, Jules Dassin, Elia Kazan, John Randolph, Karl Malden, and Joseph Cotton crossed from its stages to Hollywood's sets, along with thousands of writers, costume designers, lighting technicians, makeup artists, and others who left Federal Theatre to work across America in film and theatre. Government theatre brought the youthful radicals of urban agitprop troupes together with the old vaudevillians displaced by the new movie palaces together with the summer theatre actor or stagehand together with rising theatre stars. Federal plays collapsed theatrical histories and divisions of race, class, and aesthetics in frugally staged productions often celebrated by critics. Federal Theatre yoked the commercial producer with the university administrator; it rippled the smooth surface of establishment taste in New York, Chicago, and Seattle; it housed radicals, liberals, and conservatives in a mishmash of plays, paperwork, and people. To use C. Wright Mills's term descriptive of the set of institutions through which artistic, intellectual and scientific work is carried and distributed, Federal Theatre was an important part of the *cultural apparatus* of the New Deal, the American Popular Front, and, indeed, the twentieth century. It was one hell of a big mural.

While often broadly traditional in its production choices, the Federal Theatre Project also took chances that commercial theatre did not. Its playlists and production schedule also reflected the broadly Popular Front ethos of its administration and its New York–centered operations. The WPA arts projects in general and the Federal Theatre Project in particular explored the conditions of the disenfranchised and the working class. Its Negro Units made possible plays that explored racism and African American life, although many of its Negro Unit productions were traditional entertainment fare that included minstrel shows. Not only did Flanagan choose an adaptation of Sinclair Lewis's antifascist *It Can't Happen Here* for a dramatic opening simultaneously in 18 cities, but also the FTP collected and distributed the lists of antiwar plays, while antifascist themes influenced major productions.

As its self-proclamation as a "people's theatre" reveals, the FTP was firmly centered in a Popular Front–influenced artistic movement. The American Popular Front movement's pro-labor, antiracism, and antifascism sentiments connected artists and intellectuals with the working class, African Americans, and second-generation immigrants of a broad labor movement, and émigrés fleeing European fascism. It joined together labor and the liberal New Deal. At the Seventh World Congress of the Communist International (Comintern) in 1935, communists were directed to work with antifascist movements, and thus with Popular Front organizations. As Michael Denning has shown, this broad social movement came together in the "cultural apparatus during the age of the CIO" that produced a Popular Front–influenced mass culture, what Denning termed "a laboring of American culture."[5]

With its goal of permanence and its mandate of relief, Federal Theatre turned to children's theatre as a neglected site that could be developed in order to build support for the theatre and for the FTP. Developing a people's theatre, after all, necessitates building its audience. From her work in American theatre and her observations of European and Soviet national theatres, FTP director Hallie Flanagan theorized that a truly national theatre would need to build a broad-based American audience. Socializing and educating children to appreciate the theatre as a site of civic engagement constituted a critical aspect of her overall vision. Traveling in Europe and the Soviet Union, Flanagan had seen European theatre directed toward children, and she early emphasized the need for a vibrant children's theatre within the FTP. Children's Unit director Jack Rennick wrote in 1936, "If America is ever to have a great theatre, she cannot begin too soon to train and establish an audience that will appreciate, demand, and support the best."[6] Separate children's theatre companies were formed and adult units regularly performed children's plays. In addition, FTP marionette companies and amateur groups performed extensively for children.

The stories of its children's units are the tales of the FTP in miniature. Generally well accepted and often wildly popular, the children's plays these theatres performed nonetheless took on controversial cultural issues that not surprisingly mired the plays in controversy. Relying often on traditional fairy- and folktale narratives, writers updated scripts to reflect contemporary concerns. Children's units were targeted by political opponents of the New Deal. Budget cuts and project strife affected every aspect of their runs. But if the children's units broadly form a symbol of the FTP, the children's productions, with their simple narratives and didactic missions, offer federally funded representations of children and of childhood that richly enhance our understanding of the anxieties about nationhood and identity that broadly focused the activities of a Popular Front culture that would have a lasting effect on the twentieth century.

Dreaming America centers on this particular corner of the sprawling mural that was the Federal Theatre Project. Representations of the child and childhood in the FTP children's plays stage the hopes and anxieties of a nation destabilized by both economic collapse and technological advance. For while the relation of the child to the American ideologies of self and nation had always been important in American public discourse, the chaotic Depression years made fears about nationhood, cultural identity, and economic and technological progress particularly acute, while children were viewed as the inheritors of an uncertain future.[7] A declining economy and the first stagnant birthrate in three centuries yoked the national economy to the individual family. Profound disagreements over appropriate models of education and parenting, as well as over issues of ethnicity and class, constituted fundamental arguments over democratic values and social norms. The very newness of fascism and communism, particularly in the face of capitalism's seeming collapse, raised fears about the viability of the American political and economic system and the potential of the American future. As the focus of Depression-era adult anxieties and hopes and as the embodiment of vigor, dynamism, and growth, children carried great symbolic value both as the future of America and as the America of the future. Nursery and nation were inextricably linked.[8]

The Depression and the Popular Front

The seeds of Federal Theatre's political roots and the beginning of its end lie in a rhetorical moment of leftist unification. In August 1935, the Soviet Union adopted a stance of accommodation toward the liberal democracies of the West at the Seventh Congress of the Communist International. The move came in recognition of growing fascist aggression in Europe; it set aside international class revolution as the primary Soviet objective in the face of threats from Germany, Italy, and Japan. Calling for a united opposition to fascism, this "Popular Front" no longer heralded fascism as the last gasp of a dying capitalist order; rather, it attempted to ideologically unite the liberal bourgeoisie to the cause of fighting it. Communist rhetoric ceased to imagine liberal democracies and their institutions as enemies to be destroyed, and treated them instead as allies to safeguard. All communist parties of all nations, including the United States, were ordered to adapt themselves to the international new line.

This change mandated radical leftist support of the New Deal and its policies. The American Communist Party's support of the New Deal is evident in the 1936 presidential election, in which Earl Browder characterized the Democratic and Republican candidates as a choice between democracy and fascism. Talking about, writing about, and dramatizing revolution was replaced by the celebration of democratic traditions; the workers were replaced by the people.

Popular Front activities united on three major planks: antifascism, antiracism, and pro-labor. Émigrés from Europe brought antifascist politics to working-class jobs and to the arts. A broad emphasis on a new ethnic Americanism and civil liberties created new articulations of African American social, artistic, and political identities. As the broad political temper turned toward the left, during periods of both sectarian revolutionary fervor and Popular Front solidarity, labor made enormous gains. Strikes in various industries politicized workers early in the decade, and with the passage of the Wagner Act in 1937, which secured the right to collective bargaining, and the formation of the Congress of Industrial Organizations in 1938, labor gained the strength to negotiate with industry on a much more equal footing than had been previously possible.

By the end of the decade, art, culture, and politics would be polarized, and irrevocably marked, by the House Special Committee on Un-American Activities (Dies Committee) investigations into subversive activities. Purportedly to examine right-wing groups as well as left, the Dies Committee hearings were a systematic effort not only to link Communism with un-Americanism and thus to discredit it, but also to discredit labor, leftist politics in general, and the New Deal in particular.[9]

The Dies Committee hearings would mobilize right-wing hostility to the left around the fear of Communism. They were held from 1938 to 1944; in 1945 the Dies Committee became a standing Congressional committee—the House Committee on Un-American Activities, or HUAC.[10] In *Naming Names*, his study of the HUAC Hollywood hearings of the late 1940s and early 1950s, Victor S. Navasky pinpoints the ideological position of most in the 1930s who would be called to testify a decade or two later. He writes that they

> believed (rightly or wrongly) that those they were asked to name had, like themselves and [Larry] Parks, originally joined the Communist Party out of motives of social conscience at a time when it was in the business of fighting racism and depression at home and fascism abroad, and if there were Soviet espionage agents, which these people doubted, they operated outside the Party apparatus; that although they had supported the Soviet experiment and believed Lincoln Steffens that it represented the future, "and it works," they were patriotic Americans.... [11]

In its assault on the left, the Dies Committee targeted labor leaders, organizations committed to peace and racial equality, and artists and intellectuals. The Dies Committee was publicly committed to discovering communism leading and directing all leftist activity.

The Dies Committee hearings raised questions about the political tenor of the FTP. Accused of Communist influence, FTP administrators were unable to persuade Congress to renew funding and the project was summarily shut down in 1939. The Dies Committee investigation ended the Federal Theatre Project and encouraged a kind of national amnesia about its existence for more than thirty years. But this amnesia would have been impossible without a similar assessment of thirties leftism in general. For more than forty years, American analyses of thirties Popular Front culture presumed that international and American Communism dominated the intellectual and organizational activities of the Popular Front. The failure of Communism, then, was synecdochic of the failure of leftist culture, art, and politics in the thirties.

The difference between two seminal works that study the period, Richard Pells's *Radical Visions and American Dreams* and Michael Denning's *The Cultural Front*, illustrates how readings shaped by changed scholarly, political, and cultural interests in turn shape intellectual understandings of the decade's political currents. Examining different facets of the era's leftism, the two texts perceive different patterns and pronounce different evaluations. One consigns it to failure; one asserts its long-lasting cultural impact.

Pells's 1973 study analyzes the Popular Front through its intellectual cultural production, particularly in written works, documentary photography, and film. Envisioning the left as being driven by its intellectual component, he argues that its politics served as a metaphor for psychological and spiritual renewal:

> This persistent evocation of death and rebirth, the messianic feeling of being present at the dawn of a revolutionary age, served to compensate emotionally for the confusion and terror of the depression. But such apocalyptic sentiments did not lend themselves easily to logical plans or rational thinking. Instead, they led to an analysis of American problems that was primarily moral, psychological, and cultural. . . . [12]

Pells argues that writers and philosophers attempting to conceptualize and represent the conditions of the Great Depression took recourse in creating unifying metaphorical relationships for the problems they wished to depict and change: the relationship of self to society, of the human to the machine, of the nation to its people were ultimately depoliticized by this process. In other words, intellectual commitment to leftist political change remained cut off from the realities of social conditions and ultimately ineffective. Reading texts such as *Axel's Castle* and *The Exile's Return*, he argues that Edmund Wilson and Malcolm Cowley, among other writers, saw economic catastrophe as an opportunity not only for a shift in aesthetic values but for the moral and spiritual rebirth of the American intellectual:[13]

> Yet the notion of a collapse beyond human control, of an end to everything men had known or anticipated, did not lead only to hopelessness. In the midst of tragedy there was for some a kind of euphoria—a mood of utopian optimism that was as unideological as the opposite sense of impending doom. If the old order was dying, the new was being born.[14]

With his emphasis on intellectual idealism, Pells reads Depression leftism through the arc of its idealistic fervor, and sees the early years of the thirties as a time of great promise and excitement, and the later years as a crumbling of united purpose as the reality of the Soviet pact with the Nazis pierced a willfully blind ivory-tower vision.

Michael Denning's *The Cultural Front* shifts the focus from intellectual idealism to what he calls the "laboring of culture"—the influence of labor gains and the rise of the CIO on cultural production. Beginning "with the question that has long dominated the cultural history of the Depression: Why did the left have a powerful, indeed an unprecedented impact on US culture in the 1930s?" Denning analyzes artistic engagements with leftist issues in light of second-generation ethnic populations, material practices, and social realities.[15] He writes that "for most critics and historians, the answer is embodied in the image of the 'fellow traveler,' the individual artist or intellectual attracted to the Communist Party and the Soviet Union in the face of a collapsing economy and rising fascism."[16] But Denning argues that the center/periphery model of Communist / fellow traveler is inadequate:

> The broad social movement known as the Popular Front was the ground on which the workers theaters, proletarian literary magazines, and film industry unions stood: it was, I will argue, a radical social-democratic movement forged around anti-fascism, anti-lynching, and the industrial unionism of the CIO.[17]

It was, he further notes, "the result of the encounter between a powerful democratic social movement—the Popular Front—and the modern cultural apparatuses of mass entertainment and education."[18]

Denning's "laboring of culture" acknowledges the intertwining of mass entertainment and social movements and thus loosens the cultural production of the thirties from the charge of being driven either by an elite band of acknowledged intellectual leaders following a failed idealistic political vision or by Soviet communism. He traces the influence of its artistic and intellectual texts on later works and redefines the thirties as seminal to a movement, rather than anomalous and negated by the post–World War II political climate. He furthermore asserts the importance of changes in the economic and social makeup of America's working populations and the increased visibility of working-class African American and ethnic Americans. Pells's moment of disenchantment and fall corresponds to Denning's moment of success—the latter half of the decade and the birth of the CIO.

Denning's model is useful to my study of Federal Theatre Project plays for three reasons. First, it locates these productions in a culture of affiliations and loyalties that are embedded in and yet simultaneously escape the binary of political left and right. This positioning liberates a reading of the plays from the narrow left-wing/right-wing political binary that views the project as simply politically out of step with the political orientation of the congressmen who would, in the end, kill its funding. Second, it describes the late thirties, when these productions were performed, as a time of vigorous artistic engagement with leftist issues, and not, as would accounts such as Pells's, as a hangover from the ideologically fervent early Depression years. Thus the plays' commentary is more relevant to their times. And third, it provides for a theatre audience of ordinary Americans who were interested in the issues driving leftist politics even if they were not committed to a particular political party.

This model explains that the American Communist Party's shift from sectarianism toward coalition building brings communists into a mass social and cultural movement united by the causes of antifascism, antiracism, and pro-unionism or labor—and not driving that movement. It further comments on the cultural movement's broad interest in discovering an American essence underlying domestic and international political, social, and economic changes that historians Warren Susman and Alan Trachtenberg have both pointed out. This underlying concern with national identity mobilized cultural production, Trachtenberg writes:

> There was consensus among a broad range of Americans, regardless of political association, right, left, or center, that the "American Way of Life" (the phrase itself first came into popular use in these years) was endangered by economic failures at home and Fascism abroad. The Depression indicated that the nation had strayed from its true path. . . . At the turn of the century, Progressive reformers had argued for new institutions, a rethinking of the concept of democracy. . . . In the 1930s, however, the cry was not so much for change as for "recovery," a return to basic values, to fundamental Americanism. What is special about the American people? What are their characteristic beliefs, their folk history, their heroes, their work patterns, and their leisure? More than ideological politics or the pragmatic social theories of Dewey, the keynote of the 1930s was the idea of Culture, a search in the everyday life and memories of "the people" for what was distinctively American.[19]

If this search for Americanism was fundamentally conservative, it was also created by the destabilizing population shifts and social changes that Denning charts. It was as much a focus of those seeking to become "American" and learn "the American Way of Life" as of those bemoaning its attenuation and seeking to revitalize it. The search for Americanism is thus allied to and deeply embedded within the leftist tilt of the era. It helps explain not only Flanagan's focus on developing regional theatre and dramatizing matters of social concern, but also the focus of projects across Federal One—from the slave narrative collections of the Federal Writers Project to the post office murals of the Federal Art Project to the folk music collections of the Federal Music Project. Equally, it animated opposition to federal art and its ability to control the rhetoric of national identity. Therefore, the consensus that there was an endangered "American Way of Life" that needed to be simultaneously discovered and preserved only intensified the struggle over whose "American" would be enshrined.

Enter the Dies Committee.[20]

The Depression and the Federal Theatre Project

Almost exactly six years after the stock market crash of October 29, 1929, the Federal Theatre Project produced *It Can't Happen Here*. By 1932, the far-reaching economic crisis that would become America's Great Depression had become apparent in the precipitous drop in the gross national product, the millions of unemployed, the shutting down of banks; that crisis would become imaged in "Hooverville" shantytowns, long lines for bread, and dapper apple sellers.

The brainchild of Harry Hopkins, then Roosevelt's head of the Federal Emergency Relief Administration, the Federal Theatre Project originated in 1935 as part of the New Deal's vast public employment program—the Works Progress Administration (later the Works Projects Administration).[21] The FTP was one of four parts of Federal One, as the arts projects were collectively known. Federal One also included the Federal Art Project, the Federal Writers Project, and the Federal Music Project. Hopkins tapped his Grinnell College classmate, longtime friend, and then director of the Vassar College Experimental Theatre, Hallie Flanagan, to direct the government's venture into theatre.

Flanagan's work to that point suggests that she was an odd choice for the position: she had little large-scale administrative experience and was not familiar with Washington and its political maneuverings. The first woman to receive a Guggenheim fellowship in 1926, she had used it to travel extensively in the Soviet Union and Europe, studying contemporary productions and theory; the book that resulted from this experience, *Shifting Scenes of the Modern European Theatre*, was published in 1928.[22] As director of the Vassar Experimental Theatre, she produced drama that showcased her cutting-edge theatrical interests. Drawing on staging concepts developed by Erwin Piscator and agitprop theatre, *Can You Hear Their Voices*, her 1931 dramatization of the plight of farmers in Arkansas, foreshadowed the Living Newspapers that would be the FTP's most original contribution to American theatre.[23] According to a *New York Times* reviewer, the production was a

> series of black and white vignettes . . . capped by small blackouts and interwoven argumentatively with the stark facts of Congress's inaction thrown at you from printed slides on a huge white screen. Dominating the picture was the barbed lampoon of the quarter million dollar debutante party which startled Washington at the height of the drought.[24]

As Jane Mathews notes, the final screen comes down "as the prison-bound father sent his sons to Communist headquarters in the hope that they could 'make a better world.'" The play was performed across the country as audience members in Poughkeepsie, New York, collected clothes and money for the farmers.

Flanagan was interested in social theatre, and from the beginning of her tenure as FTP director, she envisioned a decentered national theatre responsive to regional particularities as well as political and social realities. "Our most urgent task is to make our theatre worthy of its audience," she wrote in 1936. "It is of no value whatever to stimulate theatre-going unless, once inside our doors, our audience sees something which has some vital connection with their own lives and their own immediate problems."[25]

Flanagan envisioned an American theatre that would invigorate what she perceived as a moribund institution. As Mathews notes:

> As she studied conditions in the commercial theatre contributing to unemployment, Hallie Flanagan rediscovered an ailing, frequently irrelevant institution that seemingly had come of age artistically and socially too late. Like most enterprises at the turn of the century, the commercial theatre had succumbed to the monopolistic, profit-making devices which were a part of the economic revolution transforming America. The list of such practices was long: gambling in theatres as real estate; syndicates fostering a cross-country touring system; a monopoly booking system; the "star" system; long-run shows that destroyed repertory; type casting that stifled an actor's development; the staging of the "tried and true" rather than the work of a new playwright with ideas. The result was predictable—an art stumbling toward maturity had been transformed into a primarily commercial enterprise.[26]

Flanagan envisioned the FTP as permanent, and set in place institutional practices and administrative divisions that would provide a central clearinghouse for the distribution of plays, encourage young writers, develop new theatre, and educate a new generation of theatre-goers. She imagined a theatre of many different forms, writing in *Federal Theatre* (and in the final line, alluding to *Dr. Faustus*):

> The trapeze performer hanging by her heels in the circus, the toe dancer describing an airy arc, the vaudevillian whose inspired ineptitudes console us for our own—all of these are necessary in the many-colored pattern of Federal Theatre. It need not always be Lenin's blood streaming from the firmament.[27]

Although Flanagan believed in social theatre, she intended to provide a national theatre that reflected diverse American tastes.

The FTP was organized as a series of decentered units answerable to the national director in Washington. Five assistant directors were responsible for theatre units in their territories, which were composed of a number of states. As Flanagan noted in her "Report of the First Six Months" in the FTP periodical *Federal Theatre*, "All Federal Theatre projects are responsible, through the director of the Federal Theatre in Washington, to the director of Professional and Service Projects, of which the four arts project make up one unit under the Works Progress Administration."[28] Because of this organization, each unit director had to be not only answerable to Flanagan but also sensitive to the WPA administrators responsible for the same or similar geographical locations.

Following auditions to determine the number of unemployed theatre personnel, units were set up in the 31 states where unemployment of theatre people was deemed sufficiently high to make productions possible. Most activity was in major cities: New York City began with more than 5,000 on the payroll and 49 producing groups; Boston began with 33 producing groups, Los Angeles with 32, Chicago with 14, and Seattle with 5.

There are two primary narratives of the Federal Theatre Project history. The first declares the project a failure from the beginning and details the manner in which units were hampered by staff and budget cuts and WPA meddling.[29] Because the project was mandated to spend 90 percent of its budget on labor and only 10 percent on productions, any cut in funding created serious problems for the productions. Funding cuts were often long-rumored, generating unease among casts. Particularly in New York, unions struggled against both funding cuts and government control. As Flanagan noted, the FTP was tied to Actors Equity, the American Federation of Actors, the International Alliance of Theatrical Stage Employees, with its many locals, the Union of Wardrobe Mistresses, the Union of Electrical Engineers, the Union of Scenic Designers, and others. Although Flanagan claimed, "A series of conferences extending over many months has resulted in friendly co-operation from these unions," such was never the case. The New York City project had nearly as many difficulties from the unions as it did from its right-wing critics.[30]

The amount of bureaucratic effort required to put on a play was often daunting. For salaries and other funds, state directors had to submit forms in sextuplicate—and each copy had a color of its own. Resigning in August 1937, Walter Hart, assistant to the head of the production board in New York, wrote, "Every time a play is produced by the Federal Theatre, a major miracle has been passed. After passing 95 miracles, one begins to tire."[31] By that time the list of people who had resigned supervisory positions was long and included not only Elmer Rice, but Joseph Losey, Rosamond Gilder, Jaspar Deeter, Thomas Wood Stevens, Gilmore Brown, and Frederick McConnell.[32]

Across the country, censorship marred the FTP's attempts to bring a diverse theatre to the stage. In New York, the first Living Newspaper, *Ethiopia*, was ordered shut down by the White House before it opened; regional director Elmer Rice resigned in protest. George Sklar's *Stevedore* was barred from Boston, though it had been staged in Seattle. The wife of the WPA director for the Seattle area supposedly thought the Negro Unit production of *Lysistrata* was obscene, and the play was closed after a sold-out opening night. In Chicago, both Meyer Levinson's *Model Tenement* and Paul Green's *Hymn to the Rising Sun* were closed by the city and state WPA directors, respectively.[33]

This first narrative has been complicated by Judith Brussell's remarkable dissertation detailing the scope of investigation of FTP personnel.[34] According to Brussell's research, Division of Investigation agents were investigating, at the direction of the Department of Justice, supervisors of all the federal arts projects to find people for potential criminal prosecution. She describes how people's names entered the intelligence community via often unsubstantiated charges—hearsay, informers' accusations, and anonymous accusations—and thereafter circulated among the DOI, the Justice Department, and the House Committee on Un-American Activities. A chilling document, her dissertation charts how the DOI

> was converted within five years [1936–41] from an agency established to investigate economic fraud to an intelligence agency which hunted alleged Communists and Nazis on the federal payroll. The first nation-wide organized campaign against suspected "Red" artists in 1935–1939 helped to fuel the long-standing persecution of persons in the arts and show business in America.[35]

But Brussell writes that her dissertation is "a tribute to the thousands of people who made the Federal Theatre Project the richest outpouring of diverse theatre that the United States has ever witnessed."[36]

Contrasting with this first narrative of crippling adversity is one that tells of the project's enormously successful outreach. Federal Theatre shows entertained thousands in affordable performances. Circuses and vaudeville, marionette shows, religious theatre, and foreign-language theatre productions were mounted on all types of stages. For example, in Oklahoma, productions played to those dispossessed by agricultural crisis living in squatter camps;

the project also operated a theatre at the School for the Blind in Oklahoma, where blind actors performed under a blind director for sighted audiences. Not including radio shows, which averaged 3,000 a year, the Federal Theatre offered about 1,200 productions.³⁷

Much of its fare was classic, comfortable, and familiar. Units across the country performed Shakespeare, Molière, and Gilbert and Sullivan. Units also performed the contemporary drama of Susan Glaspell, Maxwell Anderson, Elmer Rice, Paul Green, and George Sklar and Paul Peters. George Bernard Shaw gave his plays to the project and Eugene O'Neill provided his at reduced prices. The FTP was of course too broad a coalition to come to consensus about what types of plays it would stage; though in *Federal Theatre*, an article attributed to Michael Garnett insists:

> Born out of the sternest of all realities—necessity—our theatre should be an instrument for disseminating knowledge of reality. We should not waste time and opportunity writing or producing plays that have already been done, or plays paralleling in form and content the usual products of Broadway and Hollywood, no matter how good. We should have no time or temper for passive contemplation or passive reflection. Neither should we become "arty" or high-browish. There should evolve an absolute and organic union of our art talents with the life of the nation, with the interests and aspirations of the people. And this unity should be reflected in every word written and every scene acted by Federal Theatre workers.³⁸

Garnett's argument reflects more the idealism invested in the idea of Federal Theatre as a new national theatre than the difficult reality of its administration.

FTP scholar Lorraine Brown writes that nine of every ten workers came from the relief rolls; she further notes that about fifty percent of the labor was actors, and the rest were writers, designers, directors, musicians, dancers, support staff, booking agents, and research workers. According to Brown, in Federal Theatre's first two years, its funds amounted to about 25 million dollars,

> half the cost of one battleship—for which the Federal Theatre Project presented over 42,000 performances of drama, comedy, vaudeville, marionette, and musical reviews, and circuses to an audience in excess of 25 million people. This audience was located in cities and hamlets, and in villages and remote crossroads, and gathered in leased theatres in many selected major cities. Only a small portion of this audience was ever called upon to pay admission charges at the box office.³⁹

Though the FTP did bring theatre to the hamlets and villages and remote crossroads, it was by and large concentrated in the largest cities, particularly New York City, with its large, established theatre community. Not surprisingly, it was the New York Project that would focus the controversies that would bring the project—puppet shows in Oklahoma for squatter camps and all—down.[40]

Robbins uses Rivera's sixty-three-foot mural to symbolize the outsized canvas of thirties politics and art. The mural is also a trope organizing the sprawling narrative of his film. This study of FTP children's plays takes a similarly expansive view. Rather than situating the plays in the narrow context of Federal Theatre, I examine their connections to other media, culture, and politics to situate their singular histories in the big, busy, complicated mural of Popular Front culture.

Chapter One
FEDERAL THEATRE PROJECT DREAMS
Raising an Educated Audience for a Permanent American National Theatre

Children's theatre was central to the Federal Theatre Project not only in terms of productions, but also in terms of research and administrative organizing to bring together current educational, psychological theories to its work building a system of national productions for children. My first chapter examines the apparatus of federal children's theatre, tracing twentieth-century developments in children's theatre. It then locates the development of a theatre for children in the context of an emerging child increasingly understood to be deserving of the rights and benefits of middle-class childhood regardless of class or ethnic status. Examining key linguistic and visual representations of the child and childhood in labor movement history, the chapter concludes with the realization that the working-class child held a position of heightened rhetorical power as Federal Theatre prepared to stage what would become the most controversial of its productions for children.

Chapter Two
"WE SHOULD HAVE CALLED IT *RUMPELSTILTSKIN*"
A Labor Fairy Tale Gets Real in *The Revolt of the Beavers*[41]

My second chapter examines arguably the second-most famous FTP controversy—the first being the censoring of the Orson Welles–John Houseman labor opera *The Cradle Will Rock*—though it is probable that the second-most famous controversy helped to ignite the first. On May 20, 1937, the New York City Children's Unit opened its spring play *The Revolt of the Beavers*. With Group Theatre member Elia Kazan as director in initial rehearsals, the play was written by two FTP playwrights, Oscar Saul and Lou Lantz, who had been part of the Workers Laboratory Theatre (WLT), which had been incorporated wholesale into the FTP as the One-Act Experimental Theatre.[42] A number of cast members also came from the WLT. Kazan would bow out, and the play opened with Peter Hyun, also of the WLT, and Lewis Leverett of the Group Theatre as co-directors.

The play provoked a public discussion over its Mother Goose Marxism, as *New York Times* reviewer Brooks Atkinson characterized it—and police deputy chief Byrnes MacDonald castigated it. With Atkinson's review and a letter to the editor from MacDonald calling for censorship, other papers gleefully picked up the controversy: "Police Gnaw at W.P.A. over Beavers Play" reads the headline to one newspaper article.[43]

The New York and then Congressional uproar over *The Revolt of the Beavers* raises two interesting questions that seem oddly divergent. Given the temper of the times, why was there such an uproar over a pro-labor, and even pro-Marxist, children's play?[44] Equally interesting is another issue: the Federal Theatre Project was not considered to be a wildly venturesome dramatic enterprise, yet the play was not deemed sufficiently controversial prior to its opening to cause undue concern among FTP officials.[45] Why not?

Using materials archived at the Library of Congress and the National Archives, I examine the controversy that surrounded the play. Using a series of press releases that bear in their editing process the signs of the conflict between a leftist New York FTP and Washington's WPA, I follow the production through its opening as well as the controversy that opening generated in the press. Noting that the play was not only criticized in the New York press but was also a point of focus for the Dies Committee investigation of the FTP, I examine its political implications in light of the symbolic value of the child. I then examine the manner in which FTP officials attempted to depoliticize the play's politics through an appeal to genre. Finally, I look at particular moments within the play in light of other stories of urban childhood, such as Sidney Kingsley's play *Dead End*, and Michael Gold's novel *Jews Without Money*.

Because the New York City Children's Unit was designed to serve as the model for other children's units and to lay the groundwork for a permanent national children's theatre, *The Revolt of the Beavers* had a wide-ranging impact, particularly since the unit's productions had begun splendidly.

Capacity crowds saw its first production, Charlotte Chorpenning's *The Emperor's New Clothes*, which was in turn taken to orphanages and hospitals. In the late summer of 1936, Dorothy Hailparn's *Horse Play* played five times a week in city parks. *Flight*, a Living Newspaper–styled play about the history of flight, fulfilled the unit's stated goal of educating its audience.

The unit had received rhapsodic letters from teachers and local business and education leaders who had been given complimentary tickets, as well as from parents and children who had seen the shows. In a city unit plagued with production problems ranging from union strife to casting difficulties, the children's theatre initially seemed like the one unqualified success. This overall success perhaps made its one moment of real notoriety that much more memorable.

Chapter Three
"I LOOKED HIM RIGHT SQUARE IN THE EYE"
Being African American in *The Story of Little Black Sambo*

Versions of the 1899 Helen Bannerman picture book *The Story of Little Black Sambo* were produced in Seattle, Philadelphia, Miami, Newark, Cincinnati, and Chicago. Some of the productions were for puppet theatre and some for children's theatre, with adaptations credited to various playwrights. Playscripts for the productions remain, though in the case of the Seattle Children's Theatre and the Newark puppet theatre, playscripts are all that remain in the Library of Congress FTP collection.[46]

I examine productions to argue that Federal Theatre produced a radical representation of the Sambo character in Chicago against the backdrop of established racist minstrel characterizations and forms of plantation mythology within other versions of the story. By using accepted minstrel characterizations and forms, some federal versions of *The Story of Little Black Sambo* subvert the family security that provided one of the real pleasures of the book's plot. I argue that these plays provide a parable of white-on-black violence faced by American blacks; through their use of minstrelsy, they stage African American family ignorance and neglect as its cause. A Charlotte Chorpenning—Shirley Graham production in Chicago, on the other hand, creates a primitivist modernist aesthetic that introduces a brave and clever Sambo liberated from traditional racist caricature.

I briefly analyze the use of the black mammy stereotype in *Brer Rabbit and the Tar Baby* to examine how the mammy character's differing relationships with white children and black children suggest lack of intrafamilial maternal concern. By changing the Uncle Remus figure of the book to a black mammy figure who plays the dual role of storyteller and mother to the Brer Rabbit children, the play overtly contrasts her delighted embrace of white children with her violence toward her own. This minor detail of plot and character informs the staging of planned violence to the Brer Rabbit children by Brer Fox and suggests that violence is an expected and natural aspect of black family life.

I situate the plays within the framework of the FTP's often contradictory positions on race by looking briefly at *Turpentine*, a black–white collaboration between J. Augustus Smith and Peter Morrell that examines the plight of African Americans working in Southern turpentine camps, and at archived minstrel show scripts of the project.

The racial justice broadly imagined by the left in the 1930s was one of political, social, and economic equality mobilized against the spectacle of oppression personified by the lynch mob. Particularly in the urban north where, as Denning notes, the left was a constellation of "young plebians, the radical moderns, and the anti-fascist émigrés," both the modernist co-opting of black aesthetics and culture in the previous decade and the massive African American migration to the unionized north positioned African American social and artistic concerns to take rhetorical prominence in a leftist movement organized around the "brotherhood" of class and racial equality.[47] With a unionism that championed the cause of the black worker, the anti-lynching movement galvanized the left.

The FTP provides remarkable documentation of both the triumphs and the failures of leftist rhetoric of racial equality. The FTP's commitment to building a black theatre was unprecedented. The project developed African American theatre units in major cities and in smaller places such as Hartford, Connecticut, and Durham, North Carolina. Taking the suggestion of actress, theatre organizer, and Communist Rose McClendon, who would co-direct the Harlem-based Negro Unit in New York, the Federal Theatre Project organized along racial lines with separate Negro Units in major cities that had African American theatre populations.[48]

The units to a large extent segregated black and white performers and audiences, but provided productions for African Americans to stage, perform, and watch that were cheap and—more unusual—paid the performers every time.[49] For the first and only time in American history, African American audiences in cities with Negro Units had steady access to professional theatre acted by African American performers. Though plays were sometimes shut down, boundaries between what was acceptable theatre for black performers and what was not were crossed with productions of *Lysistrata*,

Macbeth, and the social protest plays *Stevedore* and *Big White Fog*. Social and economic issues facing black Americans were dramatized, though often as imagined and written by whites. Numerous produced and collected FTP plays focused attention on America's oppressive racial politics and the need for collective action across racial lines to redress injustice. In practical terms for black performers and audiences and projects, the FTP's commitment to African American performers changed the trajectory of their presence on the American stage.

Chapter Four
"SHADOWS OF YOUR THOUGHTS ARE MARCHING"
Anti-Fascism and Home-front Patriotism in Federal Theatre's
A Letter to Santa Claus and Hollywood's *The Little Princess*

The Federal Theatre's strongest antifascist statement would be in the liberal voice of Sinclair Lewis's adaptation of his novel *It Can't Happen Here*. The book had been bought by Metro-Goldwyn-Mayer, but the film studio dropped it after a script was produced. Lewis, with the help of Paramount screenwriter John C. Moffit, turned it into a play at the request of the FTP's play bureau, which also suggested its Federal Theatre multicity openings.

Of much briefer duration, and staged only in Chicago, was the children's theatre's most imaginative theatrical engagement with antiwar and antifascism issues. In December 1938, the Chicago unit produced a two-week holiday series of free matinees of *A Letter to Santa Claus,* a one-act play written for Federal Theatre by Charlotte Chorpenning. Chorpenning, a number of whose plays were produced by the FTP, planned the play for a stadium production; although it had to be scaled back, *A Letter to Santa Claus* had a full orchestra and a cast of seventy-five.

But *A Letter to Santa Claus* is no lighthearted Christmas pageant. Antiwar sentiments and the bewilderment of a nation's people on the brink of entering a terrible, global conflict infuse its story.

As the shadows of war stalk the children on stage, *A Letter to Santa Claus* pleads for a united effort to stand against and thus avert coming war. Yet, as the link between domestic and military strife suggests, in *A Letter to Santa Claus* the causes of war are not outside the boundaries of home or nation. Although much more obliquely than *It Can't Happen Here,* Chorpenning's play raises the spectre of a fascistic domination at home. Lowell Swortzell, whose collection *Six Plays for Young People* reprinted the play, wrote in its introduction:

> *A Letter to Santa Claus* is of interest not simply because Chorpenning wrote it . . . but mostly because of the anti-war sentiments that permeate almost every scene. References to hunger, poverty, and the "shadows" that cross the land (these appeared literally on a large screen as armed soldiers on the march) convey a sense of national disillusionment. . . . If her compassion results in impressive propaganda more than drama, it also makes the play a chilling social document, and unlike any of her other works. The "shadows" Chorpenning projects here are borne of personal fears; no antics of performing vaudevillians nor an attempted happy ending can erase their meaning, then or now. Surely there has never been a Santa Claus play for "Children Only" written with such a deeply felt and disturbing subtext.[50]

Although antiwar and antifascist messages were perhaps embedded in other children's plays, and certainly in *The Revolt of the Beavers*, *A Letter to Santa Claus* and the Philadelphia production of *Bunk, Bullets, and Babies* were the only two plays that explicitly criticized fascism and war as threatening to children and families.

It Can't Happen Here was staged by the FTP because the major Hollywood studio that had the option dropped the project. This chapter explores differences between the antifascist/antiwar statements of *A Letter to Santa Claus* and the frankly jingoistic Hollywood approach to fascist aggression and coming war in its 1939 Shirley Temple vehicle *The Little Princess*. In both play and film, though to very different ends, children make an explicit connection between a child's unerring sense of morality and the home-front response to a war that unifies a nation. Children trope an ideal citizenry who actively work to resolve the conflicts that lead to war.

Chapter Five
WISHING ON A STAR
Pinocchio's Journey from the Federal Stage to Disney's World

Pinocchio was Federal Theatre's most popular children's production, and perhaps its most popular production overall. Yasha Frank's follow-up to his popular *Hansel and Gretel* was a rhyming play in which dialogue was kept to a minimum and the scary parts of the book excised or lightened. *Pinocchio* drew standing-room-only crowds and moved from city to city in the last two years of the project. While not a Popular Front play, *Pinocchio* became a symbol of the Federal Theatre Project itself when the Project lost its funding. Thus, more than any other play, *Pinocchio* demonstrates the importance both of federal children's plays and of the representational power of the child. This chapter, then, bookends this study with an examination of Frank's *Pinocchio* and Disney's within the context of popular culture magazines with articles on parenting and advertisements that sold products by playing on parenting anxieties. It explores ways in which the family was imaged within the community and held as an ideal to be kept separate from a larger community. It also describes the visions of parenting that animated parent–child relationships. Positing that the parent–child relationship became the locus for diffuse adult economic and social anxieties, this chapter examines *Pinocchio*'s narrative of Gepetto's redemption as a resolution of those anxieties.

Conclusion
DEATH OF A DREAM

Summarizing the major themes of this project, I return to compare the final staging of *Pinocchio* with the film version of Federal Theatre's end in *Cradle Will Rock*. I examine how the film transforms the dead puppet figure from the hero of the children's play to the ventriloquist's dummy in order to illustrate the collusion between ordinary Americans and business and political interests that brought about the end of the Federal Theatre Project. While this shift in symbolic focus creates a stirring historical resonance and makes a strong political statement, the fact that the dead figure was the protagonist of a children's play highlights the relationship between children and politics, a relationship that the film's obscuration makes equally resonant for today.

CHAPTER 1

FEDERAL THEATRE PROJECT DREAMS

Raising an Educated Audience for a
Permanent American National Theatre

> One of the Federal Theatre Project's most successful ventures was its Children's Theatre. Representing an entirely new approach to presenting live drama to young audiences, the children's units operated on the two-fold assumption that children needed a theatre, and that the theatre needed the children. Hallie Flanagan . . . recognized that this largely neglected audience was, in fact, the potential audience of the future and needed to be "educated to appreciate the theatre as an artistic form."
>
> —*Federal One*, a publication of the Research Center for the Federal Theatre Project, George Mason University, October 1976

In a 1936 article for *Federal Theatre*, Children's Unit director Jack Rennick quotes an educator to clarify his units' goal. "If America is ever to have a great theatre, she cannot begin too soon to train and establish an audience that will appreciate, demand, and support the best." It is "with this objective in mind" that the children's theatre of the FTP came into being.[1]

During her Guggenheim-funded travels, Hallie Flanagan had seen European theatre directed toward children, and as FTP director she emphasized the need for a vibrant children's theatre. Children's theatre units, separate from the adult units, were formed in New York City, Los Angeles, and Cleveland, Ohio.[2] Adult units performed children's plays regularly in Chicago, Boston, Newark, New Haven, Hartford, Norwalk, Denver, Tampa, Miami and Jacksonville, San Francisco, San Diego, and Portland. In addition, FTP marionette companies and amateur groups performed extensively for children. The FTP also funded and took over an already established theatre by and for children in Gary, Indiana, the only unit in which child actors performed plays for federal theatre. Otherwise, performances in all cities were acted by adults.[3]

Casting this way was practical, since all but 10 percent of the FTP employees had to be on relief (and 90 percent of the budget had to be spent on salaries). Not only were casts large in order to employ as many people as possible, but also they were adult in order to employ the people who had to be providers. Casts were often huge, particularly in such cities as Los Angeles and Seattle, where former vaudeville performers could provide comic relief and perform circus interludes (such as would be seen in Seattle's *Brer Rabbit and the Tar Baby* and Los Angeles's *Pinocchio*).

The New York City children's theatre was designed as a model for the nation, and as such undertook a number of administrative tasks designed to undergird a system of national productions for children. It spent an enormous amount of bureaucratic energy setting up playlists and productions. Administrators sent out surveys to educators at public and parochial schools and settlement houses to determine children's story preferences and theatre knowledge. They formed a consultant group "comprised of professors from New York University and Columbia, the educational director of the Boy Scouts of America, the Superintendent of Schools for New York City, and such well-known leaders in the world of children's entertainment as Dorothy McFadden of Junior Programs, Inc., and Paul Wing of the National Broadcasting Company."[4] Unit personnel requested research information from the Moscow State Central Theatre for Juvenile Audiences, where, after watching children, observers had determined standards based on age for performance length, the duration of each act, and intermissions. Soviets also sent materials for suggested book reading by the children and for test questions to be answered by attending children.

Although the FTP never classified the plays according to suggested age groups for audiences, Rennick explains the corresponding age and theatre-type divisions in his *Federal Theatre* report. He describes three groups: ages 5 to 8, 9 to 12, and 13 and older. For the youngest viewers, he writes: "The young child is quickly bored and becomes restless with too much exposition. The play must have a great deal of color and action to hold their attention. The play can be as fantastic and as imaginative as you wish, but the imagery must not be obscured." For the middle group, he adds, "in this case we can begin to evolve plot structure." He describes the oldest as the most difficult group. "The majority of them refuse to have anything to do with subject matter that they claim is 'for the kids.' Here we must begin to do plays with a definite social awareness; we should begin to develop the faculties of discrimination, criticism and thought." He closes, "In the selection of plays for all age groups, entertainment value must be taken into consideration, but each script must contain some educational value."[5]

Regular audience surveys were also taken at a number of performances. (Both the plan of devising theatre for specific ages and the practice of audience surveys would come into play during the controversy that arose surrounding the New York Children's Unit production of *The Revolt of the Beavers*.) And in a report titled "The Children's Theatre," Rennick noted that the New York Unit also surveyed "the financial condition of children in 220 centers with a total attendance of 200,000 children." The survey found that 10 percent of the children were unable to pay any admission, 15 percent were able to pay five cents or less, 43 percent were able to pay 10 cents or less, and 32 percent were able to pay 15 cents or less.[6] In this context, Rennick's report presents the children's theatre goals:

> The Children's Theatre aims to present two general types of plays. The first includes plays which are imaginative, humorous or fantastical in nature. The second and more important type (neglected by children's theatres in the past) is the play with a heightened sense of realism which will help the child to an awareness of himself and his place in the world about him. In all plays there must be an educational and cultural value, and above everything else, the play must be presented to attract and retain the interest of the child.[7]

Partly in response to budget cuts, the New York Unit produced a "Children's Autumn Festival" at the end of October 1937, for which some of its more popular plays were restaged. The festival was the culmination of months of planning; FTP officials solicited support from a number of community leaders who would sponsor the festival. Following eight days of performances, the festival concluded with a conference for the sponsors.[8] Minutes from a meeting on September 29, 1937, show that planning committee members included dance troupe leader Tamaris, J. Augustus Smith, director of the Negro Unit, and marionette unit director Remo Bufano. More than 7,500 people attended the festival, which was sold out for ten performances while hundreds of parents and children were turned away.[9] The festival featured puppet shows, restagings of *Horse Play* (by the Negro Unit), *Pierre Patelin, The Emperor's New Clothes,* and *Jack and the Beanstalk,* music by the Federal Music Project, and a vaudeville show for children that included "the 'All-American Minstrels,' complete with interlocutor and end men."[10]

The FTP Children's Units were committed in philosophy and in practice to reaching the children of America; they took plays to settlement houses, hospitals, and schools; their repertory included fairy- and folktales, biographies, educational plays about such subjects as hygiene and nutrition, and new plays written for the FTP. If an administrative separation between children and adult productions served to oppose two types of theatre, audiences never recognized such an opposition, for these plays so carefully researched and so explicitly directed at children were always attended by children and adults alike, with the latter composing 75 percent of *Pinocchio*'s overall audience.[11]

Flanagan never quite gave up on the dream for a national children's theatre. Records show that on October 3, 1938, scarcely six months before the FTP would be closed, Los Angeles children's unit director Yasha Frank submitted a survey of the schedule for the "Theatre for Youth which we discussed several weeks ago." Frank writes:

> It incorporates a program which indicates the national characteristics of Federal Theatre Project. It plans to co-operate with the various related governmental agencies; with the other cultural projects; with National Youth Administration. It follows the fundamental trend which your policy more and more clarifies—to identify our work with the life of the community—to infiltrate into the cultural and educational and practical way of life of our fellow Americans.

The document lists nine major program categories: Shakespeare, motion pictures, safety campaign, patriotic programs, concerts, circus, marionettes, summer conference, and youth theatre bureau. It basically outlines a way to provide the theatrical opportunities in the main cities to audiences throughout the country and lists possible cooperative ventures. Stating that the production of children's plays in small projects is impractical, Frank proposes that motion pictures be enlisted:

> I propose a series of motion pictures on 16 mm sound supplemented and enhanced by living material in which living actors perform the expository and key situations in the play. I have completed a shooting script of my play *Pinocchio* with just such a treatment in mind. Small traveling units of five or six people could road-show these productions effectively.[12]

Frank's proposal imagines an artistic and technological marriage for a national theatre committed to all of its citizens.

Federal children's theatre was a significant development in an endeavor that had expanded throughout the early twentieth century. Beginning mostly with settlement house activities, theatre for children was considered by most educators to be important for the development of children. However, exactly how to create plays for children and what children actually wanted out of theatre remained untheorized in the early thirties and only slowly popularized throughout the decade. "It is well documented that children, when left to their own devices, will turn to things mimetic," write Roger L. Bedard and C. John Tolch in their introduction to *Spotlight on the Child: Studies in the History of American Children's Theatre*. "Yet for children to go to the theatre, or even to participate in formal drama or theatre activities, adults must not only sanction the activity, they must also design and implement such programs."[13] In the first two decades of the twentieth century, theatre for children was primarily an educational tool in the hands of teachers and social workers rather than of the theatrical community, and not a particularly important tool at that.

The first significant theatre for children was the Children's Educational Theatre, which was started in 1903 (and continued to 1909) by the Educational Alliance, which "operated for the purpose of teaching better communication in a new language and American ways to the Russian and Polish immigrants who inhabited that section of the (New York) City."[14] Settlement houses, in fact, led the way in organizing children's theatre as a means to teach immigrant children how to be "American," keeping children away from vaudeville and providing socialization as much as education. Alice Minnie Herts, who started the children's theatre for the Educational Alliance, said she "saw the great opportunity not to impose upon people from without, but to help people create an ideal from within."[15]

Professional theatre companies mostly ignored child audiences; even when they experimented with productions for children, these were accessible only to children in large cities and at a cost that precluded much of the population from attending. At the turn of the century these productions were mostly variety shows and vaudeville-influenced comedies.

The Junior League for the Promotion of the Settlement Movements, formed in 1901 to provide socially meaningful activities for wealthy women, began organizing children's theatre productions as early as 1912; by 1924 the Chicago League had voted to make theatre for children their focus. "Children's theatre in one form or another was the pet project of nearly every 1920s Junior League," write Janet Gordon and Diana Reische.[16] Organized theatre for children, in its inception and early development, was primarily something provided to children of disadvantaged backgrounds. By the 1930s, however, the renamed Association of Junior Leagues of America not only produced plays but also held national conferences on children's theatre, cooperated with local school districts, and sponsored some professional productions.[17]

The King-Coit School and Children's Theatre in New York taught children literature, history, painting, dancing, drawing, and acting after school and on the weekends and produced critically acclaimed children's theatre that was an acknowledged part of the New York theatre scene from 1923 to 1958. Well-known actors who sent their children there supported it, and first-rate critics reviewed its productions.[18]

In 1930, one of the most influential people working in children's theatre published her first book, *Creative Dramatics: For the Upper Grades and Junior High School*. Winifred Ward, working in the Evanston, Illinois, public school system, would shape the direction of children's theatre. *Creative Dramatics* was used by FTP play bureau workers as a guide for choosing plays to be included in a list for distribution to schools, institutions, and children's groups. Ward's "creative dramatics" was a theory of how drama could be used to stimulate children's interest in learning. Highly influenced by pragmatist John Dewey's educational theories, her creative dramatics stressed the experiential nature of learning and how the process of creating plays and oral presentations would benefit the whole child. She believed that education should not focus on the teaching of information, but rather should be designed to instill democratic values, develop children's self-confidence, and provide meaningful information useful to them; drama was a means to secure these ends.[19]

The Changing Social Value of the Child

If children's theatre grew out of early-twentieth-century progressive educational efforts in settlement houses, a progressive emphasis on the child similarly changed the social value, and thus public perception, of children. Labor and labor reform leaders drew upon a cultural move toward increasing protection for the middle-class child to claim a similar protection for the working-class child. The victimized child—who was in material practices denied the right of "childhood"—was used to subsume the markings of class and ethnicity. My book demonstrates how its FTP children's plays draw on such conceptualizations of childhood and children to evoke a particularly powerful nexus of innocence and victimization—as well as the symbolic fluidity of the working-class and laboring child to mediate class and ethnicity—and bring it to their productions.

In her seminal *Pricing the Priceless Child: The Changing Social Value of Children*, sociologist Viviana Zelizer charted the shift in social value of the child from economically useful to "economically useless but emotionally

FIGURE 1. Boy Sweeper, Lincoln Cotton Mills, Evansville, Ind. Carding Machines: Floor Slippery. (See report for conditions.) Location: Evansville, Indiana[20]

priceless" during the early twentieth century. Drawing on methodologies used in earlier studies of historical shifts in attitudes regarding children and childhood such as Philippe Aries's *Centuries of Childhood*, Zelizer examined what she termed the increasing "sacralization" of children by analyzing such institutional practices as legal definitions of the child, child labor and insurance practices regarding children. Her study argues that shifts in social attitudes precede shifts in institutional attitudes. She explicitly argues that studies examining shifts in children's economic valuation that posit causal relations determined by pricing and market forces ignore the process by which "values shape price, investing it with social, religious, or sentimental meaning."[21]

Zelizer's chart of the child's progression from useful to economically useless but emotionally priceless undergirds current understandings of historical shifts in child valuation and in studies of children's literature and representations of children in art of the Industrial Revolution. She notes that labor and child labor reform rhetoric adopted, and by its adoption expanded, the idea of a universalized, protected childhood. Representations of the laboring and working-class child within labor and labor reform movements inflect the early-twentieth-century discourse of childhood with class concerns. This inflection mediates dominant fears about the working class, comments on the socially constructed nature of constraints to full democratic participation, and critiques an American Dream that promises equal opportunity to all. Labor's claim to a right to childhood and reformers' efforts to expose the dearth of a working-class childhood inserted class and ethnicity into a universalized model of the protected middle-class child that, as a symbolic figure, performed such necessary cultural work that it could—without erasing—carry the inflection. Ethnicity and class were subsumed by the child. If a historical perspective charts shifts in the symbolic function of the laboring and working-class child, it also shows how powerfully the innocent child animates the shifts.

Denning writes that immigrants and their children composed two-thirds of the population of America's major cities by 1930. His chart of CIO affiliations and loyalties proposes an alliance of second-generation ethnic workers in mass-production jobs and radical specialized workers whose support of the CIO and whose movement into the arts created "an iconography and rhetoric of class."[22] Labor rhetoric in the thirties attempted to unite under the aegis of Burke's "the people" a complex network of ethnic loyalties and nationalisms. Denning writes:

> Popular Front public culture sought to forge ethnic and racial alliances, mediating between Anglo American culture, the culture of ethnic workers,

and African American culture, in part by reclaiming the figure of "America" itself, imagining an Americanism that would provide a usable past for ethnic workers, who were thought of as foreigners, in terms of a series of ethnic slurs.[23]

This reclamation project was an attempt to unite millions of industrial workers with the middle class in an "urban civic culture." Its threat to an established social order was not communism, but the powerful alliance of working and middle classes united for labor causes.

Examining discursive moments in labor and labor reform history where children and childhood performed key symbolic work for labor and its causes reveal the manner in which labor reform argued for a protected status for laboring children. I take three moments from a forty-year history to broadly sketch this trajectory: the text of an 1893 speech by labor leader Samuel Gompers, selected photographs taken by Lewis Hine, and accounts of the murder of Ella May Wiggins during the Gastonia Loray Mill strike to explore the representative power of laboring children.

An 1893 speech by Samuel Gompers, president of the American Federation of Labor, at the International Labor Congress in Chicago, called forth the bodies of laboring children as signs of economic, social, and civic injustice and demanded for these fleshly bodies salvation:

> Save our children in their infancy from being forced into the maelstrom of wage slavery. See to it that they are not dwarfed in body and mind or brought to a premature death by early drudgery. Give them sunshine of the school and playground instead of the factory, the mine and the workshop. We want more schoolhouses and less jails; more books and less arsenals; more learning and less vice; more constant work and less crime; more leisure and less greed; more justice and less revenge; in fact, more of the opportunities to cultivate our better natures; to make manhood more noble, womanhood more beautiful, and childhood more happy and bright.[24]

The speech's slide from childhood to manhood and womanhood and back again demonstrates how laboring children both occupy a place at the loom, the assembly line, and the mine, and figure as the disenfranchised whose working-class status excludes them from the social, civic, and juridical benefits of American democracy. The state of childhood and the bodily activity of skilled and unskilled labor become conflated as one site of oppression; thus, reform of the laboring class is figured as the salvation of the child.

The rhetorical power of Gompers's speech lies in its conflation of civic and family responsibilities and its insistence that public duties toward children will effect change on personal and institutional levels, and will finally transform American manhood and womanhood as well. Thus, a parental, domestic control over the values children receive and the activities in which they are permitted to engage is explicitly linked to a civic responsibility to shield "our" children from early drudgery. If children are shielded from the mills, the mines, and the factories, then manhood will be become "more noble," "womanhood more beautiful, and childhood more happy and bright." By posing schoolyard sunshine against workplace darkness, and then creating a striking series of oppositions through which the sunshine of the school is equated with books, learning, leisure, and justice and opposed to jails, arsenals, vice, crime, greed, and revenge, Gompers explicitly links civic responsibility to children with civic responsibility *of* and *to* the adult, and finally, to the social body figured by noble manhood, his beautiful womanhood, and their happy childhood.

Gompers reconstructs a class-based, economic struggle as an assertion of labor's right to America's public institutions. The child figures as the developing American to whom democratic educational opportunities must be offered and also as the laboring class that might rise to a position of economic and social privilege. The emotional logic of Gompers's speech reproduces a model of citizenship as a network of family responsibilities within the labor struggle. Its assertive communal possessive, its striking series of oppositions (encompassing moral, ethical, philosophical, and social concerns), its iconographic—noble, beautiful, and happy—American family, join to position labor itself as the communal family that creates ideal Americans and rids American society of pervasive social ills associated with the poor, the working class, and the immigrant. Change begins with the child.

This turn-of-the-century expression of labor's "family values" countermands a contemporary middle- and upper-class sense that immigrants, the impoverished, and the laboring class were not like decent, hardworking Americans who deserved the benefits and privileges of democratic society. Gompers asserts noneconomic goals of personal fulfillment and social democracy, separating the laboring from the labor on behalf of the working-class frail, toiling like slaves. He describes a kinder, gentler Marxism, where occupation of democratic processes, as opposed to revolution in the streets, tacitly results in economic and social parity for the working class.

Similarly, the figure of the child led organized labor and the child labor reform movement to ecstatic heights of rhetorical fervor in the late nineteenth and early twentieth centuries. In 1908, Indiana Senator Albert J.

FIGURE 2. A typical spinner. Mamie -------- Lancaster Cotton Mills, S.C. Location: Lancaster, South Carolina[25]

Beveridge wrote in his introduction to Bessie Van Vorst's exposé *The Cry of the Children*:

> When our people know that more than a million American children are dying of overwork or being forever stunted and dwarfed in body, mind, and soul; when they know that we are pouring into the body of our citizenship two hundred and fifty thousand degenerates (at the very lowest estimate) every year who have clouded minds and a burning hatred of the society that has wronged them, and that they have ballots in their hands . . . we may hope for an end of this national disgrace.[26]

Two years earlier, socialist John Spargo had warned in *The Bitter Cry of the Children* of the peril to a young growing nation embodied in the stunted forms of its laboring children.[27] "It is not only the interests of the children themselves," he wrote, "that are menaced; even more important and terrible is the thought that civilization itself is imperiled when children are dwarfed physically, mentally, and morally by hunger, heavy toil, and unwholesome surroundings."[28]

In visual contradiction to the rolling rhetoric of child labor reform language is Lewis Hine's photography for the National Child Labor Committee (NCLC) between 1908 and 1918. The emotional language of child labor reform opposes the apocalyptic savagery to enlightened civilization, or of verdant bloom to withered blight. Contrastingly, in Hine's factory photos, clean lines, multiple lighting sources, and classical composition and subject positioning balance aesthetically even as the photo itself displays the technologized science that enables its reproduced "truth." Yet Hine's factory photographs construct and circulate representations of children dependent upon the immersion of the photograph within progressive rhetoric. They oppose child and machine in order to consolidate values associated with children and childhood—innocence, naturalness, and energetic growth—and thus to critique the celebration of technologized business that enabled rapidly industrializing America to employ children. The relationship of the laboring child to the adult laborer to labor causes the child's victimization to demand a consideration of the relationship between human subject and machine. By presuming a protected and increasingly sacralized middle-class childhood for those whose primary marking had been ethnicity and class, by presuming a universal right to childhood, the rhetoric of the child labor reform movement presumed revolutionary social change.

Former botany teacher Lewis Hine's mission for the relatively new National Child Labor Committee was informed by the progressive idea that the application of knowledge and science to social problems would make economic self-interest give way to community interest. Hine took thousands of photographs of children at work. He often used duplicity to gain factory entrance—pretending interest in the machinery, or to be a postcard salesman—while he surreptitiously photographed. He measured children's heights against his suit buttons and recorded the measurements later. To document birthdates, he went to homes and looked in family Bibles. The photos, often with Hine's accompanying observations, were published in National Child Labor Committee pamphlets and in *Charities* magazine (among others); they served as supplements to Hine's written reports, and as posters for national exhibitions. Each child was placed, named, and aged; each factory was named and located. When Hine began his work, little was known about the numbers or about the conditions of working children. While the 1900 census revealed that 1,750,178 children were working, this didn't include the number of working children under the age of ten who weren't recorded. They worked primarily in textile mills, glass factories, mines, and canneries, on the streets and in the sun, and at home. States themselves then set standards: generally minimum ages of 10 to 12 and maximum hours of about 10 a day. And if the laws were loosely drawn and full of exemptions, enforcement was concurrently lax. In 1910 in North Carolina, where 75 percent of the spinners were children, there were no inspectors. Hine considered textile mills to be the worst offenders of child labor laws; textile mill owners and operators considered children prime laborers. While in Northern factories the population of working children in mills had decreased to less than eight percent, in the South, where numerous mills were Northern subsidiaries, the percentage of children had shot to 25 percent of all workers, an increase of 300 percent during the 1890s. Perhaps because of this cheap and abundant labor pool, the number of mills grew from 180 to 900 between 1880 and 1904.

Hine's photos display how the values of machine culture structure their presentation of child labor. In *Shifting Gears*, Cecilia Tichi argues that "gear and girder machinery," the highly visible structures and engines of the rapidly industrializing world, not only dominated early-twentieth-century technology but also powered imaginative interpretations of the natural world and the human as well as of relationships between the organic and inorganic. Early-twentieth-century machine ideology projected a natural world of integrated component parts by presuming an analogy of structural principles that integrated systems designers and systems of labor.[29]

The early-twentieth-century machine was technology made visible, and recognized by its prefabricated component structures—wheels and ball bearings and pistons, girdered structures and ordered systems; it was energy harnessed and put to work. In its mechanized harmony, it structurally imagined order and efficiency against the background of a world of flux. Yet flux is the condition of growth from child to adult. The biological progression of the human being thus figuratively opposes a stable industrial system, even as the rapid pace of early-twentieth-century industrialization suggested a powerful force whose containment was uncertain. With their miniature laboring bodies, the children in Hine's photos for the NCLC showed the frightening counterimage of the dominant machine, and their rhetorical power was heightened by the doomsday fervor of child labor reform rhetoric.

Hine's NCLC factory photos often centered the child, but the meaning of the child's body is derived from its placement against the background of machinery.[30] In numerous photos, the bodies are dwarfed by the long clean lines of a vast mechanized system; in others the small and homely devices to enable the children to perform their labor overtly emphasize small stature, unfinished bodies. The machine imagery in these photos not only threatens to overwhelm the subject and draw away the viewer's eye, but (particularly in an era when educational theory associated learning with imaginative free play) visually connoted the deadly repetition of tasks that the photo's momentary flash cannot capture. Work itself is thus represented by the machine whose physical dominance within the photo's frame suggests its power.

If machine imagery opposed the child's body and contained within its form the idea of industrialized labor, its compositional values provide many of the photos' aesthetic pleasures. To the machine's straight edges and clean lines, Hine added multiple lighting sources. A hand placed on the machinery or eyes looking directly into the camera draw the viewer's eye from the balance of form and light, and it is the smallness of the request for attention that invites an emotional participation and response. Furthermore, the compositional lines take the representation of work that the machines embody outside of the photos themselves, and reproduce in the worlds of other photos. So the straight lines of a fence and the shadowed doorway of the factory entrance suggest, in their analogic compositional form, the deadening force of the machines just outside the frame, both physically and metaphorically. Against this force, the ebullient body of the child is circumscribed.

The energy and tension of Hine's photos, and thus their overt plea for viewer participation to effect a change, comes from opposition: the opposition of darkness to light, of the straight clean line of the machine to the soft folds of a little girl's dress. The photos directly implicate the factory machines—metonyms for a social mechanism animated by greed—in the foreclosure of possibilities evident in the exhaustion, the ragged clothing, the dwarfed bodies of these working children. Their individual bodies, often awkwardly positioned against and dominated by the adult-sized mechanisms of work, suggest the impossibility of control, the impossibility of making one's own fortune, the impossibility of a mobility that would render all equal.

These photos assert a humanity for the working class against the increasingly technologized and proudly "rationalized" workplace. The rhetoric of technologized business in the early twentieth century created labor in technology's image. It classified those who worked the machines with them—cogs in the wheels designed, managed, and made efficient by the Veblen engineer and the Taylorist time manager—small, replaceable, dehumanized.

If Gompers's speech rested on protecting—and protracting—a childhood separated from adulthood, Hine's photos fuse adult and child in the opposition of human to machine. With the child laborer's haunting face in the foreground of *A Carolina Spinner,* taken at Cotton Mills, South Carolina, it is understood that the laboring child will grow into the laboring adult unto generations, trapped in a narrow, constricted world. Yet if this photo raises sympathy for the exhausted girl in the foreground, surely it also calms fears about the threat implied by a united working class. The photo explicitly appeals to a culture of patrician benevolence that exists side by side with capitalism. This girl, and the women stretching out behind her, needs help. She is small. She is weak. She is isolated and alone.

In 1906 NCLC co-founder Alexander J. McKelway wrote, "the golden age of the world ... is still in the future ... and the central figure on that canvas is that of the little child."[31] What makes Hine's photos powerful now, and perhaps most powerful to the middle and upper-class viewer at whom they were directed, is that the child embodies the dark side of the American celebration of technology—the fear that indeed its celebrants are not ubermensch engineers designing and implementing their rationalized system of control, but rather the dehumanized matter upon which these systems are imposed. Hine's photos spoke to the need for labor reform even as they ameliorated a fear of a powerful working class, and attested to a structure of familial relations outside of work. While he was still working for the NCLC, photos of working-class children were circulated to garner support for strikers whose poverty and/or immigrant status made their cause of little interest to most Americans. The opposition of the victimized child to the alienating machine so central to Hine's photographs became crucial to labor's use of children to assert a humanity that management practices attempted to victimize.

The children Hine photographed in 1908 at the Loray Mill in Gastonia, NC, would have been in their late 20s in 1929 when mill workers walked out over management practices they collectively termed the "stretch out." The term described newly conceived labor practices that made employees work harder and faster—to the point of exhaustion—and that disrupted the schedules workers had devised to take care of family emergencies or even regular family needs. The practices included production counting machines, motors on individual machines, and the introduction of "scientific engineers" whose time and motion studies attached a minimum wage to a specified amount of production. Production levels were raised as workers were forced to increase output to maintain wage standards.

The Gastonia strikers were the only workers in a wave of Southern walkouts who were organized by the Communist Party's dual National Textile Workers' Union. Because they were said to be Communist union members, the impoverished workers were hysterically reviled in the Gastonia newspaper, and in most of the statewide press, as pro-Soviet, pro-racial-equality Americans working, or rather, not working, to undermine the fabric of the community, the state, and the nation.

The Gastonia strike drew international attention and support in the left-wing press. Of particular focus was the martyrdom of balladeer Ella May Wiggins, shot in the back by Loray Mill vigilantes while she was riding home from a rally in a truck bed. Wiggins wrote and performed more than twenty songs chronicling strike events. Her death orphaned her five children, the images of whom were widely circulated in the left-wing press. Journalist Margaret Larkin chronicled Wiggins's funeral for both *The Nation* and *New Masses* and ends the *New Masses* article:

> As the first clods of wet, red earth fell on the coffin, Kat Barrett sang one of Ella May's best loved songs:
>
>> "We leave our home in the morning
>> We kiss our children goodbye
>> While we slave for the bosses
>> Our children scream and cry."
>
> Eleven year old Myrtle, who had been a "sight of help" sheperded the four littler children at the head of the grave. The tiny ones did not know what was happening at the grave side, but Myrtle knew everything. Her small shoulders dropped; her thin face was full of grief and worry.
>
>> "It is for our little children
>> That seem to us so dear,
>> But for us nor them, dear workers
>> The bosses do not care

FIGURE 3. Gaston-a, N.C. Boy from Loray Mill. "Been at it right smart two years." Location: Gastonia, North Carolina[32]

> But listen to me workers
> A Union they do fear
> Let's stand together, workers
> And have a Union here."[33]

Wiggins's most popular song was "Chief Aderholt," which describes the shooting of the town's popular sheriff during an unauthorized raid on the union's tent committee. But it is through "Mill Mother's Song," quoted above, that she is presented to America, as an anguished working mother whose wages are too low to provide a decent home for her children and whose union activities are driven by family needs.

Wiggins was described in the *Daily Worker* as a "fearless class fighter," but University of North Carolina President Frank Porter Graham said, "her death was in a sense upon the heads of us all." Castigating the politics that had inflamed and enabled the mill-employed vigilantes, he added that "Americanism . . . was not riding in cars carrying men and guns that day, barring the common highway to the citizens of the state." Rather, "Americanism was somewhere deep in the heart of this mother who went riding in a truck toward what to her was the promise of a better day for her children."[34] Ella May's motherhood, and thus her place within the sanctity of the American family, is signaled by the presence of her helpless children, innocent victims of their mother's politics. Her daughter Myrtle's grief and worry is a violation of her childhood, but its very newsworthiness is an assertion of her right to that childhood. Myrtle's too-early adulthood justifies Ella May's fight and shifts the tragedy of her death from the workplace to the home.

The death of the Gastonia striker and the plight of her motherless children made national, indeed international, news. Such interest highlights the rhetorical intensity with which the battle between the mill owners and the fledgling union and its striking workers was circulated. It was this rhetoric that allowed the strike, which as far as production was concerned was over almost before it began, to provide such a historical moment and to reverberate beyond its early events as a coherent story of labor struggle. While the *Gastonia Daily Gazette* and other North Carolina newspapers demonized the workers and the Communist union as synecdochical of a dread "Red menace" threatening to destroy the American way of life, the *Daily Worker* cast the strike as symbolic of the global struggle against capitalism. It denounced the mill owners and "their murderous vassals, the police, and private thugs and gunmen" who were "preparing one of the most monstrous blood-baths for workers in the history of the country."[35] Ella May Wiggins was a "Fearless

Class Fighter" murdered by the "mill owners' gangsters . . . because of her tremendous influence on the workers."[36]

Northern newspapers, sympathetic to the strikers, often characterized the events in Gastonia as emblematic of the South's violent primitivism and inability to provide democratic governance and protection for its citizens. As Susan Duffy, a literary scholar writing on strike plays, notes, "The Gastonia textile strike of 1929 ripped open the political animosities of the region and, like the Scopes Trial of 1925, became the cause célèbre of the liberal press in the nation. The South was perceived as another country, where people spoke differently, lived differently, and thought differently."[37]

Through representations of Ella May's children, however, members of the national and international press tried to transcend difference, even as the documentary impulse of their work is itself located in recording difference. Visual representations of laboring and working-class children had arisen primarily from the social documentary photography of Jacob Riis and late-nineteenth- and early-twentieth-century attempts to discover the sociological environment and behavioral characteristics of the poor and working class by living among them and recording their world. Following Riis, Stephen Crane and Jack London, photographers and writers armed with class superiority and a hodgepodge of sociological and psychological theories about this distinct and separate class in so-called classless America went to live among the tenement dwellers and factory workers. Taking on the identities of their subjects as they worked and lived among them, they wrote stories that appeared in such popular periodicals as *Harper's* and *Scribner's*.[38] Historian Mark Pittenger writes that in their excursion into the world of "the primitive poor," the social journalists shared a common perception that the poor lived in a "domestic 'Dark Continent' whose denizens were effectively a primitive and 'unknown race.' . . . The images they produced of that country's inhabitants tended to reinforce an overwhelming sense of otherness. Unskilled laborers, tramps, and street people looked, talked, thought, felt, and (it was more than once remarked) smelled differently than 'we' did."[39]

Children bridged this world of difference because, in no small part due to the efforts of labor and labor reform, childhood itself become culturally recognized as an inviolate and protected space. The implications of this universalized childhood can perhaps be seen in the decreased use of race and ethnicity, as well as class, as stigmatized difference during the twentieth century. In the coming decade, the racist policies of Nazi Germany would create an ensuing backlash in America wherein democracy came to be equated with ethnic tolerance; in the wake of Nazi persecutions and assertions of Aryan superiority, American racism and ethnocentrism became increasingly publicly stigmatized. Anthropological theories of Franz Boas and Margaret Mead, which stressed innate racial equality and difference of culture, were used to combat Nazi ideology.[40] Labor and labor reform rhetoric focused on the child did not by themselves change the discourse of ethnic relations in America. But they worked the ground.

CHAPTER 2

"WE SHOULD HAVE CALLED IT *RUMPELSTILTSKIN*"

A Labor Fairy Tale Gets Real in *The Revolt of the Beavers*

In the unprepossessing "Children's Theatre—1937" file of the Federal Theatre Project Collection in the National Archives lies a series of prepared press releases for the Federal Theatre Project's most controversial children's play, *The Revolt of the Beavers*.[1] Opening in May 1937, the production of *The Revolt of the Beavers* followed Charlotte Chorpenning's enormously successful adaptation of *The Emperor's New Clothes*, Dorothy Hailpern's *Horse Play*, and Oscar Saul and Lou Lantz's Living Newspaper–styled *Flight* to the New York project's Children's Theatre stage.[2] Between fluffy releases remarking upon the difficulty actors had adjusting to roller skates and describing the play's street game of "potsie" were those that linked *The Revolt of the Beavers* to the astonishingly successful contemporary labor strike tactics of the new Congress of Industrial Unions.[3] A May 18, 1937, release exclusive to the *World-Telegram* reads:

> The furore created by the wave of sit-in strikes has led to considerable speculation as to the origin of labor's new tactic. Who started the first sit-in strike and why is the question that a couple of WPA FTP playwrights, Oscar Saul and Lou Lantz, undertake to answer in a new play. . . . There is evidence that the quaint custom of sitting down until the mountain comes to Mohammet began in the animal kingdom.

Other releases directed to targeted newspapers dropped the whimsical approach. For the *Daily Worker*, the FTP's Department of Information wrote:

FIGURE 4. Paul, Mary, and Windy. *Revolt of the Beavers (New York City, New York):* George Mason University. Fenwick Library. Special Collections and Archives

Now it is the Federal Children's Theatre which takes up the cudgels for democracy on a new front . . . written so simply that a six year old child can understand the events and directed in the style of a whimsical fantasy, the play is nonetheless a clear exposition of conflicts in modern society. Although intended for children, it is an Aesop's fable that adults will appreciate.

Again for the *Daily Worker,* an April 23 release begins:

As part of its program in building a progressive children's theatre in this country, the WPA Children's Theatre carries on extensive correspondence through its research department with similar organizations in foreign countries. . . . Of considerable interest has been an exchange of letters with L. Markaviev, director of the Theatre of Young Spectators in Leningrad and Honored Artist of the Republic.

The release then details a Soviet study of child audiences to classify children's theatre before announcing the upcoming opening of *The Revolt of the Beavers.* An attached note reads, "Not too bad as a piece of writing. But let's play dirty and withhold this from Washington. I'm afraid they would be terribly shocked."

This deliberate censoring of materials from the office of the National Director, and quite possibly from the WPA, is not repeated, though an unsigned, handwritten attachment to a release noting that the play "illustrates current problems of government and economics in a simplified fashion" suggests concern over the play's political content. The attachment reads:

Not so good. Editorializing again. Also puts us on the spot by saying the play illustrates current problems in government and economics. Publicity for this unit should always stress the fact that it is a *Children's* Theatre presenting plays that interest, amuse, and entertain kids [italics mine].[4]

Publicity could not, in the end, stress that fact enough. Seventeen performances after the curtain rose on *The Revolt of the Beavers,* it descended for the last time.[5] "Meet the Chief," its brightly decorated poster had proclaimed, with a picture of a colorfully clothed, fat, grinning beaver. A "fantasy seen through the eyes of a child and embellished for adult consumption with social satirical trimmings" trumpeted yet another release. But the play was publicly branded by *New York Times* critic Brooks Atkinson as "Mother Goose Marx," and the resulting fervor in the city papers, coupled with the FTP's timid response, shut down the production.[6]

The Revolt of the Beavers tells the story of two poor nine-year-olds who are swept away to a fantastic forest where all of the animals talk and all are nine years old except the babies—"and they grow up very fast," explains one beaver. Paul and Mary find echoes of their own poverty and helplessness in the beavers' lives of toil for the tyrannical Chief, who controls the bark-producing "busy busy busy" Wheel and is thus privileged to wear a blue sweater and roller skates, eat all the ice cream he wants, and sit in a barber's chair pulling levers while the other beavers are forced to work on the Wheel without being able to eat from the bark they produce. The children join the beavers in protest against the Chief's exploitative working conditions. When the Chief refuses to respond, they help the animals stage a successful revolt so that everyone who works will share in the profits of that labor. Atkinson wrote in his review that

> The first lesson in labor warfare is staged against some whimsical settings and in imaginative costumes. . . . The style is playful; the mood is gravely gay and simple-minded. Many children now unschooled in the technique of revolution now have an opportunity, at government expense, to improve their tender minds. Mother Goose is no longer a rhymed escapist. She has been studying Marx; Jack and Jill lead the class revolution.[7]

When Atkinson's review caused a deputy police commissioner to refuse 1,400 free tickets for children "on the grounds that members of the Police Athletic League would be persuaded towards Marxism as Atkinson predicted" and to write to the *New York Times* demanding that action be taken to "suppress or at least censor" the play, FTP officials moved swiftly.[8] Without attempting to change the script to make *The Revolt of the Beavers* palatable to its critics, they closed it down.[9] Jack and Jill would not be leading the revolution on Uncle Sam's dime.

While FTP director Hallie Flanagan explicitly articulated a commitment to socially relevant theatre, the political reality was that FTP administrators could ill afford a controversy over the supposed Communist content of a children's play. Congressional funding was due to expire at the end of June and would be continued only by a nod from that legislative body whose support for the arts projects of Federal One, and particularly the theatre project, remained tenuous at best. Additionally, the public outcry over a staunchly pro-labor, Marxist fantasy play for children focused scrutiny on a project in turmoil. Rumors were flying that the WPA would be imposing budget cuts and the New York project's lively theatre unions were staging protests.[10] The New York project found itself in the uncomfortable position (to which it would become all too well accustomed) of being under the scrutiny of Congress and attack by its own unionized employees. Those employees included supervisor of the Children's Unit Jack Rennick, who was active in the Workers Alliance.[11]

Other events added to the tension. The war in Spain had mobilized Popular Front support. A sit-down strike in Flint, Michigan, in February had rallied labor. During the run of *Revolt*, workers at the "Little Steel" plants of the Midwest went on strike. At Republic Steel, workers trying to set up a picket line under the Steel Workers Organizing Committee were fired on by the Chicago police. Ten people were killed, seven shot in the back, as police fired on, beat up, and teargassed the crowd. Footage of the action would be shown at congressional hearings conducted by Senator Robert LaFollette that began July 2, 1937.

It was at this politically tense juncture that *The Revolt of the Beavers* opened, acknowledged by an FTP brief prepared for the House Committee on Un-American Activities as "the only Federal Theatre Project play at which the direct charge of 'communistic' has been leveled by anyone other than a Dies Committee witness."[12] The play's red tinge was not simply in subject matter, however. Writers, directors, technicians, and numerous cast members had come from New York's vibrant leftist theatre world.[13] Saul and Lantz had both been playwrights for the Workers Laboratory Theatre, and cast member Perry Bruskin had performed with the WLT's mobile Shock Troupes, which staged skits and short theatre at union events.[14] *Revolt*'s co-director Peter Hyun had become the WLT's Evening Troupe manager in 1934. With restructuring advice from playwright John Howard Lawson, WLT changed its name in 1935 to the Theatre of Action and its focus to full-length plays; after a financially disastrous season it was incorporated almost wholesale into the FTP as the One-Act Experimental Theatre, and from there diffused.[15]

Possibly named after a recent Artef Theatre (Arbeiter Teater Verband) production *The Revolt of the Reapers*, which also showcased actor and future director Jules Dassin, *The Revolt of the Beavers* was initially to be directed by Group Theatre member Elia Kazan.[16] Kazan temporarily joined the Children's Theatre to direct the play and led rehearsals in November. For reasons that are not known, Kazan bowed out and was replaced by fellow Group Theatre veteran Lewis Leverett (whom Kazan would years later denounce as a Communist to the House Committee on Un-American Activities).[17] Samuel Leve, who would later work with Orson Welles's Mercury Theatre productions, designed the costumes.

By most accounts visually stunning, complex, and colorful, *Revolt* delighted the children in its audience.[18] "It was so imaginative, so different from any children's theatre at that time," actor John Randolph (who, credited as Mortimer Lippman, played one of the Chief's toughs) recalled years later in an interview. "It still to this day would be considered an extraordinary work . . . that was inventive and beautifully directed and beautifully acted by very good actors. . . . "[19] Action was scored to Oscar Waltzer's original music.[20] Beavers roller-skated in brightly colored costumes under a cartoonishly dominant Wheel.[21] *Revolt* played to full houses of adults and children. The children who saw the play gave vigorous approval. They cheered the Working Beavers and booed the bad beavers; they waited by the backstage door in order to pummel the actor who played the Chief. These cheers and boos and pummelings were not heard in the public outcry over the play's Communist content, but the *New York American* critic noted that audience children "voted it a grand time and the grownups found it passably amusing," adding that "If there is any underlying significance to the story . . . the children probably will not see it."[22]

But an FTP commissioned survey designed specifically to test whether audience children understood the class implications of the play or not discovered that they did see an underlying significance. The surveyed children had no difficulty articulating the play's meaning: "Don't be selfish"; "It doesn't pay to be mean"; "Not to try to [be] a boss over anyone else"; "To show how hard they worked. Also to show that they are just human [*sic*] as us"; and "To be kind to animals" were only a few of the responses conscious of the play's social implications. More oblique, perhaps, but no less interesting socially conscious responses included "How children were wanting to have the whole world be 9 years old and happy" and "The way the big people can act to make them look like children."[23]

If the children equated the play's Marxist and pro-labor political and social economies to the moral vision of "don't be selfish," negative adult public response to the play reads like another simple equation: pro-labor sentiments equal anti-American Communism.[24] This quite clear adult/child perceptual binary, mischaracterized yet anticipated by the FTP press release, lays out competing views of American labor as simple as the play's didacticism and locates them in a child morality situated against an adult politics.

Actions derive meaning from being understood within a narrative structure that both demands them and provides a contextualizing interpretive framework. Specific actions make sense in a larger narrative structure. If children understand class solidarity and resistance to oppression as "don't be selfish," they might also be able to see the morality of joining a union to change the balance of power in labor–management strife. If this is the case, then the very genre of the play, the fairy tale, makes the narrative of labor empowerment a defining cultural one and vastly amplifies the threat posed by the story of a group of beavers defeating an evil chief into an American cultural narrative that gives moral coherence and power to the working class.

The play grapples with a number of issues confronting public perception of labor and its struggles. While Beaverland is clearly a fantastical place, the events that structure the play coincide with familiar strike narratives of early-twentieth-century American labor struggles. Paul and Mary, whose ungrammatical language and ragged clothing mark them as members of the American working class, are, in the context of Beaverland, visiting beings from another world who are drawn into the struggle. It is the fact of their childlike acceptance of likeness with the beavers—whose labor struggles are unfamiliar to them but whose want coincides with their own—that enables the children to engage with the struggle on the side of the oppressed. As children, the two envision *The Revolt of the Beavers* not in abstract ideological terms, but in human emotional terms. "We're sad, and the beavers are sad, and we're for the beavers," says Mary.[25] Identification with the beavers, then, springs from the realization that the beavers have the same feelings the children experience.

From identification comes action. The Chief cracks down on the workers, and banishes Oakleaf, because the beavers have formed a Club for Sad Beavers to Get Glad. The WPA Children's Theatre Club was inaugurated at the opening of *The Revolt of the Beavers* when more than three hundred children were enrolled, according to a May 26, 1937, report. Numerous letters from the study conducted into children's responses mention the children's delight at being club members.[26] Children who were members of the Federal Theatre Project's Children's Theatre club could thus easily translate what is in the play a thin cover for a union or workingman's club for adults into the kind of club that gave them membership in the FTP's children's theatre.

Historical representations of working-class and laboring children long associated with labor and child labor reform movements significantly expanded the idea of the protected child out from her protected middle- and upper-class space. The new social value of the child in part constructed by the labor movement's focus on children in labor issues created an explosive site where child and the labor movement meet. The resonance of *The Revolt of the Beavers* in 1930s culture, the manner in which it participates in a complex and often contradictory leftist cultural politics, has as much to do with shifts in the symbolic value of the child as with the political content of the play in its own historical moment. While early scholarship by Lorraine Brown, Jane DeHart Mathews, and others posits *Revolt* as a potent example of the FTP's naïveté about the American political tenor and the questionable freedom of government theatre to explore political and social issues, the representations of children within labor and child labor reform movements illuminate not only *The Revolt of the Beavers* controversy, but the increasing cultural power of the figure of the child. As childhood was increasingly seen as a separate and protected state regardless of class and ethnicity, the values and rights of middle- and upper-class children were subsequently extended to children whose state of childhood had previously been marked by ethnicity and class. In the twentieth century, working-class, working, and immigrant children were recast as children rather than little workers and immigrants. This universalization of childhood to include those who had been culturally stigmatized by class, ethnicity, and immigrant status—this removal of the taint of heritage—affected American determinations of class and a person's right to citizenship and democratic possibilities.

The Revolt of the Beavers opens with Mary and Paul, looking for wood in a vacant lot near a city.[27] The children are arguing about whether they can believe an earlier assertion by their teacher that beavers can talk. The first words of the play are Paul's scoffing, "I don't care if he is a teacher—I don't believe it!" Mary defends the teacher with the undeniable logic that "My father says he's smart enough to be a Professor—and you gotta be very smart to be a Professor." Paul scoffs, "Yeah! He thinks just because we're nine years old he can tell us fairy tales! Well, I don't like 'em—and I don't believe 'em!" As stage directions call for him to pick up a piece of wood, go down on one knee, and take aim at an imaginary enemy, Paul continues, "I like real stories about cops and robbers—and cowboys and Indians—Where they go bang! bang! bang!"[28]

Paul equates childhood with being lied to, and fairy stories with the deceptions practiced upon children. The children's argument, ostensibly about the reality of fairy tales, questions the relationships between fantasy and reality and between adults and children. It poses the world of dreaming against the world of action and questions the efficacy of opposing the two. Furthermore, it posits children as capable of imposing their will upon their world, of ordering a system of belief as opposed to being passive recipients of an adult weltanschauung—or the blank page on which the social subject is written. Even Mary's acceptance of the teacher's ideas, because she must argue for it against Paul, constitutes a choice.

Gendered desires regarding truth and fiction set the terms by which the play asks to be read. Mary wishes for the teacher to be truthful and the tale to be true. When Paul refuses to believe in the talking beavers, Mary says, "Just the same—I bet you wish you had a wishing stone and could have three wishes." Paul picks up a stone and wishes upon it (without effect) to

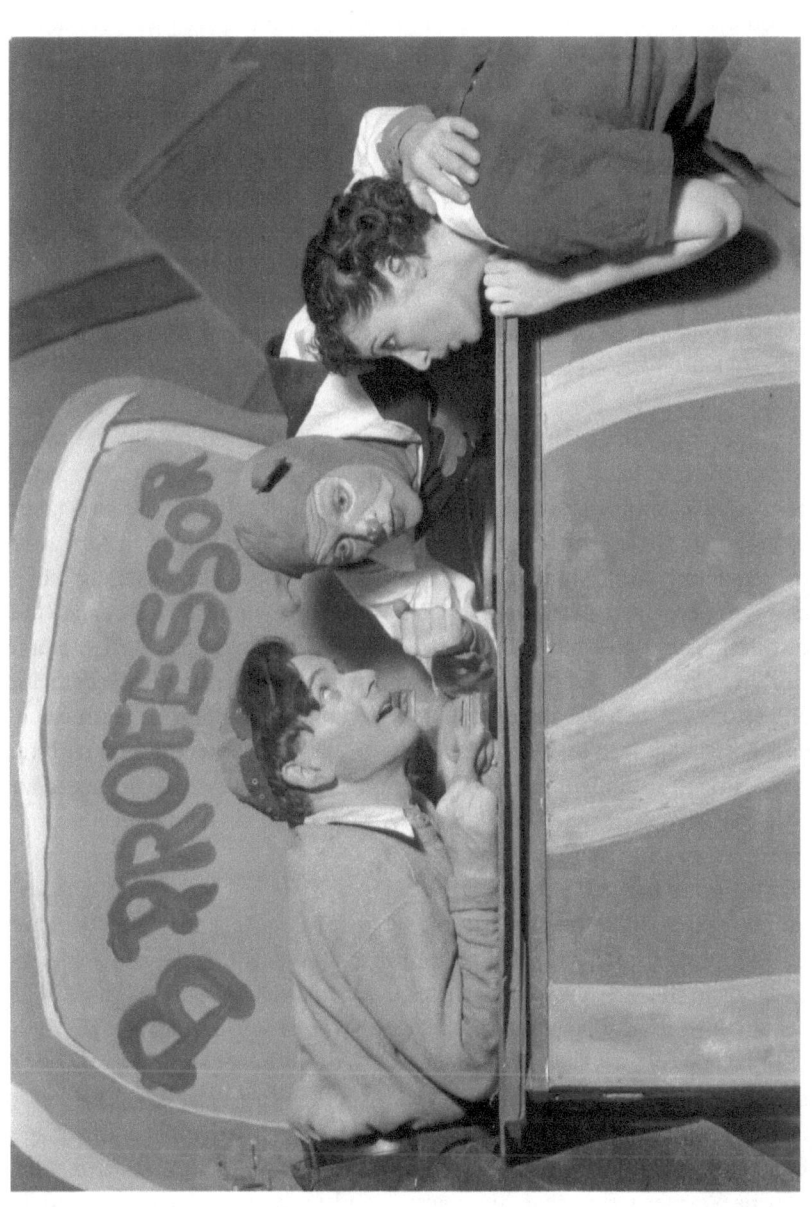

FIGURE 5. Paul, Professor Beaver, and Mary lean their heads together. *Revolt of the Beavers* (New York City, New York). George Mason University. Fenwick Library. Special Collections and Archives

demonstrate the impossibility of such magic, but Mary refuses to give up on the powerful allure of wish fulfillment. "Well if I had a real wishing stone, I would never be sad—'cause first I would wish for a big piece of chocolate—and then I would wish my father got a job—" At which point, Paul interrupts:

> You know what I would wish for? A blue sweater and a pair of skates. And d'y' know what else? I'd wish that everybody in the whole world was nine years old. Then I'd never be sad. 'Cause then I could go to the candy store and just imagine—Mr. Berger would be nine years old, and I would say, "Mr. Berger, I haven't got a penny—gimme a piece of candy, will ya?" And he'd give it to me! And then I would wish to be as free as the wind! So I could do whatever I want—Fly away and have a good time.[29]

The opening dialogue suggests that fairy tales, gendered female, are those which are told to small children too young to understand the difference between truth and fiction. Real stories, on the other hand, are also tales, but they are those which, according to Paul, narrate events of historical or contemporary social conflict. While Mary's lines emphasize the strength of a desire to perpetuate a belief that evidence does not support, Paul's create the distinctions between storytelling and childhood that the play will explore. Children are they, according to Paul, who cannot differentiate between truth and falsehood, between stories told to entertain that contain no truth value, and stories that lead to action, and embody societal norms through realistic reenactment. Paul's scoffing furthermore insists that fairy tales belong to an old order, that their signs, the signifiers of an old power—wishing stones and magic words—are now empty and hollow.[30]

If it turns out, indeed, that fairy tales—and the teacher's fantastic assertion—are true, then the play asks the audience to believe that fairy tales are not escapist fantasies woven for children too innocent of the real world to understand the difference between truth and tale-telling. Through his disbelief and obvious distance from the "reality" his real stories portray, Paul both critiques the verisimilitude in which he places his belief and raises the idea that stories that do not describe the reality of life can also be real. This argument questions whether what is is what will be and whether belief can shape the material conditions of subjective reality. In *From the Beast to the Blonde*, Marina Warner writes that "the marvels and prodigies . . . all the wonders that create the atmosphere of the fairy tale disrupt the apprehensible world in order to open spaces for dreaming alternatives."[31] If *The Revolt of the Beavers* is a fairy tale, then a shift in consciousness might be in order.

Publicity for and responses to the play blurred genre distinctions; called a fable, a fantasy, and a fairy tale, *Revolt* partakes of all three. The fantastic is evident in its whimsical staging and in the character of Windy, with his three buttons for winds, "hot," "cold," and "medium." Its animal characters bearing human characteristics and its overt didacticism characterize it as the fable. And as a quest tale in which the clever peasant hero vanquishes the evil villain, even if the quest is for "a good time," *Revolt* argues for fairy-tale status.

Defenses of the play as appropriate for children defined it as a fairy tale. In the Dies Committee brief, a child's magazine editor is cited to deny the play's subversive political character:

> Mrs Alice K. Pollitzer, now on the editorial staff of "Story Parade," a publication sponsored by the Association for Arts in Childhood, saw *Revolt of the Beavers* and said: "The play is, in my opinion, no more Communistic than Christian. Does anyone want to teach children that entrenched greed is desirable? The moral of this play is just that . . . entrenched greed and cruelty are not desirable. That is the theme of many of the old, classical, accepted fairy tales for children. . . ."[32]

Pollitzer's defense rests on the implicit understanding that fairy tales are open-ended and contain multiple readings; it privileges a universal moral lesson concerning the exigencies of historically located motifs, plot, and narrative structure. Pollitzer does not deny the Communist content—in fact, she compares it to the heavy Christian didacticism of so many nineteenth-century fairy tales for children—but suggests that rather than making a revolutionary class struggle morally comprehensible, a transhistorical moral lesson situating Communism as opposition to greed somehow wipes out the politics. Her comments suggest that the fairy tale has historically served to impart socially sanctioned values and norms, to socialize children; they imply that locating *The Revolt of the Beavers* within the sanctuary of genre diffuses any possible political message.

In her defense of the play in her autobiography, Flanagan also identifies the play as a fairy tale:

> In almost all fairy tales the poor child, the Cinderella, the Jack-and-the-Beanstalk, is abused by the selfish stepmother or the bad giant; always the hero or heroine triumphs in the end. It seemed to me natural that in the fairy-tale pattern brought up to date the beavers had a bad beaver king whom they drove out so that all the beavers could eat ice cream, play, and be nine years old.[33]

Defending the play on the basis of its genre, Flanagan allegorizes the play's overtly Marxist class dynamics as feudal European social hierarchies. She and Pollitzer both attempt a cleansing by genre. Indeed, the press release to the *Daily Worker* for the play quoted at the beginning of this chapter clearly targets the lessons of fables to adult audiences, noting, "Although intended for children, it is an Aesop's fable that adults will appreciate." The defense and press release together suggest that as a genre, the fairy tale is considered more appropriate for children than the fable or fantasy.

The idea that fairy tales speak to children rests on an "innocent" childhood imagination dependent upon an absence of political sensibility. This idea is immersed in the cultural production of ideal childhood as an inviolate space unmarked not only by adult politics, but by commerce, consumerism.[34] Childhood itself is a fairy-tale world, one separate and fused; this equation invests the fairy-tale genre with innocence and childhood with creativity and a marked protection from being capable of reading the adult world and thus being drawn into it. Children cannot read symbolically other than on moral lines admissible to the state of childhood. As symbol, childhood becomes extraordinarily powerful, absolutely inviolate, and creatively unbounded. As a genre, the fairy tale absorbs the truth value associated with childhood innocence.

As a play whose overt Communism attempts an explicit politicization of children, as opposed to the classical, established narratives and motifs whose historicity both denies their cultural immediacy and strengthens their appeal as universalized moral lessons, *The Revolt of the Beavers* hammers at the boundaries of childhood and adulthood; clearly it was characterized to the children as innocent of politics, though slyly marking those politics for adults. Indeed, in an earlier version of the play, as Paul argues with her about the reality of fairy tales, Mary retorts, "The teacher once told me that some real stories are so full of lies that they're fairy tales, and some fairy tales are so full of truth that they're just like real stories."[35]

Posed against the mimicry of Paul's use of the piece of wood as an imaginary firing arm, the optative becomes the mood for action that creates change. As the dialogue concerning the wishing stone suggests, it is as a framework for dreaming that the fairy tale enables change; Paul, seemingly the rebel against an established mode of tale-telling for children, is actually the conformist to a world of narrative deception through his belief in cops and robbers.

Folk tales cease to circulate and fairy tales lose their vexatious qualities when the relationships they draw lose any but the most distant symbolic connection with socioeconomic realities. The lines of *The Revolt of the Beavers* controversy, particularly as an updated fairy tale, are drawn in its connection between the fantastical, utopian longings, and the contemporary political and social conditions, of the oppressed. But they are also drawn in the disjuncture between the mythical, universalized "folk" voice of classical and many new fairy tales and the contemporary (and so rendered by such movies as *Dead End*) voices of its politicized children. And hence, they are drawn in the disjuncture between literary or dramatic production that is comfortably subversive and one that is deliberately revolutionary. These lines are further drawn by the connection between the fantastical and utopian longings of a clearly defined political system—in short, by the very lack of creativity of its fantasy, by its rote Marxism. The frustrated disdain of Atkinson's review stems in part from the play's singularly unoriginal political stance—not from the radicalism of the politics, but from the conservatism of its fantasy, the funneling of a free-flowing creative imagination into a channeled political course.[36]

Theorist Jack Zipes has written about the proliferation of leftist fairy tales for children in the Weimer Republic, noting that they—and new writings in general—were banned during the Nazi era that privileged old fairy tales as Aryan relics. A number of individuals involved in New York's leftist theatre were German emigrés; whether or not the ideas these emigrés brought influenced Saul and Lantz in the writing of *Revolt*, the theatre trends of the Weimer Republic would have circulated within the New York leftist theatre scene.[37]

The Revolt of the Beavers takes part in a German tradition of progressives writing proletarian fairy tales with utopian implications. "The proletarian fairy tales were intended to compel young readers to think about their impoverished living conditions and the potential they had to change them through political action," writes Zipes. "That is, they were innovative exercises in raising political consciousness, and the style and content of the tales differed greatly, although there was a common denominator: the principle of hope. The purpose of all of the writers was to instill a sense of hope that a new, more egalitarian society could be realized if people recognized who the true enemy was—namely capitalism in various disguised forms—and learned to work together to defeat that enemy."[38]

The uneasy location of the play itself, within the genre that its opening dialogue and action asserts is false, and the gendered disavowal of the fairy tale's truth, questions childhood's separate status even as it mocks realism and the authority of an experienced past to determine the future. While Paul trumpets his pragmatic realism, Mary stubbornly argues against him, first on the presumption that the teller deserves recognition as an authority, but then, more importantly, that the fairy tale will fulfill her desires.[39]

The children's urban street patois was a familiar one to the play's adult audience of every neighborhood from its prominent class coding in the popular gangster films of the early thirties. Its particular diction and syntax was the aural representation of the tenement that in *The Revolt of the Beavers* loomed as a painted set piece behind the actors introduced in a vacant lot. In plays ranging from Elmer Rice's *Street Scene* to Arthur Arent's Living Newspaper *One-Third of a Nation* to Sydney Kingsley's *Dead End,* and in novels describing a proletarian childhood of which Michael Gold's *Jews Without Money* and Henry Roth's *Call It Sleep* are perhaps best known, the tenement represents both a stunning American indifference to the humanity of its workforce as well as the ethnic complexity and diversity of the urban working class. In 1921, Gold had written in "Towards Proletarian Art" in the *Liberator:*

> I was born in a tenement. That tall, sombre mass, holding its freight of obscure human destinies, is the pattern in which my being has been cast. It was in a tenement that I first heard the sad music of humanity rise to the stars. . . . When I think it is the tenement thinking. When I hope it is the tenement hoping. I am not an individual; I am all that the tenement group poured into me during those early years of my spiritual travail.[40]

As Denning notes, the novels of growing up in ethnic, working-class neighborhoods written during and after the Depression changed stories of the ethnic other from "exotic regionalism" to a "national tale of daughters of the earth and native sons." He writes:

> By the later decades of the twentieth century, the immigrant saga and the Great Migration had become a central part of American mythology, and the streets of the Lower East Side, Harlem, and Little Italy lovingly recreated in Hollywood films and television miniseries. The emergence of various symbolic ethnicities in popular culture and the ritual invocation of immigrant grandparents by politicians made Ellis Island as sacred as Plymouth Rock. By the time of Francis Coppola's *Godfather* trilogy and Don Bluth's animated epic of the Mousekowitzes, *An American Tail,* the story of the ghetto had become quintessentially American.[41]

The tenement makes its appearance as a looming cityscape behind the vacant lot of *The Revolt of the Beavers'* opening scene, but the play participates in the dramatic and literary exploration of the tenement world both in its often subtle invocation of ethnicity and in its visual analogy of cityscape and industrial wheel.[42]

That world received great attention as the numbingly brutal setting of Kingsley's *Dead End*.[43] Kingsley's play contextualizes the ghetto formation against which *The Revolt of the Beavers* poses its workers' paradise and explains settings and rituals embodied in the FTP play. *Dead End* takes place in New York at the point where a street meets the East River, a location that gives its name both material and metaphorical connotations. A group of children swim in the river, described in the stage notes as "A brown river, mucky with floating refuse and offal. A hundred sewers vomit their guts into it." As background scenery, tenements and a single new and expensive apartment complex visually evoke class difference, an allegory of class that suggests the dynamism of urban class relations and draws the city itself into the conflict.

Dead End parallels two narratives. In the first, an out-of-work architect who has returned to the slums in which he was raised meets and in the end kills a childhood friend who got into trouble early and ended up a notorious gangster. In the second, a leader of the child gang that gathers at the wharf is sought by police after he wounds the father of a rich child the gang is teasing. Crippled by childhood rickets, architect Gimpty sits drawing every day at the wharf where the children play. A tall stranger hanging out at the wharf turns out to be notorious gangster "Babyface" Martin. Disguised by plastic surgery, Martin has returned to the tenement where he grew up with Gimpty to see his mother and his old childhood sweetheart. Against the story of Gimpty, the children's actions and language gain narrative coherence. Their taunts are vicious and their insults repetitive: their language can hold no dreams.

The parallels between adult and child plots are clarified in the dialogue between Gimpty and Griswald as Gimpty tries to persuade the wealthy man to drop the charges against the boy:

> GIMPTY: Yeah . . . Martin was a killer, he was bad, he deserved to die, true! But I knew him when we were kids. He had a lot of fine stuff. He was strong. He had courage. He was a born leader. He even had a sense of fair play. But living in the streets kept making him bad. . . . Then he was sent to reform school. Well, they reformed him all right! They taught him the ropes. He came out tough and hard and mean, with all the tricks of the trade.
> GRISWALD: But I don't see what you're driving at.
> GIMPTY: I'm telling you! That's what you're sending this kid to.

If in the opening dialogue of *The Revolt of the Beavers* Mary imagines a world where children's wishes for good things come true, Paul describes a social structure wherein communal sharing and social equity derive from a child's sense of fairness. But it is a short step from demanding candy to the criminal behavior of just taking it and, as Gimpty's assessment of Babyface indicates, a child's sense of fair play is corrupted by an unfair world. Paul's early preference for "real life stories" already asserts for him the urban class identity familiar to thirties' audiences through *Dead End* and cheap pulp fiction. In a decade that privileged collective action, the gangster was, paradoxically, a prized figure of rugged individualism. As noted in *From Caste to Class*, the gangster "was a Darwinian product of his environment . . . as well as a Romantic hero in conflict with it." The gangster "must be destroyed, but, metaphorically more important, so must the environment that produced him."[44] Paul's penchant for guns, for cops and robbers and cowboys and Indians, signals not so much a boy's sense of adventure in social conflict as the seeds of social rebellion. If as a boy named Paul he is unmarked by class or ethnicity (though he is visually marked by both class and ethnicity in the FTP production), his presence in the vacant lot gathering wood, a tenement activity shown in both *Jews Without Money* and *Dead End*, suggests his dangerous working-class potential. He is further marked after the release of *Dead End* by his streetwise New York syntax.

After Paul and Mary's argument, they are joined in the woodlot by Pinky, Skeeball, and Sally, three other children who are pushing a baby carriage in which to put wood.[45] After they leave, Paul says, "Gee, poor Skeeball—he never has time to play." Mary replies, "Yeah, they make me feel awfully sad." Mary quickly falls asleep, and once he realizes she isn't listening, Paul says:

> I wonder could there be a real fairy tale, like the teacher said. Huh! Just imagine! A beaver comin' out of the woods. Gee! I'd like to see that—If it was really true. That would be some fun. A real fairy tale. Gee!

And then he too falls asleep.

As music signals the segue between reality and dream, a skating beaver rolls onto the stage and awakens Paul, who in turn awakens Mary just as the beaver has skated out of sight: "Mary! Mary! Get up! I just saw a beaver—a real live beaver—with skates and a blue sweater and pants!" Mary replies, "Gee! I wish I'd have seen him!" and Paul answers, "Pants and skates and a blue sweater—and I bet he could talk! If he skates that means he can talk, doesn't it, Mary?" Mary's answer knows not the meaning of equivocation: "Sure! I told you they can talk!"

Allegory as dream is as old as *The Dream of the Rood*. But in this post-Freudian narrative unfolding as the processes of a dream, *The Revolt of the Beavers* invites the adult viewer to supply the analogic structure of dream and interpretation. It asks the audience member to perform the analyst's task of undoing the dream in order to recover its meaning. Freud's whole understanding of children's dreams as simple wish fulfillment is here playfully invoked to contrast the simplicity of the children's tale, and the obvious wish fulfillment embodied by the blue-sweatered roller-skating beaver, with the more complex configuration of the adult dreaming process in which, for Freud, that which the dream is about is not what the dream is about.[46] Latent content is not manifest content. As with the *Wizard of Oz* two years later, a Freudian understanding of dream processes structures a double reading of the *Revolt*'s narrative, a double reading that reaffirms the separation between childhood and adulthood yet, by providing for adult pleasure in the rich spectacle of its simple wish fulfillment, concurrently denies it.

Drawing on the narrative strategies of Freudian dream theory, political allegory, and the fairy tale, *The Revolt of the Beavers* constructs for a child audience an overarching narrative through which to read class and political issues, even as it teases adults with fantasized political and social implications. In following a tradition of socialist and Communist proletarian writing for children in Weimer Republic Germany, in genre and mood *Revolt* stood apart from the standard aesthetics of American proletarian theatre and literature. Left-wing playwrights and novelists concerned with theorizing and producing a form and content that expressed their politicized radicalism and their solidarity with the working class had settled on realism to describe the overt message of a worker's rise to class consciousness. In its depiction of character and its plot alike, *The Revolt of the Beavers* closely follows the model of American leftist theatre, a model that its dream structure to some extent critiques.[47]

As Paul is excitedly telling Mary about his vision of the roller-skating, blue-sweatered beaver, they are greeted by the voice of and then find themselves in the personified presence of the wind. To "wind effect and whistling," Windy arrives on stage and announces, "Boy, am I glad. This is my first rest in a long time."[48] When Paul asks Windy if he can be as free as the wind, Windy replies,

> You can't do that! You know what would happen if you did whatever you wanted? They might lock you up in jail—and then could you fly away, like me? No! And why? Because you ain't the wind. There's only one wind—and that's me. (points to vest) Does that prove it? And that's what I came to tell you. You can't do that.

Windy, who was played by the old vaudevillian Charles Willett, escapes the economic and social systems of which his constant travels have made him aware. He controls the weather and by so doing stabilizes potentially catastrophic events. Seemingly the *deus ex machina* in other plays, Windy in *Revolt* merely references his capabilities, though the "machinery" that brings him to the stage makes his role obvious. In *Revolt*, however, he will be conspicuously absent until the conflict is over.

When the children beg him to take them away, Windy agrees to take them to the woods and asks them if they want a hot, a cold, or a medium wind, and the children choose medium. Once they get to the woods, they immediately find their choice of the middle satirized by Professor Beaver, whom they find sleeping on a pedestal in the middle of the woods. When the children awaken the Professor, he sleepily tells them that if they are good beavers and go away, he'll sing them a song. "Once upon a time," he begins. "Once upon a time":

> My favorite instrument is the fife / But I'm also fond of the fiddle
> I sit on the left and I sit on the right / But my favorite spot is the middle
> I like to get up in the early dawn, / I'm fond of the morning light
> There's nothing I like as much as the morn / But the beautiful beautiful
> night—the night. . . . [49]

The Professor might not know in verse which way to go, but as soon as he realizes Paul and Mary are human beings, he warns, "Get out of Beaverland! You'd better get out. Right away!" When the children ask why, he says, "Because there's a lot of trouble in Beaverland and you might get right in the middle of the trouble!"[50]

The children's choice of a middle wind lands them right in the middle of trouble as certainly as the Professor's inability to choose a side and commit himself to action will not keep him out of it. Symbolizing a vacillating, weak intellectual class, the Professor is nonetheless powerful, even if he doesn't recognize his power. He is, he informs the children, smarter than a teacher and "the biggest Professor in Beaverland. The best storyteller too." Upholding the Marxist dictum that capitalism is inimical to the creation of art (storytelling), the Chief has told the Professor to keep out of Beaverland because the Chief "doesn't like stories and he hates songs. He said I was always bothering the beavers with my stories. . . . "[51] Now he might as well be dumb, the Professor confides: his banishment has made him very sad. The children also discover that the Chief has banished and made sad an entire group of beavers, the Barkless Beavers; the Chief "bent them over and chased them out of Beaverland." The Barkless Beavers "have nothing to eat, no place to go—and they're always crying."[52]

FIGURE 6. Professor Beaver tells a story. *Revolt of the Beavers* (New York City, New York). George Mason University. Fenwick Library. Special Collections and Archives

The valiant Oakleaf pops out of a rabbit hole and provides the beaver-of-action counterpart to the Professor's ivory-tower-ostrich act. Oakleaf identifies the source of the mysterious, threatening whistling that has just made itself heard [or something to that effect] as the toughest beavers in the woods, the Chief's gang, known as the Whistling Club. Hearing Huff, Ruff, Tuff, and Gruff of the Whistling Club coming, the children and Professor hide in the rabbit hole while Oakleaf disguises himself as a toadstool. After the toughs leave, Oakleaf tells his story. "One night, I borrowed the Chief's skates—but I forgot to tell him about it. When he found out he got very mad and called me a 'skate-stealer'—and he said, 'Why didn't you ask me?' So I asked him." "What did he say?" Paul asks. Oakleaf answers:

> No! You know, Paul, all the beavers are sad, very sad—and me, too—so I got mad and said, "Why don't we make a club for sad beavers to get glad?" So all the beavers said, "Yaaaaaaaaaay!" But when the Chief heard about it he said, "Oakleaf, you're trying to bust up Beaverland—Get out and never come back! Not even in a million years!" And you know what he told the whistling clubs? "If you catch him, hit him until he cries!" And why? Why? Just because I didn't want the Beavers to be sad!

To this, the Professor responds, "Oakleaf, I told you a million times not to do anything that'll make the chief mad! If you'll leave him alone and just act nice, he'll become a good chief." Oakleaf asks, "Then why did the chief make you sad? No matter how good the beavers are, he makes them sadder and sadder every single day."[53]

The word "sad" has by now covered a great deal of ground. The Professor is sad because he is banished; the Barkless Beavers are sad because they are not only banished but bent over and without work; the Working Beavers are sad because they are made to work on the Wheel without any bark to eat. With its rhyming opposite glad, sad provides an easily understandable analogy to the opposition of liberated to oppressed and locates the condition of oppression as an emotional response to material conditions. The beavers have already named their suffering with the same word; all that remains is for them to discover that if united they can similarly share in gladness.

Paul decides to go punch the Chief in the nose and the children persuade the Professor to accompany them, though he pleads, "But no fights. Let me do something! I'll tell the Chief a story—not a plain story but a story with a moral, to show him how mean he is—and then he'll turn into a good Chief, and he'll make the beavers glad and let Oakleaf come back into Beaverland."[54]

As the curtain rises on the second act, Working Beavers are engaged on the "Busy Busy," the giant wheel that dominates the set. The beavers sing,

> Busy, busy busy, busy, / strip strip strip, strip
> busy busy, busy busy / clip, clip, clip clip . . .
> If you ask us why we're giving/our attention to the bark
> that's how beavers made their living / since the day they left the Ark. . . .
> But the Chief of all the beavers / he gets all the bark we make.
> All he does is pull the levers / while we work until we ache. . . .

The Chief whistles for lunchtime as an elaborate ceremony of lunch is prepared around him. First his table is brought out, then his napkin and silverware, and finally his two-course lunch is both passed down the line of his gang to him and taken back up the line from him. As he eats, one of the beavers recites the poem he has composed about the Working Beavers' hunger:

> I used to love my lunchtime / I used to sit and munch
> a piece of bark at lunchtime / I'd crunch and crunch and crunch
> But now I don't like lunchtime / I have no bark to crunch
> and what's the good of lunchtime / If you haven't got no lunch?[55]

The Chief jumps behind a chair when the Professor calls out that he has two human beings with him. "Are they big or are they little?" he asks. "They're nine years old!" answers the Professor. Stage directions for the Chief note that he is relieved and comes out from behind the chair. To impress Paul and Mary, the Chief makes his Scaly Brothers do drills as he shows them his roller skates and blue sweater. Informing them that he is the "fanciest and smartest" beaver in Beaverland, the Chief invites them to ask him questions.[56]

After several questions, Paul says, "All right, I'll ask you. What's the idea of making all the beavers so sad?" The Chief says, "What d'ya mean, I make them sad." The Chief at this point tells them to stick to questions about Beaverland, but Paul and Mary ask why the beavers can't pull the levers and keep the bark. "Then they'd own the Wheel and the bark! And it's my wheel and my bark! What d'ya mean asking me that! I'm getting sore! Y'better ask me something else!"

In a corresponding temper, Paul asks him why his belly is so fat while the beavers are so skinny. In an amusing response, the Chief responds without irritation, "My whole family has fat bellies. (puzzled) Don't y'like it?"[57] The meeting just goes downhill from there to the point where when the Professor tells his story—which is about Oakleaf—the Chief becomes enraged and, as Huff holds Paul's arms, punches him three times on the nose. Then the Chief tells the Scaly Brothers to "hit 'em all, even the girl." When he tells the brothers to kick them out of Beaverland after beating the trio up, one of the Working Beavers warns the Chief that they too are getting sore. At that, the Chief rages,

> So now you're sore, huh! How would you like it if the Barkless Beavers worked on the Wheel instead of you—and you were the Barkless Beavers, walking around all bent over in the cold woods. Hey caw-caw birds! Go tell the Barkless Beavers to come to Beaverland right away![58]

The curtain drops as the frightened beavers resume their work on the Wheel. As this scene with the Chief suggests, he embodies not only the fat-cat capitalist, but a certain big-bellied fascist leader. The Chief's thuggish nickname, his fat belly, his paramilitary style and that of his thugs, and his extraordinarily violent suppression of workers' rights evoke fascism through Mussolini's person, his *fasci*, and his regime's notorious brutality against Italy's leftist and worker's groups. And by so embodying both capitalism and fascism, the Chief makes the two inseparable.

As the second act begins, angry and bellicose, the Working Beavers are prepared to fight to keep the Barkless Beavers from taking their jobs. Even an exhausted Professor comes back to warn against the Barkless Beavers. Again, the intellectual class is criticized for its inability to use its educational advantage to help the working classes, as the Professor is fully supporting beaver-on-beaver violence to keep the Barkless Beavers out. When the Barkless Beavers arrive, Paul and Mary realize from their sad song that they are the first beavers the children saw in Beaverland. As the Working Beavers remind each other to hit the Barkless Beavers hard, Mary faces the group and insists, "You can't hit them. They look too sad." Paul also steps away, but asks Mary, "Hey Mary, didn't we promise Oakleaf we would help the beavers?" A Working Beaver interrupts, "If we let them into Beaverland—then we'll be the Barkless Beavers, walking around bent over, always crying." Oakleaf argues, "I got a scheme! They deserve to be in our Club for Sad Beavers to Get Glad."[59] As members of the club, he tells the Barkless Beavers, "Y'gotta tell the Chief you ain't gonna work on the Wheel unless all of us work on it, too." The beavers further insist that their conditions will include allowing Oakleaf, the Professor, and Paul and Mary back into Beaverland.[60]

The Chief and his men appear and the Barkless Beavers refuse to march into Beaverland as Paul blurts out that they are all members of Oakleaf's club. The Chief tells his gang to kill Oakleaf and then, when the Barkless Beavers refuse to resume their status, the Chief says, "So you Barkless Beavers are getting brave, too? Talking behind my back?" "Yeah, we ain't bent over no more," says a Barkless. "We're going to stick together with the beavers in our club!" The Chief cries, "Scaly Brothers! Chase them out of Beaverland and let them be the Barkless Beavers for a billion years! No! Forever!" As the Working Beavers go to the Barkless Beavers' aid, the Chief keeps the two groups separate with the various factions of his gang.[61] He has the gang grab Paul and Mary and the Professor and march the Working Beavers back into Beaverland, saying:

> And the rest of you beavers, get into Beaverland. And from now on, a new rule! Any beaver that gets wise, I'm gonna lock him in a cave for a long time—maybe forever! And you human beings and Professor, I'm gonna teach you the biggest lesson there is! And the lesson is—For a hundred years—you're gonna get killed every day starting tomorrow—lunchtime!

Mary wails, "I don't wanna be killed! I came to Beaverland to have a good time!"

Scene three opens with Paul, Mary, and the Professor tied to a stake, surrounded by sleeping members of the Chief's gang; it ends with the Chief and his gang defeated. The Chief sets his men on the beavers, who respond with Zippo guns, slingshots, and bean shooters. When Huff fires a "bango gun" to terrific effect, the Chief calls out, "Gee whiz! It went off by accident. Hey, Huff, take it away. It's dangerous. Y'want someone to get hurt?" The fighting and noise resumes, according to stage directions, with even the Professor shooting a pea shooter into the Chief's eye. Oakleaf offers the Chief a negotiated settlement: if he gives up, he won't get bent over. But the Chief renews his efforts and Oakleaf calls in the Barkless Beavers, who swarm over a platform at his call. The gang is soon overcome and Oakleaf and the Chief fight hand to hand until the Chief is overcome. Then the whole gang and the Chief are passed down a line and kicked so they bend over. As the beavers celebrate, Windy arrives to take the children home. But Mary pleads, "We want to have some fun first, Windy." He answers, "O.K. Let's have a good time, first then I'll blow up a big medium hurricane and blow you home."[62]

The play ends with the beavers' "Victory Song":

> ... To all the beaver's [sic] now belong
> All of Beaverland
> ... There's bark for every beaver
> Who swings a cleaver (At this point, the leading players step forward in a
>   line)

> Or pulls a lever
> There's not a Barkless Beaver
> In all of Beaverland (repeat)
> So hear our voices singing
> With joy they're ringing (and as the cast moves forward, "with dignity" to the footlights)
> This message bringing
> To all the world we're singing
> About our beaver's Beaverland

The song would seem to end with all beavers holding hands together, equally spaced in a line on the stage. As all are equal, all share in the dignity of communal work that generates benefits for all in a Beaverland without a controlling Chief. But this joyous situation is not for Beaverland alone. The beavers bring their message to the world.

The Revolt of the Beavers provides a particular historic moment through which the changing social power of the symbolic child can be assessed. The play's heavy-handed attempt to explicitly link children's theatre to adult political issues is not so much failed leftist theatre as a drama of the emerging possibilities posed by a universalized and protected child extended to the working class, the poor, and the ethnically marked immigrant. In the public response to *The Revolt of the Beavers*, economic and political structures are conflated with issues of nationalism and citizenship, while labor's claims of legitimacy within the American capitalist economy are encoded as threats to the American system of government and "way of life." The play does construct an assault on the American system's way of life—though not in terms of its allegorical communism.

The controversy surrounding *The Revolt of the Beavers* reflects this struggle for the loyalties of the middle class and suggests the threatening power of the Popular Front alliances of disparate workers, union leaders, and artists that succeeded politically and artistically in the early and mid-thirties; it furthermore suggests that it was in ethnic and working-class cultural formations that radicalism remained powerful.

As Atkinson's review, the deputy police commissioner's letter, and later the House Committee on Un-American Activities' response make clear, the contemporary public reading of the play is one in which a dialectic of Communist class warfare erases both the labor narrative and the moral/ethical struggle the children in the audience clearly recognized. This public reading was not, of course, monolithic. A *New York Post* article published June 2, 1937, spoofed the deputy police commissioner's response; tongue firmly planted in cheek, reporter Earl Wilson wrote:

As if by coincidence, the Boy Scouts of America said they would launch an investigation. They want to be sure that there is no reflection upon the carefully-nurtured principles of scoutcraft in the beavers revolution, they said. If the beavers were to give the Scouts a different view of citizenship than they already have, it would be very dangerous and menacing to the welfare of the country, they pointed out, firmly.[63]

In its playful language and juxtaposition of reality and fantasy, Wilson's article satirizes the dull literalism of the commissioner's criticism. By imagining that Boy Scouts would launch an investigation on the premise that new ideas might shatter the edifice of their old, he satirizes as well its antidemocratic conservatism.

Nonetheless, the predominantly negative press reaction, the continued interest of the Dies Committee in the play, and the FTP reaction to the criticisms that were lodged illustrate a broad public rhetoric that adheres the laborer to the worker and to violent Communist revolution. The *Saturday Evening Post* reported on the existence of *The Revolt of the Beavers*, and the New York controversy, on June 26, 1937, weeks after the play had closed. Quoting from the Atkinson review, the *Post* writer continues,

> For the sake of the visitor from Mars, we explain that the Adelphi Theater is not in Moscow but on Fifty-fourth Street, New York, and that the Federal Theater Project is a division of Harry Hopkins' WPA, operated by the Federal Government under an Administration which uses the name Democratic, and paid for out of relief funds voted by Congress. It has produced a long series of undisguisedly revolutionary plays, with the knowledge of Mr. Hopkins and his superior, Mr. Roosevelt . . . The fact that the Reds had taken over the project has been published repeatedly.

The column continues with the description of a boy in France being stoned to death by a "gang" of children with the introduction "The children of France are not so unschooled in class hatred and the technique of revolution as American children are, as yet," and concludes:

> *The Revolt of the Beavers* might reach childish minds more effectively if it were to incorporate the stoning to death of a boy who had a bicycle. Beavers are remote to the young proletariat of New York, but they know a stone or a bicycle when they see one. Mrs. Flanagan and her playwrights still suffer a little from the rigidity of the Communist mind.[64]

When Hallie Flanagan testified before the Dies Committee, thirteen pages of her prepared brief dealt with *The Revolt of the Beavers* and attempted to vindicate the play largely through an explanation of the goals and achievements of the children's theatre in general. As the committee's interest and the tenor of Atkinson's review suggest, the play's class-consciousness was perceived by some, and publicly denounced, as anti–American democracy and pro–Soviet Union Communism. The public focus on Communism highlights the extent to which labor gains were suspected of being inherently antithetical not only to American capitalism, but to democracy and, indeed, to America itself. It further highlights an American fear of Soviet might. In the wake of the Depression and its seeming negation of all the promise capitalism had offered, the threat of the Soviet Union was indeed real. Not only was Communism a young idea, the Soviet Union, with its social engineering and its Five-Year Plans, appeared to be a system on the go, moving with an efficiency and a rhetoric of progress that had been touted by most boosters of every American main street as a particularly American energy.

A vibrant labor movement matched a threatening Soviet power that was characterized much as an earlier America had been. At the same time, intellectuals viewed contemporary America as much morally and spiritually exhausted as economically unsound. Richard Pells writes:

> At bottom, this urge to do more than merely restructure institutions reflected a profound loss of faith in the American Dream and an effort by intellectuals to discover some new value system that might fill the void. The United States seemed to be suffering from a decline of energy and morale, a fall from grace.... The nation, once so adventurous and expansive, was no longer living in a world of infinite possibilities. Biologically, economically, psychologically, it was running down. Free land had disappeared, natural resources were diminishing, population was falling, foreign markets were closing, technological progress had factored out the "human dimension."[65]

From the Southern Agrarians to such pragmatist philosophers as Sidney Hook and Richard Neibhur, writers and intellectuals turned to the idea of culture and community to imagine possibilities for a new America, a harmonious social order reborn of the chaos and confusion of the Depression.

In *Blackface, White Noise,* Michael Rogin locates the nineteenth-century popularity of fairy tales in the rise of German nationalisms, and characterizes the tales as one expression of an "effort to establish a national identity by recovering indigenous folk expressions." Arguing that minstrelsy functioned as a unifying cultural expression in a similar way as did the fairy tale in Germany, Rogin writes that "Nationalist folk expressions on both sides of the ocean mobilized the masses to overturn old, deferential, hierarchical orders."[66] Rogin's brief tracing of the nineteenth-century "fable of membership" in the middle-class production of oral tales handed down by nurses to children on one side of the Atlantic, and in the largely working-class racial subordination through racial mimicking of African Americans on the other, illustrates not so much a Herderian national soul in the recovery of "mythic modes of oral performance" but the "vehicles for new urban classes, legitimizing their right to represent a collective consciousness that could not come from aristocratic or church ties."[67]

In the 1930s in the United States, a cultural process of "folk" recovery similar to the German collection of fairy tales occurred as the widening social effects of the economic crisis created a sense of urgency about the project of national recovery. The values of Depression art displaced modernism's emphasis on stylistic innovation and artistic reinvention for a documentary aesthetics and the self-conscious social focus of proletarianism. American artists, musicians, writers, and scholars undertook a great documentary project. This project similarly sought in folk and indigenous expressions a lost origin of national unity that would serve to divorce a national history long and intimately wedded to a capitalism that had suddenly proven impotent. Like the German fairy tales, American indigenous expressions seemed to rise out of an oral history unlocated in time or in individual creative effort; they functioned as artistic expression and as unifying cultural force precisely in their anonymity and ability to perform historical, allegorical, and anthropological work. These projects include the documentary photography of the Farm Security Administration, the efforts by other federal arts projects to catalogue folktales and folk and ethnic music, and travelogues describing the lives of the impoverished, from Margaret Bourke-White and Erskine Caldwell's *Have You Seen Their Faces* to James Agee and Walker Evans's *Let Us Now Praise Famous Men*. They include the search for the "authentic" experience that led to such diverse behaviors as middle-class hoboing adventures and leftist adventures in proletarian culture. The Popular Front rhetoric of "the people" articulates this search for a national identity in "the folk."

The particular manner in which "the people" of Popular Front cultural production came to stand symbolically in relation to capitalism rests to some degree on American artistic responses to the particular historical nexus of the Depression, the progress of the Soviet Union, and the rise of Stalinism. It was an artistic assertion of a collective identity that came not from the structures of American capitalism but rather from a mythologized national identity located in community and communal relations. *The Revolt of the*

Beavers participates in the politics of this artistic movement perhaps less in its imagined Communist-styled worker's paradise than through its fairy-tale narrative and its evocation of Everychild as urban and working class.

If the fairy tale is a political expression, and as such resonates across the division of childhood from adulthood, by the end of the nineteenth and continuing into the twentieth century, its production had been for children's consumption and its political effect masked by the ideology of childhood's innocence. By observing the conventions of both adult political allegory and children's fairy tale, *The Revolt of the Beavers* lifted the mask of that ideology and its obscuration of the ever-present political. As the play did so, it violated the protected, innocent child; its politics were therefore subjected to the outrage accorded to its transgression.

With its villainous Chief and his thugs, its strike, and its chronicling of its characters' developing class consciousness, *The Revolt of the Beavers* brings a proletarian aesthetic to the stage. Though its dialogue avoids agitprop's humorless sloganeering and its structure is developed rather than episodic, in both theme and form the play is not just a fairy tale. Rennick's comment that "we should have called it Rumpelstiltskin" is well-taken, however, for if they had would the world have noticed the play's revolutionary character? Given the radical theatre background of its playwrights, and given Brooks Atkinson's interest in federal theatre and knowledge of the New York theatre world, the answer is probably yes. If working-class children had not been given such representational potency by labor reform movements, would the city have raised its voice about the revolutionary play played to New York's youngest working poor? This second question is less easy to answer.

In *The Revolt of the Beavers,* Paul and Mary are the inheritors of working-class poverty whose freedom to imagine and enact change within the dream of childhood produces revolution. At the back of the stage in the first scene of the play sits the abandoned seat and top of an old automobile, a factory-produced item so broken down that it has degenerated into its constituent parts. As capitalism's most potent symbol, as its most recognized triumph, the car, now abandoned, provides an apt symbol of the systemic breakdown of America's technologized, mechanized factory system. The Chief's looming wheel, the backdrop of the children's dream, is its analogue. Their occupation of its productive capabilities changes the world of which they dream and promises radical change for the nation whence they come. This powerful message was just the target the Dies Committee needed.

CHAPTER 3

"I LOOKED HIM RIGHT SQUARE IN THE EYE"

Being African American in *The Story of Little Black Sambo*

The following photo of three unsmiling African American puppeteers gazing down at three widely grinning black puppets represents the contradictory racial politics that plagued Federal Theatre Project Negro Units. While the image connotes African American control of theatrical representation, lines of control extended well beyond the stage and usually did not end in black hands. Though set up in 1936 following the suggestion of noted Harlem actor Rose McClendon, the Negro Units were often organized under white community sponsorship and therefore under white administrative and artistic control.[1] Separate units segregated black performers and backstage workers from other units and too often failed to offer an "alternative national Negro theatre" called for by prominent black cultural critics that would emphasize and cultivate racial pride in an African and African American heritage.[2] Even in the beginning, the failure of the FTP Negro Units to work toward this theatre is registered in a 1935 *Afro American* editorial:

> The illness of Rose McClendon, figurehead "director" of the project, leaves the entire administration up to whites, with eight of eleven executives of the production company of the other race. This condition has already been the subject of many protests by citizen's groups, who felt that capable colored theatre directors could be found if an effort were made.[3]

Instead of an African American director, the celebrated John Houseman–Orson Welles duo would take over leadership of the Harlem Negro Unit.

FIGURE 7. *Little Black Sambo (Washington, DC)*. George Mason University. Fenwick Library. Special Collections and Archives[4]

Indeed, from inception to final year of operation, when there were only ten remaining Negro Units, productions played to mixed audiences and followed scripts mostly written by whites.[5]

Productions in all cities contended with racial politics based on the political and social character of the particular African American and theatre communities and the relationship between local and regional FTP and WPA administrators and supervisors. Though varying circumstances shaped each unit's overall tenor, dictated in large part by production schedule and audience response, all of the units struggled against racism and the perpetuation of African American stereotypes that dominated white theatrical representations of blacks. And though plays consciously attempted to combat these stereotypes, they were mostly white social realism plays sympathetic to the idea of racial equality but largely ignorant about the realities of African American life. These plays used portrayals of blacks to push social justice agendas framed by white cultural experiences. A very few militantly leftist racial plays were produced by the FTP: *Stevedore*, written by George Sklar and Paul Peters, and two plays by African American playwrights written for the FTP, *Turpentine*, by J. Augustus Smith (who was African American and co-wrote with Peter Morell, who was white), and *Big White Fog*, by Theodore Ward. The Seattle Negro Unit was a marvel, creating and producing plays reflecting African America; the company performed *Natural Man*, a retelling of the John Henry folk tale, written and composed by unit members Theodore Brown and Howard Biggs, and members wrote and produced a highly praised *An Evening with Dunbar*, built around key poems and with original music by Biggs.[6] But of far greater number in the FTP repertoire were the minstrel-based comedies of the American popular stage.

The children's theatre stage seems to bear out this criticism of the Federal Theatre's racial politics. Rena Fraden notes in *Blueprints for a Black Federal Theatre* that "The Negro unit in Chicago would perform realistic plays about black life [for adults] and minstrel shows for children."[7] Many materials support this analysis. There were at least three versions of *Little Black Sambo* produced by federal theatre, two of which were for puppet shows; the Library of Congress archive holds a fourth script, an adaptation for marionette theatre by Edwine Noye Mitchell that was probably distributed by the Junior League but never produced by the FTP. Two versions of the Newark marionette theatre script by Robert Warfield that played October 4, 1937, are on file, as is a puppet version by Molka Reich that opened September 17, 1936, in Miami.[8] Scripts for a Miami production and an archived Junior League script linguistically match the visual racism and minstrel characterization of the Washington photo.[9] A production script for Seattle's *Brer Rabbit and the*

Tar Baby depicts a narrative steeped in minstrel caricature. Extant photos of the Cincinnati production of *Little Black Sambo* demonstrate that its black performers wore blackface.[10]

But the Chicago Negro Unit's version of *Little Black Sambo* as written by Charlotte Chorpenning and directed and scored by Shirley Graham reimagines the children's tale as an Africanized narrative of liberal self-actualization.[11] As written, the Chicago Sambo, like Chorpenning-scripted characters in Cincinnati, Seattle, and Philadelphia, is a poetic, responsible, clever boy. The Chorpenning–Graham adaptation, titled *Little Black Sambo* and produced by the Negro and Children's units that used African American actors, was staged intermittently at Chicago's Great Northern Theatre from August 29, 1938, to June 30, 1939. Chorpenning is also credited with the script used for a Cincinnati Children's Theatre production that opened November 5, 1938.[12] Similarly, a script and photo for the Newark production, performed by a puppet unit and not a Negro unit, indicates an unusual production that uses minstrel caricature to level a witty and provocative critique of American racism.

This chapter examines several federal productions based on Helen Bannerman's *The Story of Little Black Sambo* in the context of the American blackface minstrel tradition that pervades archived Federal Theatre materials for children and adults. I begin with an analysis of *Turpentine,* an adult play that opened at the Lafayette Theatre in June 1936 as an example of a Popular Front antiracism play whose social realist interest in the common worker and "the folk" interrogated racist caricature and whose expression of primitive lives and emotionally raw characters dovetailed uncomfortably closely with minstrel stereotypes. The chapter then turns to children's productions of *The Story of Little Black Sambo* and *Brer Rabbit and the Tar Baby* also rooted in a fascination with the expressive folk and thus the form of the folk play, to analyze these productions' complex and shifting norms of African American representation. Against the progressive Chicago and Newark productions, literary topoi of blackface minstrelsy in the Reich and Mitchell plays stage dysfunctional family relationships that provoke laughter at the danger to the small black child in the jungle.

The federally produced versions of *The Story of Little Black Sambo* offer a remarkable snapshot of American attitudes toward race. Within the context of materials that bear the marks of America's long tradition of racist caricature, Chicago and Newark federal theatre productions of *The Story of Little Black Sambo* register striking success in transforming America's most denigrating racial stereotype. In both the three-act extravaganza in Chicago and the obscure, one-act puppet play in Newark, the tale's central character is depicted as an assertive, quick-witted child who successfully overcomes his powerful assailants. Both the Chicago and Newark versions of *Little Black Sambo* focus on Sambo's capacity for fantasy to sever the name "Sambo" from its historical representational framework and insist on the universality of the title character's search for self-fulfillment. Graham's Chicago production linked the story to a reimagined Africanness, while the Newark production incorporates a popular American icon to claim the small boy who ventured into the jungles and outwitted the tigers as a symbol of racial pride.[13] Both productions overturn minstrel caricatures of African American children and families to emphasize loving, supporting relationships. By so valuing the black child, they participate in a Popular Front culture with political origins in anti-lynching and social origins in movements and organizations that broadly imagined an American "brotherhood" of class and racial equality.

"WHAT! NO PROPAGANDA?" exclaims a subhead in a glowing review of the Chicago production of *Little Black Sambo* for the *Herald and Examiner*.[14] The dig at the FTP's Popular Front politics misses the spectacular success of the Chicago *Little Black Sambo*'s Popular Front ideals. *The Story of Little Black Sambo* provides a parable of white on black violence in the era of Jim Crow. This federal transformation of the Sambo stereotype, the most widespread and demeaning figure of minstrelsy, took place against the broad cultural acceptance of its legitimacy, even as the trial of nine African American boys for the rape of two white women, known internationally as the Scottsboro Boys case, had drawn widespread attention to the deplorable conditions for African Americans in the South under the law. By the time federal Sambos were being chased by federal tigers across stages in the North and South, the Scottsboro Boys had been pursued by the Alabama jurisprudence in the public eye for six years. Although no physical evidence pointed to a crime, the nine defendants had been nearly lynched, had been convicted and sentenced to death (excepting in the case of Roy Wright, who was twelve when arrested), had had their case reviewed twice by the Supreme Court, and had become a cause célèbre and focus of numerous demonstrations, rallies, and marches. The "Scottsboro nine" had drawn together the NAACP and the Communist International Legal Defense in the formation of the Scottsboro Defense Committee in 1935. Newspaper stories in America and Europe on the trials had exposed the hunger of the lynch mob and the all-white Southern courtroom for the destruction of the young, black, male body.[15]

Blackface minstrel shows of the nineteenth and early twentieth centuries staged a division between black and white humanity that perhaps facilitated and certainly supported a juridical difference that denied American justice to defendants such as the Scottsboro nine. Scholars Eric Lott and Michael Rogin have noted blackface minstrelsy's cultural function as a negotiation tool by which racial boundaries were policed and by which new ethnic, northern, urban working-class Americans entered "whiteness." By donning blackface, both scholars have suggested, performers signaled both their fascination with and opposition to blackness and to a racially oppressed people. The blackface performance itself signaled a masquerading whiteness.[16]

The blackface routine, as described by Lott

> ... was configured at the height of its popularity as a semicircle of four or five or sometimes more white male performers ... made up with facial blacking of greasepaint or burnt cork and adorned in outrageously oversized and / or ragged "Negro" costumes. Armed with an array of instruments, usually banjo, fiddle, bone castanets, and tambourine, the performers would stage a triparte show. The first part offered up a random selection of songs interspersed with what passed for black wit and japery; the second part (or "olio") featured a group of novelty performances (comic dialogues, malapropistic "stump speeches," cross-dressed "wench" performances, and the like); and the third part was a narrative skit, usually set in the South, containing dancing, music, and burlesque.[17]

Blackface routines introduced or popularized negative caricatures such as Sambo, Zip Coon, Mammy, and the pickaninny that denigrated black manhood, womanhood, and childhood. After the Civil War, blackface minstrelsy promulgated the idea that African Americans pined for the old system destroyed by war. At the same time, however, blacks also began donning burnt cork for the stage.[18]

Lott's study of pre–Civil War minstrelsy, *Love and Theft: Blackface Minstrelsy and the American Working Class,* locates its performance at the nexus of white desire for and fear of the black male body and in the material relations of slavery, his "love and theft." He argues that minstrelsy safely facilitates "an exchange of energies between two otherwise rigidly bounded and policed cultures, a shape-shifting middle term in racial conflict. . . . " As performance it demonstrates "both a drawing up and crossing of racial boundaries." He writes:

> The very form of blackface acts—an investiture in black bodies—seems a manifestation of the particular desire to try on the accents of "blackness" and demonstrates the permeability of the color line. . . . It was cross-racial desire that coupled a nearly insupportable fascination and a self-protective derision with respect to black people and their cultural practices, and that

made blackface minstrelsy less a sign of absolute white power and control than of panic, anxiety, terror, and pleasure.[19]

Minstrel shows began to disappear in the 1920s as film began to dominate American popular culture. Rogin's study of Jewish performances of blackface in early Hollywood films argues that blackface's racial masquerade turned ethnic and immigrant groups into Americans. Like Hollywood itself, he suggests, blackface performance provided a common imagined community for diverse groups predicated on the "surplus symbolic value of blacks, the power to make African Americans represent something beside themselves."[20] Denied Americanness, then, were the negative racial stereotypes minstrelsy performed, the Sambos, mammies, Zip Coons, and pickaninnies; denied both representation and the rights of Americans was the racial group these negative stereotypes purported to represent.

As minstrel characterizations dominated both old and new American mass entertainment, press reaction to Negro Unit theatre often exposed the gulf between stereotypical audience expectations and government-funded performances that challenged American racial attitudes. *Turpentine* followed the enormously popular "voodoo" *Macbeth* to the Lafayette Theatre.[21] Both productions generated commentary about the spectacle of African Americans playing serious roles in serious dramatic productions. Calling on perhaps the only major African American representations its reporter knew, this review of *Turpentine* ran in the *Brooklyn Eagle*, June 27:

> It was Summertime in Harlem last night and turpentine in the Florida swamplands, the scene of the Negro Theater's new drama, "Turpentine." And although it was Summertime, the living was far from easy, for the Negroes who suffle [sic] and run across the stage of the Lafayette are as far removed from the inhabitants of Catfish Row as the first production of this Federal Theatre unit, "Macbeth," was from Shakespeare.[22]

If the *Eagle*'s reference to *Porgy and Bess* suggests both the paucity of a black stage tradition within which to appropriately situate *Turpentine* and an uncomfortable yoking of primitive and plantation, reviews of popular productions suggest pervasive and insidious white stereotypes of performers as well. Reviewing *Macbeth*, Brooks Atkinson wrote in the *New York Times* that "with an eye to animalism . . . they turned the banquet scene into a ball." Percy Hammond noted that "They seemed to be afraid of the Bard, though they were playing him on their own home grounds." Burns Mantle assumed the audience applauded because of its regular gaiety. Arthur Pollack relied on stereotypes of African Americans as childlike and imitative. He wrote, "It (Macbeth) has a childlike austerity . . . with all its gusto," and "They play Shakespeare as if they were apt children who had just discovered him and adored the old man."[23]

Excoriating the reviews that expressed stereotypical assumptions about African American actors, Roi Ottley wrote in *New Theatre*:

> The Broadway reviewers . . . journied [sic] to Harlem with the idea of seeing a mixture of Emperor Jones and Step an' Fetchit, with burlesque thrown in to season a palatable opinion many of their readers have of the Negro. This was best evidenced by their reviews the following morning.[24]

The malapropisms and childlike geniality that characterize blackface minstrel characters dominated African American representations on the 1930s stage and screen, competing against and often coinciding with performances that showcased the "natural" abilities of African Americans such as playing music, singing, and dancing.[25] In this context, antiracist Popular Front theatre often utilized social realist and folk play tropes to produce a new African American figure. Ottley's *Macbeth* review heralds this change:[26]

> In Harlem's opinion the Federal Theatre Project's production of "Macbeth," at the Lafayette Theatre, was an eminent success. After years of playing distasteful stereotype and idiomatic roles in the American Theater, the Negro at last was attaining the status of an actor.
>
> It is generally believed that the Negro is a "natural" in an idiom part. Broadway producers and directors have therefore felt that the Negro has no need of real direction or training. They only think of the Negro portraying Negro roles, but not an actor in the sense of interpreting universal emotions.
>
> The Negro has become weary of carrying the white-man's blackface burden in the theatre. In "Macbeth" he was given the opportunity to discard the bandana and burnt cork casting to play a universal character.[27]

In such rare cases as *Macbeth*, black actors played roles not written to describe an "African American" experience. Yet social realism plays that addressed African American conditions, with their emphases on folk and working-class heroes, still participated in racism's pervasive binary that opposes black emotionalism to white intellectualism. Social realist FTP plays such as those by Paul Green, Smith and Morell, and Paul Peters and George Sklar created complex black characterizations whose untutored magnificence was signaled by the height of their often inarticulate emotional passion. White social realist plays used black bodies to mount critiques of the status quo as envisioned by whites. Reviewing *In Abraham's Bosom*, Federal Theatre playreader H. L. Fishel writes, "Mr. Green does not give us an insight into negro psychology since he sees that for the negro which the negro does not see for himself."[28] Though sympathetic to African American oppression, white social realist playwrights too often drew on essentialist ideas of race.

When the New York Negro Unit's production of *Turpentine* opened in Harlem in 1936 with a racially mixed cast, the press thrilled to the cultural anomaly of a black man performing whiteness in a serious drama. "A Negro actor will have the rare distinction of playing a white man," noted *Women's Wear* on June 24, 1936. "Reversing a familiar order, a colored actor, Thomas Moseley, will play a Southern colonel," wrote the *New York News* the same day. "Numerous white actors have adopted black faces, but this process will be reversed," added the *Bronx Home News* on June 25.[29]

Invoking the spectacle of reverse minstrelsy, the press comments reveal the extent to which staged race was the prerogative of whites and hint at the fluttering anxiety Moseley's destabilizing presence may have caused white audiences and critics. His performance signified more than a black man "adopting" whiteface. His presentation of whiteness also calls forth a social order in which race is both reversible and interchangeable, in which black becomes white both in color and in socioeconomic status and in which the ontology of upward mobility erases racial hierarchies. In Moseley's embodied performance, in a production that insists that a black man can be a white Southern colonel, old man minstrelsy is not so much reversed as undone. The performance insists upon a racial equality where black can stage white and all can be as white. As the United States Congress was unable to muster the votes to pass an anti-lynching law, *Turpentine* suggests that the violence called forth by the black body can be appeased by the erasure of that body into a reassuring whiteness.[30]

Turpentine tells the story of black workers who are underpaid, starving, and brutalized in an isolated Florida turpentine camp. They strike for better conditions; the play ends with the white sheriff's firing into a church where the strikers are gathered.[31] Within the context of the play's politics, Mosely's performance subsumes race under class, coding white as a class position and not a racial identity and thus reproducing visually a class-based political ideology through which to read the larger narrative of oppressed workers, particularly since the cast of the play was racially mixed.[32] His performance can thus describe both the colorblind tenets of thirties liberalism and the very different but equally colorblind ones of American Communism.

As blackface and racial role reversal, Mosely's display of racial interchangeability visually recalls the tug of the old plantation system and minstrel performance. He is adopting not simply whiteface, but power within a racially hierarchized system. This mounts a challenge to expectations of the roles open to African American performance, yet the challenge is undercut by the minstrel associations of staged race reversal. If his greasepaint makes a political point, his class position recalls pointed blackface minstrel jokes denigrating black cultural aspirations as unsuccessful strivings for whiteness in the figure of Zip Coon. Mosely's character is overdetermined, and the class marked by race as staged by blackface minstrelsy undercuts the import of social realism's daring experiment. Thus, as publicly labeled racial masquerade, Moseley's performance can be read as not so much a liberating dream of America's racial future but rather as the limits of that dream imposed by the lingering traces of a conflicted racist history.

Turpentine was not popular with the black audiences of Harlem. Audience surveys suggest that the Harlem audience wanted to see plays that dealt with the issues they faced in their own community, and not the faraway struggles of the Southern working poor.[33] But *Turpentine* was unpopular within the Harlem community—though critically appreciated by the community that traveled uptown to see it—not only because of its setting in the South, but because of its depiction of poor, uneducated, "primitive" African Americans. While the leftist focus on class struggle caused its playwrights to focus on the working poor and to celebrate folk art as reflective of class vitality, representations of working-poor African Americans in the South could not help but raise the specter of slavery and its concomitant representational framework of minstrelsy and plantation mythology. *Turpentine*'s unpopularity focuses attention on the manner in which interest in "folk" plays, or plays about and reflecting the ethos of the "common man," and an untutored and expressive artistry could dovetail uncomfortably close to negative stereotypes about poor and uneducated blacks. As Henry Louis Gates notes in "The Trope of a New Negro and the Reconstruction of the Image of Black" about the Harlem Renaissance's New Negro,

> its "success" depends fundamentally upon self-negation, a turning away from the "Old Negro" and the labyrinthine memory of black enslavement and toward the register of a "New Negro," an irresistible, spontaneously generated black and sufficient self.[34]

African American cultural critics celebrated the folk play, but the "culturally willed myth" (to use Gates's phrase) of the New Negro made such celebration, particularly with rural Southern inflections, problematic.[35]

The significance of the folk play in perceptions of *Little Black Sambo* is expressed in Production Book notes from the Goodman Theatre production. Graham writes: "The Costumes of the people should be suggestive, merely, not accurate to any place or period, since the play is drawn from the folklore of all jungle peoples. . . . " Written by a Scottish white woman living in India, *The Story of Little Black Sambo* had become—by virtue no doubt of its simple characters, its human–animal interactions, its preindustrial time frame, and its jungle setting—a "jungle peoples" folk play.

But the Chorpenning–Graham production is not of "the folklore of all jungle people" any more than is Bannerman's book. The Chorpenning–Graham production features Chorpenning's pragmatic, clever, lyrical child besting tigers in Graham's Africanized setting. It draws on modernist aesthetics to herald a new American racial identity grounded in a Popular Front assertion of African American inclusion.[36] In a decade when modernist primitivism had been too often reduced to inherently racist stereotypes of African American emotionalism and irrationality, Chorpenning and Graham succeed in creating a black character who is distinctively and positively African and American. In an era when, as David Chinitz notes, "The legacy of 1920s primitivist discourse . . . left Africa, the African American, and jazz all but *defined* in terms of the primitive," Graham's production used African motifs in set, costume, and music to frame a tale that was distinctly American in its rags-to-riches narrative arc that describes how a boy's ingenious and plucky self-sufficiency wins him his heart's desire.[37] African artistry is depicted as transformative, and thus is liberated by narrative from essentializing African heritage as contributing to a stereotypical and reductive primitivism. The play lifts Sambo from the character's demeaning history.

Played out in this federal partnership between Chorpenning and Graham is a performance of what Anthony Appiah terms W. E. B. du Bois's "antithesis in the classic dialectic of reaction to prejudice." If the thesis in the dialectic is "denial of difference," Appiah argues, then a du Boisian antithesis accepts difference, positing that differing racial groups provide complementary contributions in service to human advancement. In "The Conservation of Races," du Bois argued that because race was fundamentally a sociohistorical construct, and that as each race had contributions to make borne of its particular history, then because their message had not yet been articulated to the world, African Americans should strive together to "work out in its fullness the great message we have for humanity."[38] His argument rejects assimilation to recognize that complementary racial contributions best forward human progress. In the Chorpenning–Graham production, the motifs that signal Sambo's Africanness create markings of ethnic identification that perform two primary functions. In a play that celebrates a boy's desire to articulate in

FIGURE 8. *Little Black Sambo (Chicago Illinois).* George Mason University. Fenwick Library. Special Collections and Archives

poetry his sense of beauty and wonder inspired by an Africanized landscape, they create a du Boisian celebration of African heritage. Within a narrative of liberal self-actualization, the motifs bring an African ethnicity to a universalized American boy. Thus they signal Sambo's place, and the place of African American children, within pluralistic twentieth-century American society.

The Story of Little Black Sambo is practically unavailable in school libraries today, but in the thirties, it was widely recommended by librarians and educators as a positive portrayal of African Americans.[39] Certainly when compared with the (also green-umbrella-carrying) Bumpo of *The Story of Dr. Doolittle* and the caricatures of African Americans in popular series books through the first half of the twentieth century, the characters in *The Story of Little Black Sambo* avoid the worst excesses of racism in their very simplicity.[40] Written and illustrated by Helen Bannerman for her two daughters while the family was living in India, the story seems to be set in India even as it seems to depict African Americans. Bannerman later sold the story, drawings, and copyright; *The Story of Little Black Sambo* was first published in 1899 in London as the fourth in the small sized "Dumpy" books. It was instantly successful, with more than 21,000 copies sold in the first year. *The Story of Little Black Sambo* was first published in the United States in 1900.

The original has pictures and text on facing pages. It begins simply: "Once upon a time there was a little black boy, and his name was Little Black Sambo." On the facing page is a drawing of a dark-skinned child with curly hair and brown eyes; he wears a loincloth. The story tells of how Little Black Sambo, whose parents have given him a green umbrella, blue trousers, a red coat, and "purple shoes with crimson soles and crimson linings," goes into the jungle, where he is beset by four tigers. In order to avoid being eaten, he gives all of his clothes, piece by piece, to the tigers. The tigers, in a fight over which is most grand, grab each other's tails and chase each other around a tree until they turn into melted butter. While Sambo picks up his clothes, Black Jumbo, his father, scoops up the melted butter and takes it home. Black Mumbo, Sambo's mother, makes pancakes, and eats 27 of them to Jumbo's 55 to Sambo's 169.

In the early decades of the twentieth century, neither librarians nor educators were publicly concerned about the racial stereotyping in the pictures and text of the story.[41] Yet the influence of the minstrel show on Bannerman's original drawings is unmistakable. Black Mumbo is drawn with a kerchief over her head, a dumpy head atop a no-necked body, and with a big-featured, lip-thrust face and sloping forehead. Black Jumbo is as great a caricature, drawn in classic minstrel clothing and standing with overturned wrist on hip and holding a red umbrella while smoking a pipe.[42] Both parents are barefoot, as also is Sambo.

Bannerman's drawings emphasize blackface minstrelsy visually as the name Sambo does linguistically.[43] Sambo, "a Darwinian loser and preindustrial primitive, became the nation's demeaned alterego . . . ," writes Joseph Boskin. He was to whites

> slow-witted, loosely-shuffling, buttock-scratching, benignly-optimistic, superstitiously-frightened, childishly lazy, irresponsibly-carefree, rhythmically-gaited, pretentiously-intelligent, sexually-animated. His physical characteristics added to the jester's appearance: toothy-grinned, thick-lipped, nappy-haired, slack-jawed, round-eyed.[44]

Sambo graced the minstrel stage, but he was much more. Sambo existed as artifact, image, and theatrical buffoon. Boskin writes:

> As one of the earliest minority images to be translated into a cultural form, Sambo had become a multipublic figure by the eighteenth century, appealing across the social landscape. When, in the mid-nineteenth century, the figure was presented in the minstrel theatre, its long passage into the other levels of culture was virtually assured.[45]

As Gates notes:

> By 1900, when Booker T. Washington called for *A New Negro for a New Century*, it would have been possible for a middle-class white American to see Sambo images from toaster and teapot covers on his breakfast table, to advertisements in magazines, to popular postcards in drug stores. Everywhere he or she saw a black image, that image would be negative.[46]

Drawings for subsequent American editions of *The Story of Little Black Sambo* drew upon the Sambo caricature's widespread cultural resonance. A Cupples and Leon 1917 publication, with illustrations by John B. Gruelle, has mother and son barely human, with thick white lips, round circle noses, and popping eyes with black-dot pupils. A 1908 Reilly and Britton edition that appeared with "The Story of Topsy" from *Uncle Tom's Cabin,* and drawings by John R. Neill, shows frighteningly staring eyes, enormous lips, wildly kinked hair, and pierced ears. In this version, Sambo looks like a miniature adult, with a full-formed musculature, big hands, and bowlegs. His mother is a classic Mammy caricature straight out of plantation stories, a doughy mass, with her chin hanging over the beginnings of an ample bosom, wearing a polka-dotted kerchief and matching apron. As the drawings emphasized minstrel caricature, publications changed the locale from India to a stylized Africa or generic American South.[47]

The Story of Little Black Sambo's history of egregious racist caricature obscures the book's very real charms for children. The pleasure of reading it is most obviously felt in the sweet satiation of its final feast. There are other pleasures, of course. Sambo's tiger triumph is vividly inspiring. Like the Babar books, *The Story of Little Black Sambo* speaks of a distant geographical location all the more alluring because its improbability of difference is real, an allure that extends to its fascination with the jungle and its celebration of dressing up. If the large, capacious Babar books of the 1930s (of which there was one FTP puppet theatre production in New York) invite the young reader to climb into them, *The Story of Little Black Sambo* makes itself deliciously sized for children's hands. But the almost unbearable rightness of fearsome, child-eating, clothes-snitching tigers turning into soft sweet butter for pancakes almost too numerous to count, pancakes enough to satisfy the terrible hunger that follows terror, is the pleasure of its climax. Like Max's dinner waiting when he returned from *Where the Wild Things Are,* the meal at the end of *The Story of Little Black Sambo* symbolizes the security of home. Flanked by his parents, the small boy who has ventured into the jungle and been stripped of his clothes by ferocious tigers ingests the very terror that pursued him. His mother makes the pancakes. His father brings home the butter. He is the center of his family and he is loved. It's obvious in the eating.

Most who argue that Bannerman's book with her original illustrations is not racist cite Sambo's triumph over the tigers as a feat of skill and intelligence. But the book equally poses Sambo as a young dandy whose taste in clothes is mirrored by animals. Sambo barters away the only precious things he has because he cannot conceive of them not being universally desirable. The book's simple narrative does not tell readers that Sambo is resourceful, but both it and the corresponding illustrations suggest that he is vain. What is unambiguous is its construction of a loving nuclear family that is reunited in happy plentitude at the book's end.

The Chorpenning–Graham three-act production follows the basic Bannerman story with the addition of a subplot centered on a group of monkeys. An extant playscript includes director's notes for an earlier production at the Goodman Theatre and gives some idea of staging. According to the notes, the same backdrop was used for all scenes, "an imaginative and colorful impression of the jungle, with all sorts of greens predominating, and brilliant suggestions of jungle flowers giving needed variety. . . . " The notes continue:

To this set, unchanging (except for lighting) we added for the scenes in the clearing, the hut in which Sambo lived. It was round, with a pointed roof, and set on a platform two and a half feet high, with a flight of several steps running down. . . . The roof was thatched high with dry cornstalks; the whole unit was put on rollers so that scene changes were very swift. On the other side of the stage a fire, with a large metal pot so placed that it caught the glow, added interest.

Costuming notes say:

> In the Goodman production, Sambo used a dark brown wash over his whole body (not black, which would have made him too comic)—and wore a loin cloth colored like the most brilliant tawny foundation used for the tigers. A three-strand chain of shells hung well down over his chest. Mumbo, also brown, wore a modification of a Hindu sari, with a turban not exactly like any ever worn anywhere, but very becoming to her. Jumbo wore a loose outer garment belted in at the waist, and open down the front, showing his brown body and loin cloth when he moved. His turban was also an original affair. All three went barefoot.[48]

The notes suggest a fascination with the primitive borne out by extant photos of the production. Graham Africanized the costumes, giving Mumbo an African-style headdress and Jumbo a brightly patterned loose shift and baggy pants. Though in sketches Sambo is shown in matching shorts and jacket, throughout much of the play he wears a loincloth.[49]

In addition to directing the federal production, Graham wrote its original music, described as "inserted incidental music . . . which harmonizes with the African motif."[50] As Graham noted in her "Director's Notes,"

> We stressed the Negro character of the play by the play of brilliant colors, decided use of percussions, intensity of rhythm and in a definite minor melodic line of the music. Thus, again this negroid quality came through without effort and without getting away from the naïve charm of the script.[51]

Before the curtain rises, music is faintly heard; the play begins with Sambo grinding corn near the hut, but looking off into the jungle and gradually ceasing to work as the music swells. The animals that will drive the plot, the monkeys and tigers, enter the stage and then dart off when one of the monkeys accidentally rolls a drum. Sambo works half-heartedly for a moment, then leaps up and bursts into song:

> I hear the wind. / It says it is going away. / I am going, too / We go, go, go. / Through the cocoanut [sic] trees. / Where the monkeys are, / Where the elephants are, / Where the tigers are. / I ride on the back of an elephant. / We ride, ride, ride. / Plop, plop, plop. / To the end of the world, / Then we ride, without ground, / Without tree, / Only on the wind, Only on the water, / Only in a dim place—[52]

The song's lyrics suggest the breadth of Sambo's imagination, even as it prepares the audience to consider the symbolic aspects of the trip to the jungle that the familiar storyline demands. When his mother chides him for singing when he should be grinding corn for pancakes, Sambo says his father would grind for him, "He likes to have me make songs." Early in the play, Mumbo is set against Jumbo; the former is practical, in charge of finances, and hardworking. When Jumbo returns from the bazaar, we see the future of the singing, impractical Sambo; instead of buying the food Mumbo has ordered, Jumbo spent the money on blue and red cloth for clothes Sambo wanted.

In the Bannerman book, his parents gave Sambo the colorful clothes. Against the drawing of a grinning Sambo holding his green umbrella with one arm outstretched as if in acceptance of applause, the text asks, "And then wasn't Little Black Sambo grand?" On the next page, it continues, "So he put on all his Fine Clothes, and went out for a walk in the Jungle." In the Chorpenning play, Sambo goes into the jungle because he makes a deal with Mumbo: if she will make the clothes from the cloth, rather than returning it to the bazaar and buying the food, he will somehow get eggs, milk, sugar, and butter for her. She agrees because she thinks Sambo needs not only to learn to work, but to value the food that keeps them alive. Sambo has no money, so he asks Jumbo where the bazaar sellers get the food and realizes that he can find the raw ingredients or substitutes in the jungle. Rather than a parading of finery, his journey to the jungle is a quest for items of exchange that Mumbo values equally to the clothes.

This thematic shift focuses narrative and dramatic tension on whether the child will provide for his family and keep his word, not on the child's danger. Furthermore, once in the jungle, Chorpenning's Sambo is not first beset upon and frightened by a tiger. Rather, he befriends a monkey who has been the butt of all the other monkeys' jokes. The monkey promises to get Sambo ostrich eggs in exchange for a trick of his devising for her to play on the others. As she frolics off to fetch the eggs, two tigers happen by. One asserts, "We are the finest beasts in the jungle," and the other seconds, "No one dare be as fine as we are." Sambo responds, "I never thought of being fine," and the tiger questions, "Then why have you got a black and white and yellow skin like ours?" When Sambo explains that part of his coloring is his clothes and beads, the tigers insist that he remove them, which he politely refuses to do on the grounds that he would then be naked. The tiger rejoins, "You wish to make the animals think you are as fine as we." Sambo responds, "Nobody in the world would think that, Mrs. Tiger."

This exchange introduces the distinctions between Sambo and the monkeys and tigers that will be drawn on again to interrogate similarities provoked by the child of the jungle entering the jungle and talking to the animals. It provides a significant point of departure from the logic of the picture book, which suggests that Sambo walks into the woods in his new clothes to show them off. When he gives them to the tigers one by one, it is because he and the tigers recognize that the grandeur of which all equally want to take part is located in the clothing. If Sambo's coloring is a point of recognition by the tigers, whose antagonism is provoked by a grandeur that is like theirs, and thus insistent upon Sambo's animality, then his dismissal of similarity sets him apart. Indeed, the tigers decide to watch the monkeys' response to Sambo; if they think he is fine and grand, "We will eat you in our burning mouths."

The monkeys do gather round the boy and say he is the grandest of all, but Sambo saves himself by singing a song about the animals that ends:

> The tiger walks in the jungle paths,
> The grasses bow as he goes past,
> They bend and whisper praise,
> He stands, he stands in the sun, he shines,
> His beautiful body all patterned,
> The beasts bow low, they sing, they shout, they praise!!!
> I am the tiger. You are the beasts!!
> Everything lives, everything dances, everything sings.[53]

The monkeys bow to him as "the tiger" as Sambo leads the dance to where the tigers are sitting so the monkeys are bowing and shouting to them. "They sing about us. They bow to us," says one. "They don't notice him," notes the other. Sambo's safety among the powerful jungle beasts is predicated upon dramatic and literary skills that allow him to successfully stage tiger worship.

But the tigers' jealousy of Sambo is based not on his beautiful colored clothing, which in this play he hasn't yet received, but on his glorious combination of black skin, white beads, and loincloth, which he tells them (in lines seemingly cut from the FTP production) that "I asked my mother to make my loin cloth yellow because it is beautiful like the moon at night . . . " "Take it off," interrupts a tiger. In this play, Sambo's beautiful brown washed skin, though described by the tigers as black, is the source of his beauty, their envy, and the monkeys' desire to worship.

This scene introduces a theme that weaves throughout the production: skin color as reason for pride and arrogance and therefore skin color as provoking danger. While the tigers are colored much like Sambo, they wish to differentiate him from themselves and literally to strip him of that which makes him beautiful like them. Without his loincloth, Sambo is only black, and black alone is not like a tiger. Sambo's delight in his clothes is very carefully allied with his reason for song-making; he loves beauty in the disinterested spirit of a poet and a creator. Once the monkeys worship them and the tigers relax from the threat embodied by Sambo, he asks the mother tiger for a jug of milk. She replies, "You are not grand enough even to look at tiger's milk," and a second later adds, "You aren't fit to have a drop of the milk that makes my wee wonderful tiger babies grow their beautiful stripes." Sambo tells them he wants the milk so his mother can make pancakes and sew him blue trousers and a red coat. The tigers come back to find out what the red and blue colors mean:

BOULANE: I am Boulane the tiger. I want to know what you meant by a beautiful little red coat and beautiful little blue trousers. Are you trying to find something finer than our black and yellow stripes?
DACURA: And I want to know.
RONGA: And I want to know.
BOULANE: Why do you change from colors like ours to be like a parrot or a bird of paradise? Do you think you will get more praise from the jungle folk?
SAMBO: I'm not thinking about praise.
DACURA: Everyone thinks about praise.
SAMBO: I'm thinking about how beautiful, beautiful, beautiful they are. That's all I'm thinking about.[54]

When the tigers ask him why he wants his clothes to be beautiful, Sambo replies, "I don't know. My father never told me. It's the way I am." And Boulane responds, "In your muscles that do not show, you feel that you will be grander than we." Sambo turns the tables on the tigers by asking which is the grandest of them. They argue, and the argument at one point centers on the fact that a tiger that is not present has "more white than you. If the white on your coat makes you grand, then Koumba is grander than either of you." The tigers appeal to Sambo to choose the grandest, and he says that until he sees the tiger with the most white, he cannot judge.

Sambo's triumph proceeds from his ability to befriend the animal that is not like the others and raises another theme that will be repeated: the difference between monkeys and men. The monkeys do not recognize similarity between themselves and Sambo as do the proud tigers; rather, in the face of the tigers' calling Sambo a beast in their comparison with him, the monkeys consistently refer to the family as "men." While Sambo's song is a virtual sound bite of evolution from fish to tiger that allies all the animals and only sets him apart as performer, the monkeys do not recognize the child as like creature, saying he is smarter than any monkey. The play overturns the pejorative connection between monkeys and men that underlies so much of racist caricature in American cultural production.

With his monkey friend Malinke's help, Sambo gets all the pancake ingredients except butter. He makes sugar out of sugar cane himself. But when his mother sends his father to the bazaar for butter, his father buys a green umbrella and purple shoes with crimson soles and linings for his son instead, and Sambo offers to return to the jungle for the butter. Though he returns from the jungle successful, he must fight off not only the tigers in this production, but the jealous monkeys who trap him and set him out for the tigers to kill. While Sambo is lost, his mother chants to drumbeats that she hopes will call him home:

> The drum beats
> My heart beats
> When will my child come home?
> I wait, I wait,
> My breath comes fast.... [55]

In highlighting the mother's fear for her child in lines scored by rhythmic drumbeats, the play allies Mumbo's fear for her child with the primitive and the African. In training her child to be responsible and brave, she exhibits a mother's fearful heart as she waits for her child's return. Sambo's safe homecoming brings the play to a close, with Mumbo's, "To all, the drum in my heart beats thanks" echoed by Sambo and Jumbo. The curtain falls as the family begins to eat.

Federal theatre worked on a large canvas, and so to present the Chicago production of *The Story of Little Black Sambo* as its triumphant center is to show only part of the picture. In the Miami puppet and the Junior League version of the story, the symbolic equation of food and love is subsumed under the signs of the blackface minstrelsy. Visually dominating, expelling burlesque dialect and what passes for African American humor, the blackface minstrel mouth and its association with primitive orality testifies to a gaping need, a ravenous appetite, an insatiable orifice, even as it is metonymic for the grinning, giving, bountiful servant. "Weel about and turn about and do jis so / Ebry time I weel about and jump Jim Crow" seems distant from tigers twirling round a tree into butter. But the racial burlesque that underlies Bannerman's naming and provided the source of her visual characterization overtly structures the Miami FTP production. If so much of the book's pleasure resides in participating with Sambo as that which would kill him turns into food making him stronger, these federal scripts deny the recognition and identification integral to the participation of that pleasure. As it did in minstrel shows, comedy resides in caricatured staging of the African American oppressed, in displaying and ultimately negating the threat posed by the excluded upon whom a unified American family rests.

The dependence of federal *Little Black Sambo*s on minstrel characterization and the minstrel forms—music, dancing, and verbal play—shifts the focus of the food within the story and in so doing shifts the focus of family. Their primary debt to minstrelsy is the gaping minstrel mouth painted on the puppets. As Boskin writes, "Being puppets, they wore perpetual grins against coal-black faces with wide eyes and thick red lips."[56] As the photo from Washington, DC, makes clear, this particular FTP marionette Sambo did not have fine clothes with which to parade in the jungle. He is barely dressed in overalls. His mother wears a servant outfit with bandana, and his father working clothes. Their home contains the standard portraiture of melodrama or farce; before a word has been spoken, the audience has been informed by a wealth of signs as to how to read the show.

The plays' emphases on minstrel characterizations—distortions of dialect, malapropisms, and the inversion of gender norms and gendered behavior, combined with the minstrel forms of exaggerated dance, emphasis on song, and what passes for African American verbal play—invert the family structure celebrated as the ideal. In these plays, communication is based on telling lies, threatening violence, and congratulating self-promotion. The head of the family is female, and she is a threatening (violently rather than sexually) figure. In these three-scene productions, minstrel characterization and form disrupt the narrative flow and the dependence on reassuring repetition that in the picture book builds the pleasures that culminate in the final feast. In so doing, the Miami and Junior League plays shift the emotional center from the family to Sambo's interaction with the tigers and from the family feast to the tigers' hunger. Both plays draw out the spectacle of Sambo's fear in the face of the tigers' threatening desire for him and shift emphasis at the end from shared meal to the family members' individual antics. "Jumbo does cakewalk," tersely notes the Junior League script; Mumbo flips pancakes while Sambo and Jumbo dance in the Miami version. The shift spatially breaks up the family.

The script used in the one-act, three-scene Miami version begins and ends in Mumbo's kitchen and sandwiches the jungle in between. Notes at the beginning of the scene direct "At rise of curtain, MUMBO at stove singing Negro spiritual—'Nobody knows the trouble I've seen.' Negro dialect throughout. Tigers, etc."

> MUMBO: Sambo, Sambo. Where is that pestiferious child? Sambo? Sambo Where is you at?
> SAMBO: Here I is, Mumbo.
> MUMBO: Come in here this instant. Where you been, chile? Come yere to yo' mammy.
> SAMBO: Oh, Mumbo, I was havin' do bestest time. I was in the swimmin' [*sic*] all the de morning, in de ribber.
> MUMBO: Ain't I been told you not to go swimmin' in dat ribber? You want to be et up by dem crocodiles?[57]

Sambo lies to Mumbo, saying a crocodile ate his clothes, and then bursts into a song-and-dance routine about his swimming prowess that makes her laugh. Mumbo's brief maternal fears forgotten, she laughs, "You sure is the beatenest child. I reckon you'll have to wear your new Sunday go-to-meetin' clothes effen de crocodile done et up your other ones. Anyway, I want you to go down to the market store for me and buy some shortenin' for de shortenin' bread." Sambo pleads, "Mammy, ef I sees some watermelon, kin I bring dat home, too?" Mumbo says yes, and then warns him not to get mud on his new clothes or she'll tell Jumbo to get him no more, at which point Jumbo enters with:

> JUMBO: What do I git no more of? And why? (sees Sambo—looks him over) Well, if you ain't the grandest looking child I ever did see—you sure do your pappy proud. Don't he, Mumbo?

MUMBO: Well, he sure look good, but he is the beatenest chile fer gettin' into trouble. Tell your Pappy how you done lost all your clothes.
SAMBO: Oh, I done took a swim in de ribber and a feericious crocodile et em all up.
JUMBO: Effen you ain't careful, boy, next time you'll get et stead o' your clothes. Den where'll you be? Tell me dat?[58]

Then telling Sambo to hurry because "I'se hungry," Jumbo adds, "Don't swim no more, or I'll whack you good!" while stage directions note that he laughs. Sambo exits into the dangerous jungle with "Yassum, yassum, I'll take care nothin' don't happen to me, nor my fine clothes. Won't I be grand, though (sings) all dressed up in my finest clothes from my head to my toes. Folks will stare at me, I know. Way down in the jungle."

In scene 2, Sambo stops by the river to swim to sing about his beautiful clothes in loving detail. He is quickly confronted with the first tiger, who says, "Grr, oh, how do you do, little Black Sambo, if you don't look delicious today—mum—mum—And where are you going?" Sambo replies, "Oh—how do you do Mr. Tiger. I got to do an errand for my Mammy down to the market. I'm late already—guess I better hurry—goodbye Mr. Tiger." The tiger replies, "Well, well, not so fast my little tender one. I'm also late, late for my dinner. I'm so sorry if I seem to cause you too much inconvenience, but I am hungry, and must not delay my lunch any longer. So please stand still and I'll begin at once—I promise not to hurt you any more than necessary."[59]

Until the tiger arrives, Sambo's speech has been written in dialect, but with the tiger's racially unmarked speech, Sambo (mostly) loses his own until he returns home. Not only is the dialect in the Reich script uneven, but while it follows some of the conventions for minstrel speech, it doesn't follow them all. She seems to only occasionally have followed familiar dialect substitutions: the voiced bilabial stop /b/ for the voiced labiodental fricative and substituted voiceless apicoalveolar stops /t/ and /d/ for the voiceless apicodental fricative /th/. The script doesn't delete the present tense of "to be" nor does it use the present tense to describe actions in the past. What seems to be the case is that the writer was familiar enough with minstrel conventions to indicate the genre in which the play was to be situated, but not familiar enough to successfully recreate minstrel speech. Even the mispronunciations "feerocious" and "pestiferious" seem like labored attempts to simulate distorted dialect for comic affect. But the dialect serves to construct a reading of the family dynamics by its allusion to minstrel speech and malapropism. Named "mammy" by her son, Mumbo demonstrates a nonmaternal lack of concern for her child's safety situated in the minstrel stereotype of the black mother. Mumbo invites the audience to laugh at her child's danger along with her.

Sambo offers his red coat in exchange for his life and convinces the tiger that he will be the grandest tiger: "go on down to the deep pool and look for yourself." Tiger number two says "Grrr—oh how I feel. No dinner. Oh there's Sambo—good—I'll eat you right up and maybe that will make me feel better. Oh my stomach. Hurry now. I am going to gobble you right up. Grrr. Don't stand there like a ninny. Didn't you hear me say I was going to eat you right up . . . " Sambo responds, "Oh please Mr. Tiger, please don't eat me! I'd be very bad for your stomach and besides, I don't want to be eaten." The second tiger responds that what Sambo wants "has nothing to do with it."[60]

The third tiger pauses in telling Sambo she will eat him up to ask "Did you bathe today?" Sambo's dialect briefly and incompletely returns with his answer, "Yassum, I done swum in the river today, but I wouldn't taste awful good." The tiger doesn't believe him and he persuades her that she will be even prettier wearing his purple shoes on her tail. And finally, he convinces the fourth tiger to shade himself with the umbrella, at which point Sambo cries, "Oh Mumbo sure'll lick me. Losing all my clothes. Boo-hoo." The tigers leave, but their return fighting over who is grandest forces Sambo up the tree. The scene ends with him laughing down at the tigers.

Scene three opens with Jumbo snoring at the kitchen table. He wakes and worries briefly that Sambo went swimming and lost his new clothes. Mammy says, "You sure ought to give that young one a few licks, so he'll mind," Jumbo laughs and says, "Lawsy 'magine me lickin' that young one," as Sambo returns singing, all dressed in fine clothes, with tiger butter on a palm branch and his story to tell. When he tells his story, Mumbo interrupts with, "Child, is you fabricatin? If you gave them all your clothes, how come you have all your clothes on? Orate me that." Even though Sambo actually tells the truth, Jumbo leaps in admiringly, "You sure can tell 'em, boy! Chip off de ole block, dat's wot." The play ends with Sambo singing and Sambo and Jumbo dancing while Mumbo is frying and flipping pancakes.

The Newark puppet production with its odd and unsettling script by Robert Warfield also begins in the kitchen, although in this case the kitchen is a cauldron outside of a hut where "MUMBO is stirring big pot; then moves over to basket, takes out red coat and looks at it. Comes to front and holds up coat for JUMBO's inspection."[61] The scene begins with an exchange between Mumbo and Jumbo:

> MUMBO: Jumbo! Jumbo! Look-a-heah and see ef'n dis coat looks fitten to wear. I ain't made anything so litty bit as dis heah coat in all my

life befo.' That Sambo looks so scandlous in his lil' white shirt, I 'lowed I betta make him some shore 'nuff clothes. What he wearin' right now don't come furder dan his waist. (NEGROS SONG, SINGING OFF STAGE.)

JUMBO: (Enters carrying his brass pot; sets it down) Well! Well! Mumbo, it mought'n fit him, but it shore is a bee-u-ti-ful coat. Is de tail of his shirt g'wine to show 'neath de coat? Looks kinda funny to me.

MUMBO: You is crazy man! 'Course I'm gwine to make dat chile a pair of trousers. Look! Here dy are, most done. I reckon our son'll look like a Rajah's son pretty soon. P'raps dey'll let him in the school when dey see him in all his fine clothes. Dey tell me the teachers are mighty 'ticular 'bout the 'pearance of de school chilluns, now dey got chairs to set on, stid of squattin' on de floor.[62]

After Sambo enters, pulling a dog by the tail, his mother tells him to try on the clothes. Stage directions instruct, "Sambo takes clothes and goes back of hut. Mumbo and Jumbo sing duet. Sambo returns, struts around; squats in front of dog. Sneezes. Mumbo wipes his nose." Then Sambo says, "Mammy, Ah shore is glad to have somethin' to wear besides mah little white shirt. . . . Seems like Ah was sneezin' 'most all de time." Mumbo replies, "Dat's a fact, chile, you certainly ketches cold mighty easy—maybe dese here clothes g'wine stop dat."[63]

Then Sambo catches sight of his bare feet and begins to cry, telling his mother that he won't be allowed in school without shoes. Jumbo offers to go to the bazaar "an' fetch de findin's for lil' Sambo's first man's costume. Mumbo, give me some money."

In scene two, Sambo is strolling in the jungle. He says:

Oh man! Is I happy? Yes sah! I is. I'se got me a coat, I'se got me green trousers, purple slippers with crimson soles and crimson linings and a blue umbrella. What I care ef'n school keeps or not. I'se g'wine tek a lil' walk in dis heah jungle. Ah jest can't bear to keep may purty clothes in de dark house. (TIGER GROWLS) Ah fought Ah mought meet up wid some folks to show mah clothes to, but Ah shore don't want to meet up wid any tigers.

TIGER: Good morning, little fella.

Up until this point, the script draws on minstrel caricature for characterization and malapropism and what passes for African American verbal play

FIGURE 9. *Little Black Sambo* (Newark, New Jersey). George Mason University. Fenwick Library. Special Collections and Archives.

as humor. And, as with the Reich script, Sambo is then put through the same spectacle of beasts threatening the little African American child that so delighted the Miami script, and again with the introduction of the tigers scripted Sambo loses his dialect. The Newark script, however, adds a contemporary note. When Sambo is begging the third tiger not to eat him and to take his shoes instead, he says, "You look like a sensible tiger." The tiger responds, "You bet I am. Not only am I the smartest tiger in this neck of the woods, but I am also the handsomest one!"

> SAMBO: Of course you are. But it looks like you're going to get some keen competition from two of your friends. I gave one of them my beautiful red coat and the other one got my pretty green pants.
> TIGER: Oh . . . so! I'll bet that would be Benny and Adolph. Those two guys are always cutting in on my territory.[64]

Sambo returns home and runs to his mother as she cries, "Whatever happened to you?" Sambo answers, "Oh mummy, did I have the time. I met three real Tigers." She replies, "Didn't your daddy tell you to stay out of the jungle?" (which Jumbo actually does not in the archived scripts). Sambo says, "Aw, what's the jungle? Nothin but a bunch of overgrown trees. Me, I'm brave, I'm not afraid of anything, not even tigers or jungles. Bring em on. Me and Joe Louis are brave guys." Mumbo asks him why he is carrying his clothes, and Sambo says, "The tigers took 'm off of me! They said they'd eat me if I didn't turn 'em over."

Describing a fantasy in which he beats up the tigers, Sambo continues:

> When there was just one ol tiger, he said, "Sambo, you give me your new coat or I'll eat you!" But I just laughed in his face and said, "Go on you ol' tiger, I ain't afraid of you, you better go on now or I'll bop you in the nose!"
> MUMBO: My, what a brave little boy you are, Sambo!
> SAMBO: Sure, an' a secon' ol tiger came up an' said he would eat me up if I didn't give him my new pants! But I jus' said to him, "Mr. Tiger, if you don't want me to kick you right in that ol' snoot of yours, you better run on along home to Mrs. Tiger!"
> MUMBO: And did he go, Sambo?
> SAMBO: What else could he do when I looked him right square in the eye?
> MUMBO: You sure make me proud of you, son!

> SAMBO: But then the fun started. Another ol' tiger snuck up on me behind and held my arms while his two pals took off all my bran' new clothes!
> MUMBO: My God! Then what did you do?
> SAMBO: Then I got sore. I ripped myself loose from that ol' third tiger and bopped 'im right square between the eyes with a left hook just like Joe Louis! Then I grabbed the other ol' tiger by the tail and swung him around in the air until he got dizzy, an' then I socked the third tiger with the one I was swinging around . . . [65]

As has no doubt become clear, Mumbo is a different character from the first scene, and the Sambo in these pages bears no relation to the child who entered the first scene dragging a dog by the tail. Presented first are negative characterizations in which each character performs to stereotype and the dialogue seems designed merely to forward the humorous situation these stereotypes provoke—the mammy figure whose coarseness is figured by her cauldron cooking, her ignorance of delicate sewing, and her neglect of her child's nakedness, the father figure who must borrow money from his wife to purchase the food, the child whose bare bottom is exposed as he is sneezing at his animal companion on the floor.

These caricatures are abandoned when Sambo returns home from the jungle. Mumbo becomes Mummy and listens to an excited Sambo retelling his exploits where instead of tricking the tigers, he beats them up, like Joe Louis. Instead of characters who function as stereotypes who play off of each other, Mumbo and Sambo create a close-knit mother-and-son dynamic. She listens to him and asks questions that respond to his imaginative retelling of his adventures. His exploits and his vision of himself grow in stature in response to her interest and admiration. His description seems less a lie than an imaginative retelling of a dream deferred.

Only the second African American holder of the World Heavyweight title, Joe Louis knocked out Nazi boxer Max Schmeling in the 1938 heavyweight title fight, one of the key events of the decade. Louis was a heroic figure who carried the hopes of the African American community for a symbolic blow to white racism and in the bout was pitted as the American champion against the Nazi champion—democracy against fascism—as Germany's aggression was heightening. Louis's only defeat before gaining the title in 1937 had been to Schmeling in 1935.

Though it was a less iconic event, Louis also fought and knocked out the representative of the other major European Axis power, Italian champion Primo Carnera. Later that summer, in August 1935, there was a race riot in

Jersey City between members of the African American community and the Italian-American community in which more than a thousand people armed with knives, baseball bats, bottles, and stones were involved. "The blacks in Jersey City had ridiculed the Italians for 'Mussolini Darling's' poor showing. The Italian Americans retorted by boasting about what fascist arms would achieve in Ethiopia," writes William R. Scott in a *Journal of Negro History* article about the incident.[66] On October 4, interracial fighting broke out in Brooklyn and Harlem. When Adwa fell later that month, blacks in Harlem attacked Italian street vendors and there were calls for national boycotts of Italian-owned businesses.

Louis's victory over Carnera provided the event that sparked the Jersey City controversy, but the context of this northeastern insurgency was a widespread African American interest in fascist aggression toward Ethiopia, grounded in no small part in the Black Nationalism sentiments of Garveyism and the back-to-Africa movement.[67] As Scott writes, "the Italian invasion of Ethiopia evoked an emotional attachment with the ancestral homeland which, in the opinion of some contemporaries, was far more intensifying than Marcus Garvey's vision of a free, redeemed, and mighty nation."[68]

The Newark version of *Little Black Sambo* opened on October 3, 1937, on the two-year anniversary of Mussolini's invasion. If the boy Sambo is like the fighter Joe Louis who fought the champions of both major fascist dictatorships, and the first two tigers, Benny and Adolph, are recognized as Benito Mussolini and Adolf Hitler, then the third tiger to which Sambo is forced to give not only his shoes but his green parasol is perhaps a contemporary figure as well. If so, Sambo's boast that the tiger was scared from taking his clothes from him, "What else could he do when I looked him right square in the eye?" and Mumbo's response, "You sure make me proud of you, son," carries extraordinary resonance.

Reading the first scene through the events surrounding the fights of Joe Louis shifts interpretations of Mumbo's hope that her son would be allowed to go to school. As the play opens, it might seem that she predicates educational opportunity on appearance and hopes to turn her son into a young dandy who will find the doors of the school opened to him. But read through the context of the play's latter half, education might be closed to Sambo even if he looks like a rajah's son. Mumbo's provision of clothes and Jumbo's of shoes speak of parents striving to better the conditions of their son's life.

Both the school lines in the first scene and the Mussolini/Hitler reference are removed from a second script, which is also attributed to Warfield.[69] Also removed is the reference to Sambo's "scandlous" little white shirt, which is replaced by a "little gingham skirt." In the second script, singing and dancing seems to have been added to replace some of the more controversial material. The overall structure is similar, but lines have been changed throughout and there is a much greater emphasis on singing. Sambo enters singing "Sometimes ah feel like nobody cares about me." Though Mumbo's lines about school are removed, after Sambo tries on his clothes and looks down at his feet, "He begins to whimper, 'PAPPY.' When his father asks what's wrong, Sambo replies, 'Pappy, ma feet don look right showing out so naked from under ma bran new breeches. The teacher won't let me in de school lessn'n ah have something on mah feet.'" This provokes the third song of the first scene, "Gonna Get Shoes."

As in the first script, the third tiger is dissuaded from eating Sambo by the parasol and shoes, and says, "Alright, you look pretty skinny anyway." Instead of the Mussolini/Hitler reference, the tiger says, "Oh, yeah! I'll show them mugs a thing or two. First I'll eat you and then—"[70] The dialect reappears in both scripts after Jumbo returns home triumphantly bearing the tiger butter and the truth about Sambo's tiger troubles is out. Both parents tease Sambo, drawing out his tale until he has also beaten up a rhinoceros, an elephant, a crocodile, and a lion. Jumbo then says, "Then you can go to the bazzar [sic]. I forgot to get sugar!" Sambo says, "Who, me? Me walk through that jungle with the sun goin' down? Uh-uh, I should say not! No-oo-oo." With Mumbo's response to quiet him, the dialogue returns: "Hush yo' cryin' honey. You jes' set while Mama's gonna bring back a heap o' fo' you [sic]." Then we find out that Jumbo's borrowing act in the first scene is complicated by his "Hope you made plenty [of pancakes], Mummy, case workin' twelve hours a day on that railroad sho' makes a man hungry."

The final scene, after the feast that takes place with the curtain down in the first script and offstage in the second, focuses on how both Jumbo and Sambo have a stomachache after having eaten so many pancakes. The absurd appetite in the book is here turned into a commentary about the joy of excess in a world of lack. Sambo says, "It hurts here Mummy. What yo' spec' I'se got?" Mumbo answers, "Lans sake chile. Expec' yoh can eat 169 pancakes without yo' lil tummy feeling it? (RUBS HIS BELLY)." The curtain comes down after Sambo says:

> Dis shore was a 'citin day for Sambo. Ah gits mah fust breeches an' Ah meets all dem Mr. Tigers an' now Ah eats dem, 'stead of dem eatin' me. Hoopla, an' Ah feels like Ah'd nevah be hungry again. One huner and sixty nine pancakes. Whoopee! Ah wouldn't mind meetin' tigers every day eff'n we could have pancakes right after.[71]

Given the topical cultural and political references in the play, it seems that in this final speech, Sambo is not only reflecting upon a very fine day, but asserting a new Sambo. He has bested his tormenters and *eaten* them. In the Miami script, the audience is denied the pleasure of the feasting, of the satiation that provides such full narrative closure in the picture book. In this *Little Black Sambo* we have not only the feast but Sambo musing afterward that he would be happy to take on and eat such tormentors every day.

A third script in the files was never produced by the FTP but was distributed by the Association of Junior Leagues of America, Inc. This play, which provides for "no royalty on *free* performances for *underprivileged children*" [emphasis theirs] begins in the jungle with "Large Black pot tripod L. Black Mumbo bending over pot" as Mumbo says, "Jumbo! Black Jumbo! Whar is dat no count niggah?" The exchange continues:

JUMBO: Who dat callin' Black Jumbo?
MUMBO: You knows berry well who callin' you. Don't you go pretendin' you can't reckernize the voice ob your lawful wife! What's mo' 'twas lil Black Sambo's own Mudder callin' you an' don't ferget it!

Mumbo says Sambo has been good for "three whole days" and that she wants to give him a present; she has been sewing clothes and wants Jumbo to get something from the market. After Jumbo exits, Sambo enters on a cartwheel as Mammy sings "Hush-a-bye ma lil pickaninny, etc." Sambo speaks the memorable lines "I's lil Black Sambo, I is, I is! I's lil Black Sambo, I is! Hello, Mammy!" Sambo gets his new clothes and feels so grand he wants to walk in the jungle; he is beset, gives the clothes away, the tigers fight, and he gets the clothes back as Jumbo scoops up the tiger butter. The play ends with Sambo's line "You bettah git me 'bout 169 (pancakes), Mammy, 'cause I is *so* hungry" and the stage directions "(JUMBO does the cakewalk)."

In all the puppet productions, including the Junior League script, Sambo addresses the tigers as Mr. and they in return call the boy by his first name, thus reproducing Southern black to white forms of address. This reproduction is perhaps no accident; it is perhaps not sheer carelessness that causes Sambo to lose his dialect upon confrontation with the tigers. Perhaps to oppose blackface and white speech so closely was to name too clearly the referent of ferocious hunger, an act of naming the Newark script subversively plays with and table-turning its end celebrates. Sambo's threatened body recalls nine Southern black boys facing the death penalty for an accusation of rape unsubstantiated by evidence. It recalls old Southern tourist postcards that showed black children clinging desperately to treetops and gazing down popeyed at grinning alligators on cards whose message read "Come on Down!" African American children and youth as natural prey in the American jungle is a part of U.S. cultural history.

The significance of the blackface minstrel-based *Little Black Sambo* plays lies in their continuing denial of black inclusion into the increasingly universalized protected child. By the 1930s, practically all children were recognized as deserving the rights and privileges of schooling, play, decent food, and health care. Both in adhering to and in subversively overturning the racist stereotypes of African Americans, these federal *Little Black Sambo* puppet shows, mostly forgotten and lying neglected in FTP files, detail the structure of racial feeling that enabled such exclusion.

Underscoring the complex racial representations within federal theatre is the Seattle production of *Brer Rabbit and the Tar Baby,* wherein it is precisely such mother love that is denied the mother figure. Although possessing a very different history, Joel Chandler Harris's Uncle Remus stories have, much like *The Story of Little Black Sambo,* enjoyed favor among white audiences as authentic folktales. The Seattle FTP adaptation *Brer Rabbit and the Tar Baby* by Ruth Comfort Mitchell and Alfred Allen used minstrel stereotypes and denigrating family characterizations much like the Miami puppet play had.[72] *Brer Rabbit and the Tar Baby* opened May 7, 1938, in Seattle.

As Tina Redd writes in her dissertation chapter on the Seattle unit,

> With the exception of a censored production of *Lysistrata,* Seattle's production history, critical recognition, and audience support combined, suggest that this Federal Theatre Negro Unit had achieved many of the goals established in Harlem, despite the fact that Negroes made up little more than one percent of the city's overall population.[73]

Redd also notes that initial directors Florence and Burton James contributed to the unit's early vitality and initial leftist slant.[74] They wrote, "As directors we see the theatre then as a social force in which is mirrored the contemporary scene," and with the establishment of the Negro Unit under their directorship proceeded to delight the general labor community of Seattle with their production of Sklar and Peter's *Stevedore.*[75] The James duo would leave the project, however, by the time *Brer Rabbit* was produced under the direction of Esther Porter Lane.

Brer Rabbit opens with "an old-fashioned darky of the child and laughter-loving type, [*sic*] comes down the center aisle of the theatre. SHE is dressed as in the plantation days before the war, and sings as SHE walks, in a low plaintive croon . . .)." The woman is singing "Swing Low, Sweet Chariot," and as she reaches the stage, "turns, faces the audience, and continues the croon, pleadingly—)"

> I'se feelin' so mon'fl, so sad an' fo'lorn!
> De chillen, dey's all run' away!
> I watch an' I wait, but dey sho' nuff gone . . .
> I'se longin' fo' de good ol' day!

A little girl who is lonely in the "big house" because the babies are too young to talk answers "Mammy's" lamentations. The girl answers Mammy's "Wonn' nobuddy come? Ain't dey *no* lil' chillen now' days?" by running down the aisle dressed in pre–Civil War hoopskirt and dress with "I'll come! Mammy, I'll come! Wait for me! I'll come!" Mammy "rapturously" replies "Bless de Lawd! One ob de chillen's come back!" and "flinging her arms" about the child says, "My honey-bud! Des come right erlong wif Mammy." As the two disappear inside "DARKEY FIELD HANDS (coming from the hoeing of the cotton, cross the stage, singing old time plantation melodies)."[76]

In an interview with Lane collected by George Mason University, Lane remembers the actor who played the Mammy because of her refusal to carry the portrayal to a certain point. Lane explained that the woman

> sat out front and started as a mammy telling stories out on the side to get us going on the whole Joel Chandler Harris stuff. And thoughtlessly, in those days, I had costumed her or asked her to be costumed in an Aunt Jemima red kerchief with little knots here and little knots there and she looked adorable. And then I found something was wrong, they were unhappy, she wasn't singing very well and, you know, the scene wasn't clicking. And they finally said, "Anything but that." And her mother had been a slave, her grandmother had been a slave, and even in those days, "I'll do anything but I won't put a red kerchief on my head."[77]

The cut frame is built around Mammy's explanations that babies have a language all their own that they share with animals, while what remains is the explanations themselves; in the cut version Mammy begins the story at the girl's request and the scene changes from her cabin to the woods as her voice becomes increasingly drowsy and the lights dim.

The actor next appears in act 2, which begins at Brer Rabbit's house. Miss Molly Cottontail who is "(plainly the darky MAMMY of 1) . . . stands in the doorway, talking into the house, sputtering wrathfully":

> 'Pears lak I don' got de tormintenist chillen ob de weepin' worl'! Kyarin' on dis-a-way, lak yo' nebber had no raisin! Ain' nebber *seed* yo' so rambunkshus!. Huccome yo-all so onery? I'se des plumb beat out, das what I is! I ain' drawed a peaceful bref since sun-up. Look lak de good Lawd wanter chasten my sperrit, gibbin' me all dese boddermints! I'se des daid on my feet, das whut I is! (rousing a little) But yo' hyar me! Ef de Lawd don' 'flict my sperrit, den I'se gwiter 'flict yo' hide! (She picks up a switch and shakes it threateningly in the doorway) De nex' chile whut lets out de firs' squidgeon ob a squeal, I'se gwinter to frail him if hit's de las' act!

The kind and gentle, forlorn Mammy wishing for her children to return is transformed into a violent mother figure. This characterization accords with a racist stereotyping of black women dependent on a plantation ethos that insists that African Americans display appropriate familial behaviors only under the influence of the larger "plantation family." In an inversion of normative gendered familial relations, black women are shown as violent and threatening and domineering within their own families. The mammy of *Brer Rabbit and the Tar Baby* is only nurturing to the white children, and her call at the beginning of the play is only to them and, significantly, constitutes a longing for the return not only of the white children, but for the system that produced them.

Analogues to children's theatre's conservative and sometimes racially oppressive productions are found in adult theatre files. The FTP's National Service Bureau, which had a theatre library of five thousand volumes, produced both "A List of Negro Plays" and "56 Minstrels" for distribution to theatre groups and use by Federal Theatre units in 1938.[78] In a foreword to the "Negro plays," authored by white and black playwrights, John Silvera acknowledges:

> The number of plays written for Negro actors has up to now been almost negligible; what has been done, however, gives a clear indication of the possibilities that lie within the race group. It can be truly said that by his acting, his dance, and his music the Negro has left an indelible imprint on the American stage. A few memorable characters have been created and it is these that best reflect the ideals if not the tradition of the Negro theatre. In presenting this group of representative plays, Federal Theatre attempts

to further these ideals and to assist in broadening the dramatic horizon of a gifted race. . . .

Silvera adds that though both black and white playwrights were writing about the American black experience, only white perspectives on blacks had received wide dramatic success.[79] Noting that a white-controlled theatre circulates and reifies white perception of the black American experience, he writes:

> The rich field of Negro drama has attracted both White and Negro authors but the majority of Negro plays that have received public attention have been written by White persons. Compared with his efforts in other forms of literature, particularly poetry and the novel, the Negro author has done little in this fertile field. In censuring his choice of endeavor, we must however, bear in mind the fact that writing for the stage has been subjected to commercial dictation and Negro themes find little market for expression. Federal Theatre hopes to stimulate further writing and through its National Service Bureau offers assistance on research, problems of direction and stagecraft, to authors, schools, and nonprofessional groups alike. . . .

A young African American playreader, Silvera co-wrote the Living Newspaper on American race relations *Liberty Deferred*, a production that would never actually reach the stage.[80] He writes further after the table of contents:

> Perhaps no subject in American literature is as alive and moving as that of the Negro in his relations to his own and to other races. More and more has the place of the Negro in his community, his efforts to combat repression, racial, economic and political, become the theme for dramatic presentation. Most of the plays herein presented deal with the social and economic phases of this struggle. They are important as representing a definite break with the traditional concept of the Negro as a music-hall, tap-dancing comic figure. . . .[81]

"A List of Negro Plays" contains brief descriptions for each play that include the author's name, publisher's name and address, synopsis, and playreader commentary.

This format is followed as well for each of "56 Minstrels," which contain as well "type" ("colored minstrel act for young people"), cast number, running time, and sets. If the overriding presence of social realism in the "Negro plays" gathered for distribution indicates an attempt to build an American theatre that recognizes and reflects the complexity of African American history and psychological subjectivity, as well as adherence to Popular Front social realism, the minstrel list indicates the widespread cultural resistance to that effort. The minstrels were compiled by the Music Vaudeville Service Department, which seems to have gotten most of its performances from the catalogues of the T. S. Denison & Company and the Dramatic Publishing Company of Chicago and the Willis N. Bugboo Company of Syracuse. In addition to the compilation, vaudeville performances with titles such as *Dixie Minstrels, The Dixie Dandies, All American Minstrels, Swanee Minstrels,* and even *Federal Theatre Minstrels,* titles that do not appear in the collection of minstrel acts, appeared on federal stages across the country. *Plantation Days* was performed by Negro Units in Oakland and San Francisco and by a puppet theatre in Jacksonville, Florida.[82]

The presence of federally staged and collected minstrel shows reflects the talents of those performers on the welfare rolls and the types of roles available to them historically as well as audience tastes. The conflicted attitudes that appear on the FTP playreader reports for minstrel skits reflect how pervasive was minstrelsy in the common culture. In their language and assessments, readers reveal discretely different attitudes toward the blackface minstrel tradition in American entertainment, yet all display a comfortable familiarity with the material. A "poem" titled "Nigger Baby," by Bertha M. Wilson and published by the Penn Publishing Co. of Philadelphia, is rejected by one reader, who writes, "This effort is too hackneyed for present day audiences." The reader writes the following synopsis:

> The poem deals with a little colored girl similar to Topsy of *Uncle Tom's Cabin* in which the person reciting the poem reveals herself to be white when, at the finish, she removes some of the burnt cork.

Another reader rejects the same piece with this comment and synopsis:

> One can imagine grandniece Agatha inflicting this recitation on Sunday evening guests in the parlor way back when audiences were seen and not heard, but nowadays there's the Bronx cheer to be reckoned with, therefore it would be wiser to allow this material to be placed in the limbo into which the passing of many years has placed it.
>
> The little darkie Miss tells all about her dollie, her dancing and her love of watermelon and lastly reveals she is not really a little darkie, having created her brunette complexion with ink and shoe blackening.[83]

A reader for the minstrel show "Alabama Attaboy Minstrels," by Arthur Leroy Kaser (author of 19 of the "56 Minstrels"), recommends it as a "good first part of a minstrel show." A second reader concurs, though with unexplained "reservations," writing that it is a "fairly amusing minstrel crossfire with at least one gag which is new to this reader." A third rejects the same "as material no longer considered worthy entertainment. Dialogue, puns and jokes are very old and no longer amusing." The reader characterizes it as "usual minstrel material—gags, duologues [sic] and jokes of a 'passe' period."[84]

Acknowledging racially denigrating stereotypes in FTP productions, however, does not negate the achievement of key federal plays for children in registering the expanding range of possibilities for African American representation. A second review to the one that opened this discussion, for the *Chicago Evening American,* begins

> "Yep," said the wide-eyed nine year old. "It's Little Black Sambo alright...."
> It's a play, for children, but truth to tell, the half child, half adult audience enjoyed it equally. Every one of them remembered the old, old[] story of a Jungle Sambo who wanted a red coat, blue trousers, green umbrella, and purple shoes more than anything else in the world.... [85]

Much like the audience of the Newark production, perhaps those in Chicago saw the old, familiar story—and nothing more. But it would not have been that with which they had been presented. Not Sambo, little or otherwise.

CHAPTER 4

"SHADOWS OF YOUR THOUGHTS ARE MARCHING"

Anti-Fascism and Home-front Patriotism in Federal Theatre's *A Letter to Santa Claus* and Hollywood's *The Little Princess*

By 1938, the House Committee on Un-American Activities (Dies Committee) had expanded its search for communists outward from the Federal Theatre to Hollywood. Uncritical press had given its investigations influence, but in its first turn to Hollywood the committee invited ridicule. The *Washington Post* later reported: "One of the most highly publicized charges aired before the Dies committee was that the Communists had captured Shirley Temple and made that charmer of the screen if not quite a dues-paying Red at least into an unwitting 'fellow traveler.'"[1] The *Post* article continues:

> But now the police chief of Los Angeles has confused the picture, painted in such frightening colors at a Dies committee hearing, by giving Shirley a resplendent police badge. That makes her a member of the auxiliary police force of the city and subject, like the 7,842 other badge holders, to call in emergencies. Since the Los Angeles police has often been accused by liberals and radicals of being enamored of Hitlerite and Mussolinian tactics, the little lady now faces the accusation that she is a Fascist as well as a Communist.[2]

Temple's name appeared before the Dies Committee because she was one of a number of Hollywood celebrities who had sent greetings to a French communist newspaper. And while other than this brief foray into the Dies Committee's purview, Temple remained famous for her curly mop rather than her radical politics, in 1939's *The Little Princess* she starred in a film that examines the role of war on the family, a film that arguably engages with fascist aggression in Europe and mobilization for war at home.

This chapter examines two productions for children—the Federal Theatre Project's 1938 *A Letter to Santa Claus* and 20th Century Fox's Temple film *The Little Princess*—that dramatize the difference between the leftist liberal FTP and a conservative Hollywood system. As will be argued, they enact very different moral responses to the looming threat of fascism and war. Drawing on a deeply felt investment in the child, the American play and the film reveal fundamental national concerns about democratic values, national character, and citizenship, and deeply divided ideas about the relation of family to the larger national/social body. Like Shirley Temple's screen persona, *A Letter to Santa Claus*'s companionate siblings Joe and Mary embody innocence and goodness, but the play's characterization and narrative suture very different connections between home and nation and, thus, portray very different responses to citizen involvement in a threatening global conflict.

Comparing the film and play brings together two prominent and often contradictory discourses of childhood: the sentimental Victorian fantasy of the idealized child and the Popular Front utopian longing for the radicalized future citizen. Joe and Mary subordinate the domestic sphere to the public one and nationalistic values to cosmopolitan ones. This inverts the relationship of the domestic to the public articulated by *The Little Princess*, an inversion that foregrounds the issues of home-front patriotism I explore. In both productions, however, the figure of the child is deployed to assert America's democratic ideals and citizen resolve, thus allaying anxieties about both fascist might and America's role as a global power in the production of war.

Children simultaneously provided rich symbolic material for artistic production in Germany that celebrated Nazi power and for American entertainment that warned of the rising fascist threat. In her 1988 autobiography, Shirley Temple Black remembers that her stunningly successful 1934 *Baby, Take a Bow* was banned in Berlin because of the opinion that "gangsterism and gunplay were excessively portrayed." At the same time, she notes, "Germany was then awash in pride over the epic *Triumph of the Will*."[3] If not partaking of the child-centered erotics of a Temple film, Riefenstahl's depiction of the 1934 Nuremburg rally builds much of its celebratory message on children's symbolic potential. Children figure consistently in the early crowd scenes in *Triumph of the Will*.[4] They are lifted on shoulders and pushed to the front of crowds lining the streets to see the Führer drive by; they gaze at his passing figure with wide, excited eyes as the camera isolates their faces. Riefenstahl's children enact an appropriate emotional response to the Führer's presence and particularize the future of the German Reich. Their presence attests to an ordered social body wherein a united family forms a synecdochic signifier of political, economic, and cultural order. In *Triumph of the Will* children gaze at their redeemer, the father/führer, whose patriarchal control assures their future as their static, subordinate position emphasizes the vigor of his progress.

Thus, as in *Triumph of the Will*, children's symbolic plenitude is harnessed in these pieces in order to enact national values and model citizen behavior for vaguely defined political ends. *Triumph of the Will* is an explicitly political document, but it celebrates a militaristic culture and imperial rhetoric while masking very explicit plans for war. War in both children's productions is removed from explicit cultural touchstones; in *A Letter to Santa Claus* war is one manifestation of economic strife, and in *The Little Princess* it is historicized. If in genre and culture of origin the German film fits uneasily in comparison to the two American productions for children, its presence here nonetheless highlights the manner in which Nazi discourse draws on the symbolic value of children's dynamism, growth, and vigor in service to the state. This relation to power provides an interesting comparison to the lack of legitimizing authority in the two American productions for children. It furthermore draws attention to how representations of children implicitly promise a better future, a promise particularly meaningful in the economically depressed cultures of both Germany and the United States.[5]

Planned for a two-week run in December 1938, the one-act *A Letter to Santa Claus* tells the story of two children who are frightened and confused by the "shadows" that disturb their family and community.[6] Trying to deliver a note to Santa Claus, they see the shadow of a soldier before they fall asleep on the rooftop. When they awaken, Santa is on the rooftop to deliver gifts, but the house is now surrounded by more shadows of war and social conflict. Disliking this strife-ridden world, Santa decides to leave. The children hear his call to the wind and repeat it so that they are whirled to the North Pole, where they undergo a series of character tests as Santa is traveling the world delivering gifts. When they pass the tests, Santa gives them a chant to take back to America to make the shadows go away. The play ends as audience and children chant together.

Based on the Frances Hodgson Burnett story, *The Little Princess* was released in March 1939 as Hitler was seizing Czechoslovakia. The film's Sara Crewe is the daughter of a soldier who has traveled from her home in India to a London boarding school, where she will remain while her father fights in the Boer War.[7] Temple's Sara is left destitute when her father is listed among the missing at Mafeking and his fortune is seized. As in the book, the headmistress forces her to live in the attic and work for the school. But Temple's Crewe never believes that her father is dead, and in the end she finds him in a hospital, where they are reunited under the benevolent gaze of Queen Victoria, trundling through in her wheelchair visiting the wounded. The film ends as all sing "God Save the Queen" together.[8]

Triumph of the Will provides an entry point to a discussion of the two American productions because it offers fascism's most idealized vision of the role of children in the state both symbolically and literally. From the boys playing games that prepare them for the soldier's life ahead to the children standing along the parade route as Hitler's motorcade enters Nuremburg, children figure as the ideal German citizen. This citizen is submissive to authority yet vigorous in enactment of rituals that symbolize national allegiance; this citizen's energies are marshaled by the state's call to action and organized by participation in state-sponsored societies.

In Germany, as in America, difficult economic times manifested themselves in a heightened rhetoric centered on children. The fascist celebration of purity, rebirth through submission, primitivism, and feeling over intellect found its corollary in the figure of a child. Hitler's leadership was represented as a potent tonic for a national crisis of faith. As Hans Schem, head of the National Socialist Teachers Federation, writes:

> National Socialism is the awakening of the youthful strength of the German Volk, regardless of the age of the individual. . . . All of us, spiritually viewed, were rejuvenated through Adolf Hitler and his work. . . . Adolf Hitler returned Germans to their childhood. Every event in our present economic, political, cultural and governmental life finds its parallels in youthful life-affirmations.[9]

The Nazi political order mythologized, and its spectacles often visually represented, a mysticism that characterized nature as the signifier of *blut und boden,* a spiritual connection to a national heritage born of blood's connection to the land.[10] As bodily development is imagined as a socializing process, Schem's metaphor depicts a revitalized political and economic life that connects the socialized adult to the natural child. The metaphor yokes civilization and nature, technology and primitivism, the real circumstances of the individual to a dramatic narrative of national history. Children thus symbolize not only nature but a mythologized past, even as they stand for the future citizens of the fascist state.[11]

In *Triumph of the Will* fascism's invocation of a collective will and memory is visualized to connect citizen and state in a pageant of national unity.

The film juxtaposes shots of the parade of flags and symbolic elements such as the eagle with shots of the solitary, impassioned leader and adoring crowds in order to create an expressive identification on the part of the viewer with the camera and its immersion in the orgiastic pageantry of National Socialism. The individual finds expression as part of the disciplined mass.[12] Technique and characterization thus combine to make the viewer feel as though she is a part of a present moment that proceeds, like a history, from past moments unrecorded. *Triumph of the Will* evokes a history and a historical forgetting by substituting symbol and seamless editing for historical memory and events. Like its parade of torches and flags, the film's repetition of its beautiful blond children (both in silent homage and boisterous Hitler Youth games) strips the children of individuality and orders them as aesthetic signifiers of Nazi ideology. Children in *Triumph of the Will* embody the *volk*'s perfect submission to Hitler and testify to the vigor of his power. The replication of that perfect submission renders childhood itself as abstraction, as symbol, in service of the political order. Children in the Nazi film participate in a symbolic structure wherein national identity is analogous to traditional family roles of authoritarian father and submissive, obedient children.

European fascism provoked widespread opposition in America, particularly among Popular Front artists and intellectuals. The New York theatre world and Hollywood were both centers of antifascist émigré culture. Although neither progressive nor overtly antifascist, *The Little Princess*'s engagement with the rising threat of war signaled a growing Hollywood engagement with fascist aggression. To that point, the studio system had largely avoided commentary on the rising fascist threat in order to maintain lucrative overseas markets and avoid problems with the American regulatory system. The American film industry capitulated to domestic pressure from pro-fascist groups, the Hays Office, and the Production Code Administration. Additionally, in 1933 Germany decreed that it would pull the distribution rights of any film deemed anti-Nazi. The threat was significant: Hollywood studios received 30 to 40 percent of their gross revenues from foreign markets. In 1939, 150 million Europeans were watching American films each week. Although Warner Brothers pulled out of Germany in 1934, other American studios, including 20th Century Fox, did not; it was one of three studios that exported films to Germany until September 1940.[13]

Domestic fascism and American attraction to European fascism lost popularity when Hitler consolidated power in the early 1930s and Benito Mussolini invaded Ethiopia in 1936. But though leftists and leftist liberals almost uniformly supported the antifascist cause following Mussolini's takeover of Italy in 1923, the pragmatic, experimental nature of Mussolini's regime appealed not only to certain U.S. business leaders and proponents of authoritarian governance but also to some liberals who viewed Mussolini's revolution as a new social experiment offering a redistribution of wealth and insisting on the primacy of the values of private property. To these liberals, fascism—at least initially—seemed like Americanism. Historian Charles Beard wrote of Italy in the *New Republic*:

> This is far from the frozen dictatorship of the Russian Tsardom; it is more like the American check and balance system; and it may work out in a new democratic direction. . . . Beyond question, an amazing experiment is being made here, an experiment in reconciling individualism and socialism, politics and technology. It would be a mistake to allow feelings aroused by contemplating the harsh deeds and extravagant assertions that have accompanied the Fascist process (as all other immense historical changes) to obscure the potentialities and the lessons.[14]

While such liberal assessments had all but disappeared by the time of the rise of Hitler, fascism's authoritarian politics and racist ideology appealed to the disenfranchised and the violent and the anxious at home. Fascist Italian American newspapers and organizations operated with far more support than antifascist ones. The pro-Hitler German American Bund printed a magazine for young people and published four newspapers; it held rallies that numbered participants in the thousands. The pro-fascist Silver Legion was founded in 1933 in Asheville, North Carolina, by former Hollywood screenwriter William Dudley Pelley; members of Detroit's Black Legion murdered the secretary for the United Auto Workers that same year. For these Americans, fascism's authoritarian control, supreme nationalism, and articulation of mythic destiny were deeply appealing.[15] In the pro-fascism magazine the *American Review*, Ross J. S. Hoffman, professor at New York University and self-described member of the Catholic Right, wrote:

> Obviously there is no solution but a revolutionary solution, for the tottering American political system of today is perhaps the best demonstration of those anti-authoritarian principles which have brought about the wreckage of modern society. There must be a revolution—a constructive revolution in behalf of authority, order, and justice; and there is no dodging that fact.[16]

Against the tired Enlightenment values of liberalism and the new class consciousness of communism, both of which appealed to internationalism, fascism seemed to offer a potent Americanism—a return to a mythologized America whose destiny was manifest.

Three-quarters of a century later, the resonance of *A Letter to Santa Claus* and *The Little Princess* stems in part from the poignant uncertainty of the power each upholds to ward off the shadows of war. In *Triumph of the Will* children are visually connected to power, their outstretched fingers twinned by Hitler's at the most basic level of the fascist salute. But in the two American productions the children are dangerously on their own. And the worlds of *A Letter to Santa Claus* and *The Little Princess are* dangerous. In the first, threats are manifest as shadows; moral authority and action are invested in the wisdom of Santa Claus. In the second, a fatherless child is turned out of her room and made to go hungry in an attic garret. In neither world does a parental figure offer reassurance or an authority figure offer security.

Thus, Charlotte Chorpenning staged a very different federal pageant for the Chicago Federal Theatre Project than the paean to power conceived by Hitler and Riefenstahl. Primarily known for her fairy-tale adaptations, Chorpenning wrote *A Letter to Santa Claus* for a series of special matinees staged just before Christmas in 1938; children were admitted for free to these showings. The play was planned for a stadium production but had to be scaled back for the Blackstone Theatre. For *A Letter to Santa Claus* the federal theatre ignored its mandate to use only adult actors and used two children to play the leads. According to the production book, the play was originally intended to draw on the resources of all the Chicago units—the vaudeville, ballet, white, and Negro units, and with choruses and the orchestra from the Federal Music Project. Scaled back, it still had a full orchestra and a cast of seventy-five, including acrobats, a snow ballet with thirty dancers, and the entire Chicago vaudeville unit. Almost all of its music was original. Lighting notes by Duncan Whiteside in the production book describe effects intended to emphasize color. "Whatever the scene or the particular demands of the scene, the result was the quality of a Maxfield Parrish canvas."[17] The play also featured dancing penguins and polar bears in a production that was timed to last exactly one hour.[18] It was a Federal Theatre Project extravaganza.

An elegaic meditation on the value of liberalism to animate civic, economic, and political justice, *A Letter to Santa Claus* stands alone among the FTP children's plays. Positioning its child protagonists as seekers of peace, *A Letter to Santa Claus* expresses a liberal response to international and domestic aggression that links global strife to people's daily interactions and international fascism to domestic fascism. Understanding that the strife within their home is emblematic of larger conflicts, Joe and Mary seek to rid their world of threats that they only dimly understand as shadows. No other FTP children's play asked so much of its contemporary protagonists outside of a distancing dream narrative or framework of comedy. No other FTP children's play broached the topic of war and the Depression realities of hunger and strife outside the framework of comedy.[19] Lowell Swortzell, whose collection *Six Plays for Young People* reprinted the play, wrote in his introduction:

> A Letter to Santa Claus is of interest not simply because Chorpenning wrote it . . . but mostly because of the anti-war sentiments that permeate almost every scene. References to hunger, poverty, and the "shadows" that cross the land . . . convey a sense of national disillusionment. . . . Surely there has never been a Santa Claus play for "Children Only" written with such a deeply felt and disturbing subtext.[20]

These fears were also singular in federal children's theatre.[21]

In its themes and staging, Chorpenning's play exemplifies what Julia Mickenberg has cogently analyzed as a Popular Front rhetoric that "linked the playful, nonsectarian, and antiauthoritarian consciousness characteristic of the Lyrical Left . . . to the strongly prolabor, antiracist, and anti-imperialist views of the revolutionary Old Left."[22] Popular Front cultural production for children combined the progressive emphasis on the child as a socially animating site of hope with the communist program of socializing children for a transformed society. As Mickenberg notes, this common emphasis on socializing the child "rejected an authoritarian model of adult-child relations and emphasized freedom, democracy, and cooperation as desirable traits."[23]

Chorpenning's productions for Federal Theatre, from *The Story of Little Black Sambo* to *The Emperor's New Clothes*, emphasize these values and valorize the child's potential. Her fairy-tale adaptations exemplify modernist reimaginings of traditional narratives, though they do not exemplify the radical work that would be done in proletarian and leftist children's theatre. If Popular Front cultural production for children eschewed the traditional fairy-tale narrative, with the rise of Nazism in Germany gone too was the Weimar Republic's freewheeling, often overtly political, experimentation with children's theatre.[24] Paradoxically, the authoritarian Third Reich and the democratic United States largely agreed that the most appropriate theatre for children was traditional, if not necessarily overtly didactic, and apolitical; by the twentieth century the traditional fairy tale's inherited symbols, gender roles, and narratives placed it comfortably in the delimited space of cultural production for children in both countries. Although the first New York Children's Unit director Abel Plenn dismissed "the outdated" fairy-tale plays as "harbor[ing] very few illusions for that stern realist, the post-war child," in fact the FTP children's theatre repertory was always heavily drawn from fairy tales and folktales.[25] The social realism of adult plays produced by the Federal Theatre Project was largely rejected in favor of fairy-tale adaptations for children.[26] But the cultural politics of mythologies and traditional fairy tales central to the construction of the German *volk* was obviously quite different from that of the traditionalism implied by the same tales in an ethnically diverse, immigrant America. Adaptations by Chorpenning and Los Angeles Children's Unit director Yasha Frank articulate a leftist vision of childhood, although they did not adhere to an overtly Popular Front politics or aesthetics.

A Letter to Santa Claus begins as Joe and Mary have sneaked to the rooftop on Christmas Eve to give Santa Claus a letter Joe has been writing for "weeks and weeks. . . . I couldn't get the letter to sound right. It's about the shadows," he says. Stage directions call for a shadow to appear "of a soldier (not nationalized), a little larger than life, and not too black."[27] Shadows presage strife both within their own family and outside of it and thus connect the domestic and the public:

> It isn't just us. You think it's Mother crying, and it's lots of people crying. You think it's just the milkman quarreling with the man that pays him, and it's lots of people quarreling. You think you're hungry, and it's lots and lots of people hungry. They're what you hear when the shadows go by.[28]

The soldier introduces and outlasts all other forms of conflict in the play, suggesting the primacy of aggression and military domination among all other conflicts. And yet, the first cause following the soldier is shown to be "children quarreling," with "shadows of children snatching from each other, food, etc and voices 'It's mine,' 'I want the most!' and 'I don't like you.'" Voices escalate to include industrial and class conflict, and the sound that resonates beyond the weeping and quarreling voices is the little child crying "I'm hungry."[29]

Against the fear, hatred, and aggression bound up with the appearance of the shadows is the majesty of the morally and materially bountiful Santa Claus who wants no part of the shadow-led strife. He calls out:

> Christmas music on the air
> And so I came.
> Other things are on the air.
> What you think is on the air.
> What you feel is on the air.

Shadows of your thoughts are marching,
Shadows of the things you feel, go by.
I don't like those shadows,
I don't like the world you're making with the things you think and feel
So I go away.[30]

Santa's action clarifies that the sociopolitical problems enumerated by the people's voices feed and strengthen one another and that a solution cannot be imposed from on high. Equally, his departure negates the possibility that as a moral authority he exists in some affective relationship with the people. As a beneficent figure whose actions of goodwill are not constrained by national boundaries, and as the locus of a moral authority disconnected from the exigencies of responsibility for economic, political, or social justice, Santa Claus figures as an intangible being who explicitly belongs to no one. Instead of glorifying militarism, he refuses to participate in an order that supports it: like universal values, he is transcendent.

The central trait of the play's Santa Claus is, in fact, his absent presence. Having heard Santa's call to the Christmas winds that help him lift his sleigh, Joe and Mary echo his words in order to follow him and deliver the letter he has not taken.[31] From a distance, Santa Claus puts the children through a series of tests; he listens on the radio to determine whether or not they have responded appropriately. The lessons taught by these tests range from learning to share with polar bears to learning to work together. They enact in simple, didactic terms the complicated way in which childhood innocence is both assumed as inherent to children and assumed to be the result of the process of education. Joe and Mary learn sharing as a civic virtue; they initially do want all of the gifts offered. But in seeing that the polar bears want them too, they gradually learn to accept only what they need.

The tests also point to the rejuvenating possibilities of a childlike faith in the rules of society. At the South Pole Joe and Mary want to hunt for Santa, but the playful penguins assure them they will only find him if they have fun. Joe is encouraged to slide, but he almost runs through a red flashing light. "Oh! I almost didn't see it! How would I be punished if I hadn't?" The penguins are mystified by the idea of punishment:

> NOEL: No one is ever punished here.
> NOELITA: We just all agreed together to stop when the red came on.
> JOE: What if some one doesn't stop?
> NOEL: Doesn't stop? . . . Everybody does.
> NOELITA: (With finality): We agreed on it.[32]

In a just society, penguins are rationally good.[33]

Joe and Mary enact a simple representation of childhood that enables audience members to equate civic action with innocence and moral purity. The children experience each lesson as if they had no complicating social or familial contexts. In this they are innocent. Free of hate and greed and fear, they confront adult problems with a self-reliant bravery stemming from a certainty about what is right and wrong. In this, they are good. When Santa Claus explains that he cannot banish the shadows and that the light that will destroy those shadows must come from someone else, the children go alone to rid the world of shadows. Childhood innocence becomes the basis for a goodness that will produce a just and equitable society.

Thus, the child's innocence tropes a nation's. *A Letter to Santa Claus* deploys the figure of the child to explore the role between the American citizen and social transformation. It makes explicit the link between a child's innocence and corresponding morally correct action, and the shift in political consciousness necessary for America to produce a response to European war commensurate with its self-image as a moral leader. While both the cause and effect of conflict are rooted in quarreling situated in familial, domestic terms—father, mother, children—the children appeal to the international moral authority of Santa Claus to end the strife. The children provide the link between family, nation, and the world. America, the play suggests, cannot defeat the shadows of war until it addresses the problems of economic inequality. Situating effective idealistic action in such childhood values as unselfishness and kindness, the play produces a child who stands in for the resolute problem-solving American who is in turn the metonymic mascot for the nation.

But if Joe and Mary enact a simplistic representation of childhood, the manner in which childhood innocence tropes American identity is not simple at all. Many critics have noted that representations of childhood innocence create a condition that is outside of history and knowledge, and therefore outside of accountability.[34] As a longstanding trope of Americanness, innocence is not innocent at all. Rather, it is a thematic that divorces national identity from the social and juridical injustices and inequities the nation has imposed upon individuals. It absolves a nation of accountability. But childhood innocence would not be such a powerfully animating thematic for Americanness if it just served as a deceptive cover for American participation in unjust practices and histories. Childhood innocence also emphasizes America's self-image as a nation united by ideals rather than shared history or blood. As Todd Gitlin puts it snappily, "In principle Americanness is a matter of principle."[35] Innocence is the condition of being for the ideally principled person who is never compromised by the messy context of lived experience. So while a childlike innocence will mask, for example, America's complicity in the production of arms for war and its low quotas that kept Jews from reaching safety, Joe and Mary's innocence makes operational the values of tolerance and cooperation and thus makes paramount the ideals of liberal democracy.

Contextualizing the children's actions, Chorpenning uses the opposition of light and dark imagery to suggest a dichotomy between unconscious, psychological fears and rational action. The play most vividly externalizes inner subjectivity by its use of shadows that symbolically enact the unconscious fears of the American populace. They were produced by projecting actions and tableaus onto a screen behind the stage and were accompanied by sounds: guns popping, martial music, voices raised in argument, children and adults crying. The shadows are an externalization of those primitive and irrational forces against which Joe and Mary and Santa Claus are allied. But unlike the unconscious as projected, for example, in *Emperor Jones*, the shadows in this play have become threatening to a multitude, awaiting only the hypnotizing wizard to harness their power. The light that Joe and Mary bring back from the North Pole is not the light of the cross, and their banishment of the shadows and transformation of people is not an exorcism. Rather, it is the light of the analyst, the wielder of human truth in the modern science of psychoanalysis, the light that can harness, contain, and so banish the primitive of the unconscious.

Light imagery is also used to suggest Enlightenment values as opposed to the dark psychological savagery of war. The opening scene, for example, reflects a conception of an ordered and harmonious universe. The stage directions state: "In spite of its being night, the first effect of the stage on the children must not be sombre—but mysterious, very beautiful but not depressing nor 'creepy.' A shooting star across the silver screen would be a good first thing to happen. Faint radio, Christmas music, in some house."[36] The universe is harmoniously connected by the aural and visual display of Christmas music and a shooting star, which are echoed and amplified in a later scene at the South Pole in "spires, gleaming shafts, arches, lacework, every sort of carving by wind and water in the ice, all breaking the sunlight into the prismatic colors by their facets and throwing strong shadows."[37] The South Pole is staged as a utopian space of light and form, a place brought back with the children.

Of the shadows, Santa says, "Nothing will blot them out but the Christmas light. And it can't come from me. It must come from the same place as the shadows do." He then teaches them a chant:

> Open your heart
> And shut your eyes
> And I'll give you something
> To make you wise
> Your heart shall be
> The heart of a friend
> Your eyes shall see
> How love should end.
> And now I have made you wise.[38]

When Santa asks, "How should love end?" both children respond, "In doing things, of course." They return to the city with its shadows of the "down and out," whom Joe recognizes as "the shadows of what you think and feel." Mary begins the chant and Joe joins in. As Mary speaks, the tableau changes and the huddled figures "undergo a change, lifting their heads, their faces light up . . . the MAN gets to his feet, the WOMEN stand strong and radiant. A slender pencil of light shoots across the shadows."[39]

As the first group is transformed, however, new groups enter the stage. The stage becomes filled with people chanting, but the drums and sounds of grief rise, even as more light shoots across the stage. Joe and Mary start the chant again, until there is only the shadow "of a great soldier and two figures with uplifted fists." At this point, Joe lifts his hands for the audience to come in, and as the entire theatre chants "Your heart shall be the heart of a friend / Your eyes shall see where love should end," "the last SHADOW is blotted out in streaming Auroras" and the sound of bells is heard.[40] The crowd forms a tableau: "some on their knees, some arms entwined, some lifting others to see." On cue, Santa appears, and the play ends with a chorused "Merry Christmas . . . and laughter."[41] In this theatrical mash-up, Chorpenning brings together expressionist lighting, leftist tableau, and Main Street holiday bathos in an aurally and visually spectacular finale.

As the character Santa Claus articulates, both light and shadows (essentially good and evil) come from the same place. Within this moral dichotomy, fear, class hatred, and violence threaten to undo the order of the play's world. Consequently, Joe and Mary are tasked with rebuilding social morality. And as they bring the values of rationality, pluralism, and the rule of law to the world to save it from war, they further reinforce the adherence to those same values that they have demonstrated in the polar bear and penguin games. Yet the moral authority from which salvation stems is Santa Claus, a figure with an alliance to the history of Christian religious doctrine and practice of giving. Santa's fairly contemporary role in advertising Christmas connects the character to a distinctly secular practice of giving, punctuating a Christian theology of good versus evil without reference to sin. A Christmas pageant without reference to figures of Christian theology, the play thus asserts a moral binary and overtly positions a secular Santa Claus as its supreme authority. The dialogue forces the audience to remember Santa's role as judge, thereby reinforcing a moral binary. Yet there is no messiah and no messianic return to assert both authority and judgment within Santa's role. Salvation is conceived as an international and secular project dependent upon ethical behavior, wisdom, and the rule of law. And while the names Joe and Mary connote the ordinary Jewish couple who will give birth to Christ, such naming challenges the Christian sexual taboo as the text covertly assails Christian norms of "good" and "evil."

Although she too faces a fearful world, Shirley Temple's indomitable little Sara Crewe stands in sharp contrast to the FTP children in the face of imminent war. If the FTP play deploys the child as a force of effective idealism in a public social space, Shirley Temple's screen child in *The Little Princess* enacts the code of "the little soldier" to retain her father's protective love and the sanctity of her domestic space. As in her other films, *The Little Princess* details an excruciatingly cruel reversal of fortune that Temple must overcome in order to return to her status of petted center of the household. If the children in the FTP play create a relationship of identification and otherness that tropes social change, Temple's screen girlhood constructs the child as an inaccessible force of innocence that works on adults to restore a pre-existing order.

Burnett's *A Little Princess* is not an obvious template for an antifascist film. It is structured on the theme of parental loss. As in her other children's classic, *The Secret Garden*, the restoration of order and home does not ever make up for the loss of the parent. Sara is the daughter of a wealthy young widower who brings her from India to a select London boarding school. Her father later invests all of his money in an old school friend's scheme to buy diamond mines and dies believing he is bankrupt when the scheme fails. After much misery, Sara is returned to her former splendor when the gentleman who has moved next door to the school turns out to be the old school friend who has not after all bankrupted her but rather increased her fortune and has been searching for her to give her a home. In a pivotal scene retained in the Temple film, he instructs his Indian servant, and Sara's friend, to transform the poor little servant girl's room while she is sleeping. Sara awakens to a fire, food, and sumptuous decorations. She touches everything and then steals next door to the maid's room and brings her back.

> "It's true! It's true!" she cried. "I've touched them all. They are as real as we are. The Magic has come and done it, Becky, while we were asleep—the magic that won't let those worst things *ever* quite happen."[42]

But the worst thing has already happened. The book is both an exploration of how to survive intact from such an intense loss and a description of the material relations upon which Sara's return to her appropriate class position depends.[43] Both a critique of and an apology for English imperialism and class relations, *A Little Princess* celebrates its heroine's self-reliant triumph against selfish materialism (coalesced in the grasping virginity of Miss Minchin) that nonetheless rests upon the dynamics of lower-class and other-nation servitude exemplified by Becky and Ram Dass.[44] Sara, whose wealth made her easily kind, remains loyal to her friends and thoughtful to those less fortunate than she, whether she is actually fortunate or not. Her largesse is the vehicle by which she maintains appropriate class relations with her lower-class intimates.[45]

Changes to the central character and historical context refocus central themes for the Temple version. Temple's celebrity Americanizes the Sara Crewe who grew up in India as efficiently as her outsider status (and flat accent). The film opens to a kaleidoscopic survey of major sites of British national identity, history, and pride—Buckingham Palace, Winchester Cathedral, a portrait of the Queen—before the sound of martial music introduces Sara and her father watching a parade of soldiers preparing to leave for the Boer War. War and nation frame every domestic scene. The appearance on the screen of "England 1899" in white block print locates the temporal setting of the film and provides the historical and national otherness that allows the film to function as a sufficiently distant metaphor for the United States in 1939.[46] Three settings map the spaces of home-front patriotism: the domestic space of the school, where goodbyes are bravely borne and letters anxiously read; the street, where parades and a joyous celebration on the relief of Mafeking are held; and the hospital, where injured soldiers are succored.

Like the FTP children, Temple's character must leave her domestic space in order to set the world aright. Unlike the FTP's Joe and Mary, and in some distinction to her literary forebear, Hollywood's Sara Crewe is modeled on the sentimentalized child who figured so prominently in nineteenth-century sentimental and reform fiction. As the *New York Times* review of the film notes:

> That infantile ornament of the Victorian age, Mistress Shirley Temple, enjoys what is undoubtedly her greatest role to date (since Mr. Zanuck has admitted as much in signed advertisements). . . . The late Mrs. Siddons might well envy her these scenes of tears and heartbreak, of riches and squalor, of oversentimental tenderness and melodramatic abuse. . . . [We have] a baby Bernhardt from whom tears run as from a tap.[47]

Like her nineteenth-century predecessor, Temple's Sara is the child whose love enables reform and redemption of the father, but she does not fundamentally challenge the patriarchal order that has left her open to its abuses in the first place.[48] A weak vessel, she has the strongest love of all, a love that recalls the father to the lure of domesticity while empowering him to assert his rightful place within its social order.

Thus, at the beginning of the film, when Captain Crewe deposits Sara in Miss Minchin's Seminary with little time before he leaves, tears attest to the moral, domestic space that Captain Crewe's soldiering protects. While Burnett's Sara Crewe became a stoic soldier as one of her imaginative subject positions, Temple's Sara can only let her father go by calling on the code of the soldier. Preparing to leave, her father says, "We're going to be brave, aren't we? We've fought this kind of battle before and you've never cried when I went away." Temple's character is supposed to recite a little verse, but instead she breaks down into tears. She looks at her father and sees that he is crying, too. As she and her father are crying together he says tenderly, "I'm afraid we're not such good soldiers as we thought." At this, Temple's Sara stiffens her shoulders and marches to the window, saying, "Oh yes we are. I can do it now," and recites the verse with chin lifted while her father leaves quietly. A daughter's tears and her loving embraces can unman Captain Crewe to tears of his own, but her soft resolve to go through with the goodbye ritual can gird his loins for battle.

Thus, redemption is brought to the service of nation. Not only does the domestic space of Sara's world provides a sanctified space of love and dependency, but its inviolability is intimately tied to the production of men who will preserve the nation from defeat and disintegration.[49] The domestic project of creating and preserving a feminine space serves the project of preserving nation and empire, which in turn is in service to the domestic ideal of home. This connection is made by Temple's Sara in her description of her father's reason for going to war. Captain Crewe, she tells everyone, is "making the Boers behave." Sara's feelings provide the moral impetus to action. When her father's name appears on the list of the dead, the familiar reversal occurs: the old tightwad of a school headmistress turns Sara out of her rooms and makes her work as a scullery maid to pay off the money she had advanced to the captain's account. Whereas in the book Sara accepts the reality of her situation and continues to imagine she is a princess in order to find the strength to behave as she believes she ought to, in the film Temple's Sara refuses to believe her father is dead. "Something inside tells me so," she tells Becky. "And sometimes I hear him calling for me."

Thus, when Captain Crewe has been lying sick and amnesiac in the hospital, there is nothing the doctors can do for him. Only the demonstration of his daughter's faithful love can restore him to health. Sara falls on him with kisses and tears, and although he does not recognize her and says that his little soldier would never cry and she must not either, within moments he blinks several times and shakes his head and sees his daughter crying over him. Sara's loving embrace is so restorative that Captain Crewe is able to stand and salute Queen Victoria, who happens to be at the hospital, moments later.[50] The film ends at this moment, with a close-up of a beaming Sara saluting into the camera as "God Save the Queen" ignites the soundtrack. Temple's Sara has brought her father back to life and redeemed a subject of the Queen to service. The only name Captain Crewe murmurs is Sara's, but with her tears, he becomes not only father but also loyal subject of the British Crown.

Sara's restoration of (and to) her father makes possible the ordered familial relationship disrupted by his presumed death and, though not resolved in the film's narrative, presumably rewards those who have believed in her position within her domestic community. Not only is the potential destruction of the family averted under the ordering force that is Sara, but her allegiance to an overtly patriarchal order, the code of the soldier, expands Sara's personal, familial crisis into a larger, social one.

Temple's Sara Crewe draws on the ideology of the sentimentalized child to mobilize home-front patriotism. She embodies perfect service to her father, who is not an authority figure so much as a public projection of her unswerving service to the social order. Thus, when she is strong and recites the code, he can leave to fight; and when her devotion brings her to his room in the hospital, he recovers by her tears. Furthermore, she represents the sanctified space of home/nation the war will be fought to protect. In one of the film's most affecting scenes, Temple's Sara is contrasted with a wounded soldier in the hospital. She draws close because he said he saw her father, but it becomes clear that the soldier is psychologically traumatized when he proceeds to hold up a series of paper dolls he says are brave soldiers he is making for the war. In the juxtaposition of child and soldier the viewer is shown the cost of war; in the moment between his seeming normality and psychotic actuality is shown the quickness with which war can destroy a young man. This melancholy scene is framed between Sara tap-dancing in the hospital room and her joyous reunion with her father. While it undercuts the airy optimism of both happier moments, the framing ultimately suggests that such sacrifices must be borne.

The film makes its strongest antifascist statement through the opposition of the mean authoritarianism of Miss Minchin with the generous egalitarianism of Sara. Within the boarding school's society, Temple's Sara is a triumph of democratic individualism. Her enactment of an idealized noblesse oblige of character and democratic class unconsciousness frames her relationships with Becky, Ram Dass, and three characters added for the film—Miss Minchin's vaudevillian brother, her beautiful and kind teacher, and the teacher's fiancé. No one provides a role model for this Sara Crewe. Her favorite teacher does not stand up to Miss Minchin, just as the fiancé fails to protect his lady love from the headmistress's wrath. All the adults are either weak or, as in the case of her father, absent and injured. The girls of the school are divided between admirers and enemies. Temple's Sara stands in stark contrast to everyone both in her sense of personal autonomy and in her ability to act. Miss Minchin, on the other hand, enacts the rule of a tyrant, policing the personal lives of students and employees with ruthless control. Obsessed with power wielded through money and class, she makes all the rules to suit her needs. When she needs to, she draws on the police to enforce her self-interested dictates.

The political dimensions of the personal differences are emphasized in a dream sequence in which the power relations are reversed. Sara really is a princess. As a citizen in this dream utopia, Ms. Minchin is a snitch who informs Sara that the riding master has stolen a kiss from the teacher. Sara's judicious and benevolent interpretation of their actions saves them, but the dream scene strongly highlights the film's emphasis on empathy and moral action.

In both the framing and the solution of disorder, Temple's screen child functions much differently than the FTP children. Because the disorder casts her into the role of the outsider, she is identified with people outside of her domestic space. But such points of identification do not result in a systemic change, which would be represented by her movement from the bounds of the family to the community and her recognition of her father's training of her as preparation for a communal role. Rather, scenes outside of the boarding school serve to exemplify Sara's single-minded devotion to her father. Temple's winsome child radiates an impermeable innocence that protects her from the corruption of national conflict and adult greed. If the FTP play suggests that family is always situated in the community, *The Little Princess* insists that community must be ordered on the model of the family; if Joe and Mary's movement into the adult public space of conflict rewards the community with peace, Temple's allegiance to her father and her insistence upon his fulfillment of his patriarchal role rewards her character with preserved stability.

Temple's Sara is ever the child whose triumph offers consolation for that which has been lost to the adult. Predicated upon the symbolic shift of father to national leader, and inhabitants of the nursery to national citizenry, her actions model an unquestioning allegiance to patriarchal authority and home-front support. She keeps the home safe for domesticity. As we have seen, Joe and Mary exist in a play where there is no such sanctified place. Importantly, both productions advocate for a kind of cosmopolitanism that makes room for patriotism but not nationalism. England had not yet declared war on Germany when *The Little Princess* was released, but the film's overt emphasis on war marked an unusually political moment by a 20th Century Fox studio that had long attempted to accommodate fascist Germany and Italy. There was also Popular Front sentiment to counter international and domestic fascism with the power of the movies. In 1938 a group calling itself Films for Democracy formed to make, produce, and direct films that would "safeguard and extend American democracy." Director Fritz Lang and author Thomas Mann sent letters of support; producer Walter F. Wanger joined author Sherwood Anderson, entertainer Will Rogers Jr., Rex Ingram, and labor leader Heywood Broun on the thirty-seven-member advisory board. On November 15, 1938, in the *New York Times,* the group clarified its progressive goal: "The motion-picture screen, with its daily audience of many millions, must now be used to reaffirm and popularize in dramatic form the principles of democratic government and thereby to combat the sinister spread of intolerance and reaction."[51]

Responding to the announcement of its formation, the *New York World Telegram* lauded Films for Democracy, opining:

> It is a laudable undertaking, one which merits respect and attention, because it must be evident to anyone and everyone who pretends to have any feeling for his fellowmen that now more than ever the power and influence of the motion picture should be used to reaffirm certain fundamental principles of humanity and decency. For make no mistake about it, we are in the midst of a wave of intolerance and bigotry right here which, if it is not nipped in the bud, may very easily become as ruthless and horrible as it is now in certain Fascist countries. Already certain demagogues are fanning the spark of racial hatred on the radio and other misguided bigots are slandering radio entertainers because of their faith.[52]

Noting that Films for Democracy had already garnered some famous names, the same column ended with the hope that major actors would publicly support the project to get it off to a "rousing start" and concluded by suggesting one in particular. "Maybe Films for Democracy should try to get ahold of little Shirley Temple, too. After all, she's regarded in some quarters as a pretty dangerous radical, isn't she?"

The call for a child to galvanize public sentiment around a political cause is answered quite differently by *The Little Princess, A Letter to Santa Claus,* and *Triumph of the Will. A Letter to Santa Claus* uses its children to symbolize the responsibility of each citizen to work toward peace and to resist the defeatism of conflict, a clear opposition to the visual synecdochic relation, and subordination, of family to nation in *Triumph of the Will* and *The Little Princess.* It makes no appeal—implicit or explicit—to nationhood or to patriotism. Indeed, by imposing its childlike vision, the play forces the audience to view conflict through its children's vision of the family, a family that extends through social relationships and is not bounded by national borders. Here, too, is an inversion of the family–nation relationship visualized in *Triumph of the Will,* in which familial relationships and loyalties are subsumed under the sign of the Nazi salute. The play's uncompromising antiwar stance makes the case for old-fashioned cosmopolitan internationalism and liberal ideology. But in its resolutely antipolitical presentation, it rejects the terms by which international conflict is being defined and insists upon a return to the fundamental moral values of unselfishness and kindness.

CHAPTER 5

WISHING ON A STAR

Pinocchio's Journey from the Federal Stage to Disney's World

Federal Theatre's most popular children's play was written in doggerel verse and was a production in which "everything is sacrificed to simplicity and hilarity."[1] That the newly flesh-and-blood Pinocchio would become the symbol of the Federal Theatre Project upon its demise underscores the manner in which children's plays performed work analogical to that of children in its productions—to convey an innocence outside of politics. Thus, while Federal Theatre's story of the puppet who became a real boy is outside of the Popular Front sensibility that informs other plays here, his representational power within the history of the project places him within its scope. As the changing social value of the child was introduced through a study of the visual and linguistic rhetoric centered on labor and laboring children, the FTP's *Pinocchio* provides an important bookend clarifying the power of the emotionally priceless child, and thus the representational power of children in the service of Popular Front ideals.

Pinocchio is best known in the twentieth century through Walt Disney's 1940 animated film. In the Disney version, Pinocchio may tell a few lies and play a little pool, but he is in the depths of his little wooden heart a very, very good boy. The gleeful, willful, spiteful, cricket-killing activities that made Carlo Collodi's puppet so very good at being bad are erased in the full-length animation movie. Critics lamenting the oversanitized cuteness of Disney's *Pinocchio* reference Collodi's 1883 story to emphasize representational and values shifts that Disney effected.[2] But few note that in 1937 the Federal Theatre Project mounted an extraordinarily popular stage adaptation of *Pinoc-*

*chio.*³ A letter from Walt Disney to FTP adaptor, writer, lyricist, and director Yasha Frank praises the play and predicts that many successes will follow. This letter documents at least one of the eight times Disney and/or his technical staff reportedly viewed the Los Angeles production before announcing that Disney's next full-length cartoon adaptation would be, indeed, *Pinocchio*.⁴ Disney's version differs in key ways from the FTP's production, but profound changes to lighten and sentimentalize the puppet boy and his father were begun by Frank and carried through to the Disney production. "While Frank's storyline bears no resemblance to Disney's film plot, Frank's character revisions could well have offered Disney the key he needed to unlock and revamp the novel," writes Richard Wunderlich.⁵ Certainly both productions radically revised Collodi's amoral wooden boy.

Frank's federal *Pinocchio* premiered at the Beaux Arts in Los Angeles in June 1937. According to the 1939 Boston Production Book:

> Presented at the height of the Bank Night craze in California, Pinocchio nevertheless managed to lure the same customers back to the Mayan Theatre time and again. It was quite normal for adults to see the show four or five times. Children often returned seven or eight times. The record for repeat performances was shared by two youngsters who paid thirteen return visits to the theatre.⁶

In New York, the show was standing room only for seven weeks, during which more than 80,000 people saw the play. By May crowds had dwindled to "Sold Out" only and more than 100,000 people had seen it over 125 performances.⁷ A note in the National Archives collection reveals that "Although this production was offered primarily as a children's show, box office reports indicate that adults have outnumbered youngsters five to one."⁸ As one reviewer wrote approvingly, "Grownups too will enjoy the smoothly told rhyme which would even be a bit of a spiritual treat for those who feel that their sophistication and cynicism have removed them from the boundaries of dream-tempoed fantasy. . . . Yes, the Federal theatre, once again, has justified its support by [. . .] Uncle Sam."⁹

Los Angeles was one of six California cities that originally had Federal Theatre units. According to Robert Holcomb's seminal "The Federal Theatre in Los Angeles," the Los Angeles units were able to begin production very quickly, with a vaudeville show opening December 31, 1935, two months after administrators began interviewing actors.¹⁰ Holcomb characterized lighthearted theatre as the specialty of the Los Angeles units, "a combination of music and drama that was neither true musical nor true vaudeville,"

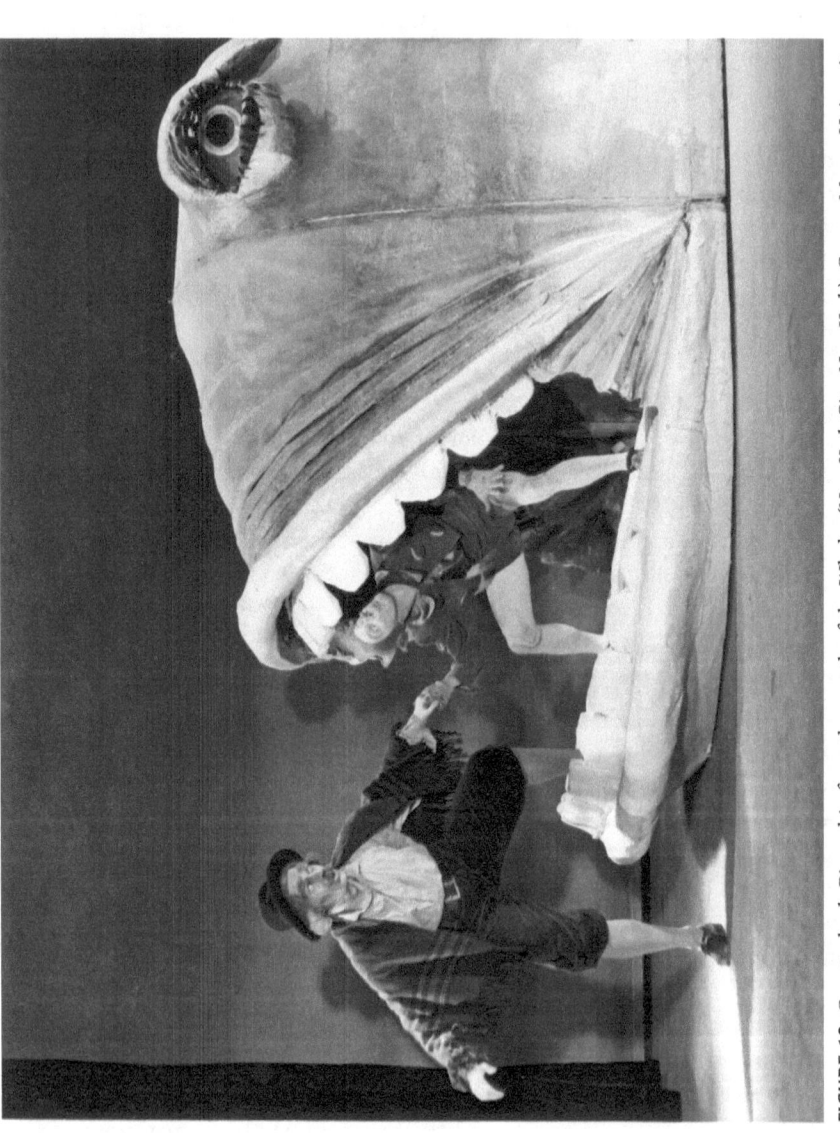

FIGURE 10. Gepetto leads Pinocchio from the mouth of the Whale. *(New York City, New York)*: George Mason University. Fenwick Library. Special Collections and Archives

he drily notes.¹¹ Vaudeville performers were integral to the circus scenes in *Pinocchio*. Children's drama was divided into "live" and "marionette" and extremely popular. More than 100,000 people attended marionette performances in the summer of 1937 at the Greek Theatre. When federal theatre was ended in 1939, more than 1,150 people in the Los Angeles unit lost their jobs.¹²

Though many have seen the Disney version, and some may have seen Frank's televised version of the FTP play in 1957 with Mickey Rooney, relatively few scholars have read the Federal Theatre Project playscript.¹³ Frank regularized Collodi's episodic, bildungsromanesque narrative structure into a three-act play, with three scenes to each act. He lightened the tone, introducing the figure of the kindly woodcutter through opening comedic interplay between Gepetto and his cat, and provided not only song and dance but a spectacular full circus performance—the cause of much praise for the play. Robert Rice of the *Morning Telegraph* explicitly compared the FTP *Pinocchio* to Disney animation:

> In it there are sequences which approach more closely the classic works of Walt Disney than anything I have seen the stage produce. There is a beautiful undersea fantasy, there is a charming marionette sequence, there is, in fact, that kind of simple, imaginative fancy running through the production that not only delights a child's heart, but touches responsive chords in the minds of an older and ostensibly wiser generation.¹⁴

Dialogue is in rhyming verse.¹⁵ The play ends with a birthday celebration for Pinocchio attended by all the characters; in this scene the audience learns that even the ones who had led him astray were only working to help him overcome greed to become a real boy.

The Disney version does draw much from the FTP *Pinocchio*. Both simplify and sentimentalize Collodi's wooden boy. Both lighten the tone of Collodi's text. Both shift its characterization of the child from amoral to good, and the tale from one of bourgeois socialization to one of the triumph of impervious innocence. And both produce a child who serves as anodyne to anxieties concerning child-raising that were circulating in Depression America. The puppet boy's federal stage and silver-screen debut showcases cultural anxieties centered on the intersection of childhood, the family, and social responsibility in the late 1930s, even as it reflects ideological differences driving productions of the Federal Theatre Project and the Disney studio.

These anxieties reflected in the stage and screen productions also circulate in mass-media representations of appropriate parent–child relations and responsibilities that reflect highly unsettled cultural territory. As Stephen Kline writes:

> ... Anxiety pervades much of the advertising of the 1930s, which overtly recognized the significance of a child's changing status within the family. Much of the anxiety concerned parents' ways of relating to children, of controlling and directing their abundant energies, imagination and creativity. Sometimes mothers fretted over their lack of control of their children's well-being; sometimes experts intruded into the scene to help resolve this sense of insecurity; and sometimes parents disputed the appropriate ways to deal with the troubled moments of childrearing. These scenes seem to speak of a more fundamental unsettledness that went beyond the disputes over childrearing practice.[16]

In their portraits of the child who will, with the warmth of flesh and blood, care for an aging father, both the FTP and the Disney studio index cultural concerns about family solvency and parent–child relationships in a rapidly changing and economically destabilized society. Stacking up the Pinocchios against the little children of parenting periodicals whose endless needs must be met by particular brands, or whose "modern" problems must be solved with "modern" parenting techniques devolved from behavioral sciences studies, reveals shifting valuations and conceptualizations of the child. On stage and screen, Pinocchio triumphantly resolves his family's problems. In popular magazines, children are the helpless victims of their parents' lack of knowledge or the victorious inheritors of their parents' careful stewardship. In both, the family was the site of catastrophic potential failure.

The FTP and the Disney *Pinocchio* each offer an alternative fantasy of the parent–child relationship, situating the child as a force whose animation—literally—can create a community, as in the case of the Federal Theatre Project, or redeem a failure in the case of the Disney version. Born of paternal desire rather than woman, both of these Pinocchios verbally contract to be good in almost their first speech act. Responsibility for success is thus resituated with the child whose very physical impermeability signals psychological and developmental plenitude. Having given life to the wood, parents pretty much complete their responsibilities, except for an epic journey to the belly of the whale begun as a search through the night for a lost wooden boy.

The Italian version of *Pinocchio* was first serialized in a newspaper in 1881–1882 and then published to much acclaim in 1883. It was translated into English in 1891 and first appeared in the United States in 1892.[17] The book offers a tale of bourgeois socialization in which the little puppet learns to be a proper boy as each of his misadventures brings him suffering. Collodi's wooden boy is an amoral brat who learns throughout the novel to do the right thing in a tale designed to instruct those like him to do the same. Collodi makes no concession to the idealized, sentimentalized child (who would become the Disney and FTP Pinocchio) who inhabited the opposite pole on the representational scale and to whom tales were told to delight. Rather he draws on a literary tradition of the child as morally unfixed by nature.

Nineteenth-century popular representations of the morally unfixed child and the sentimentalized child had to yield some ground as the twentieth century ushered in a new representation born of child psychology and advertising. As historian Harvey Graff has noted, a particular constellation of changes brought about a rise of interest in the child overall, including:

> ... "new" psychologies and concerns about social order and progress for a nation confronting unprecedented levels of immigration and other forms of growth and transformation. Children and juveniles, at once the hope of tomorrow and the fear of today, symbolize the resurgence of reform. Movements to educate and assist mothers and families, to compel and extend schooling, to promote proper play and peer groups, to restrict work and enhance health all portrayed the young as victims to be "saved."[18]

But the nineteenth-century sentimentalized child, with its capability for redemption, its purity, and its lack of sexuality, still had enormous popular appeal, as the conditions that brought it into widespread circulation, increasing urbanization, a mechanized and increasingly dehumanized workplace, continued to shape people's lives.[19]

The widespread economic displacements and uncertainties of the 1930s created enormous pressure on American families, and these pressures were increasingly reflected and created by twentieth-century sociological, psychological, and educational theories that brought a new child into being, one whose needs and drives were the focus of new periodicals dealing with parental treatment of children. Child psychologists wrote influential articles in the popular press that explained children's educational and social process as highly determined by parental actions. In the late 1920s and early 1930s, psychology was increasingly envisioned as a science, and its results as predictive and experimental. The animal experiments at the turn of the century that were used to theorize the "learning curve," or length of time it takes to learn patterned behavior, were being complicated and questioned by the behaviorism of John B. Watson that focused on the observation of outward behavior. Behaviorism was an important strand of psychological thought in the 1930s—Watson's experiments led to the behaviorism of most importantly B. F. Skinner, but also to a number of men who published studies throughout the 1930s. Fundamentally Darwinian in his understanding of the importance of adaptive reflexes, Watson came to claim that proper training could produce anything. His best known statement boasts:

> Give me a dozen healthy infants, well-formed, and my own specified world to bring them up in and I'll guarantee to take any one at random and train him to become any type of specialist I might select—doctor, lawyer, artist, merchant-chief, and, yes, even beggar-man and thief, regardless of his talents, penchants, tendencies, abilities, vocations, and race of his ancestors.[20]

Of a tenor with its times is an advertisement in *Parents Magazine* for *The New Generation: The Intimate Problems of Modern Parents and Children* that quotes Watson as saying, "Once a child's character has been spoiled by bad handling, which can be done in a few days, who can say that the damage is ever repaired?"[21] Psychology-driven articles and advertisements described children at the mercy of their parents' child-rearing techniques.

As blocked mobility caused by a scarcity of jobs and economic uncertainty caused parents increasingly to displace aspirations onto their children, advertisers raised the specter of a stagnant social mobility that poor parenting might make permanent. And increasingly, as Roland Marchand has shown in *Advertising the American Dream,* ads deployed children to prod parents to buy. The child envisioned by General Electric whose school performance is poor because he studies by dim light struggles for the bottom rung of the academic ladder against the skinny child whose mother isn't giving her Postum. Advertisers pointed the accusing finger directly at guilty parents not only for failing to ensure their own economic success, but for endangering that of their children and future generations also. Because parents' job situations were too often perceived as precarious, these increasingly child-centered ads explicitly linked ability to care for children with long-term economic security and reflected an increasingly overt emphasis on the importance of the parental role in the minutiae of the child's life. Ignorance of the cause of poor performance was no excuse ("Many a bright child is unjustly blamed for dullness"—Metropolitan Life Insurance Company warned); parents had to be diligent in discovering which product would give their child the edge in a cutthroat struggle for success.

Concomitantly, parents were warned that theirs was a uniquely historical, and uniquely isolated, position in new thirties periodicals on parenting such as *Parents*, which grew out of *Child* in 1930, and *National Parent Teacher*. Laments a *National Parent Teacher* article:

> Even if we wished to bring up our children without thinking much about it, as our great-grandmothers did, we no longer have the excellent, if accidental, educational plant of the old home, complete with limitless space of field and brook and orchard, and a small army of hired help and unhired aunts, resident grandmothers, great-uncles and spinster cousins all engaged in simple, understandable, material tasks interesting to boys and girls.[22]

Much as did advertisements, articles in popular-culture parenting manuals took a personal, familial tone that denied their participation in a system of mass production and distribution; in a society perceived as increasingly technologized where the communal ties are increasingly replaced by impersonal networks, ads and these periodical articles insinuated themselves as the voices of personal guidance to fulfill unmet needs that the very system that projected them produced.

But if the tone proffered empathy, in article after article, the magazines emphasized the scope of parental control and concern. Vigilant parents, these articles suggest, must be literate in modern child-rearing techniques and up-to-date on the latest scientific information concerning children's social, psychological, and developmental needs in order to safeguard each step of their children's development—information no old-fashioned familial or community member could give. Advertisements and articles correspondingly construct the child as the inheritor of an uncertain future whose very uncertainty the child might manifest in signs the parent is unable to read. Inarticulate about its needs, displaying them on the body and through bodily behavior, the child imaged as a process of growing, as child development, became the locus of parental anxiety. The child was subject to an increasingly wide array of psychological and sociological forces threatening the boundaries of the adult–child relation. To stabilize this structure, and to counter the increasingly destabilized child, periodicals and magazines presented a stable parent figure. But the parent, separated from mythologized American community both characterized as ideal and dispensed with as inadequate to the modern child's needs, was increasingly stranded.

Thus the parent–child relationship became the locus for diffuse anxieties due to the combined circumstances of economic instability, a perceived increasingly mass-produced social community, and the popularization of "new" twentieth-century social theories centered on the child. While the Federal Theatre and Disney versions of *Pinocchio* deploy the image of the child in different ways, both *Pinocchio*s envision a harmony of social order predicated on a cohesive innocence so powerful that it charms experience. Frank's stage adaptation and the Disney version transform Collodi's nineteenth-century tale about the education and the development of the bourgeois self into a narrative about the redemptive power of the parent–child relationship.

That *Pinocchio* is a tale told about a puppet had a particular resonance in the late 1930s. Psychoanalysts experimented with using puppet shows as therapy for disturbed children, a treatment predicated on the idea that puppets provide an unmediated access to the "hidden" of the subconscious; the puppet thus began to function within psychoanalytic treatment then as it often does in children's therapy today, as the object of psychic transference. At the same time, by the 1930s, puppets and puppet theatre were regarded as almost exclusively the province of children. The puppet figure, then, stood as figural representation of both the child's subconscious and body. If Collodi's puppet drew on the dreaming of the inanimate for the animate to figure both educational progression and biological growth of child to adult, by the 1930s, the space of that dream had become crowded with additional systems of meaning and representation.

Federal theatre's *Pinocchio* deploys the wooden puppet as a force of purity and idealism capable of creating within the production's comic world a cohesive family unit located in a larger social order. Stability within the family unit and social order is predicated on a shared responsibility for identity formation born of the intersection between paternal desire and a childhood innocence that informs that desire. Toasting a new father, Gepetto says, "Well, I've made cradles by the score. / I wish I might have made one more / That would have been a pretty one / That I'd have made for my own son / Ah, me! I envy you the joy / Of watching o'er a growing boy."[23] Even as these lines articulate Gepetto's desire, they proclaim the universal joy of fatherhood in its position of "watching o'er a growing boy." Gepetto then creates the puppet out of inanimate wood pieces after wondering aloud, "Children are not made of wood? / Good heavens I wonder if I could?"[24]

The original Pinocchio's insatiable hunger and gleeful flight from Gepetto set the tone for the problematic father–son relationship that Pinocchio's lessons throughout the serial will resolve. The FTP production removes the threat of the willfully disobedient son and the novel's grinding poverty, even as it emphasizes kindly Gepetto's paternal desire through dialogue centered on food. "A bit of cheese, a slice of veal / Now we shall have our morning meal," Gepetto says, and as Pinocchio sniffs at the chop, Gepetto cries out,

"It wouldn't do you any good / Alas! You're only made of wood." Pinocchio replies:

> Please do not despair, Gepetto / Just you wait and see / I shall be most dutiful / And good as I can be! / I'm sure that if I'm very good / We'll some day know the joy / Of actually seeing me / Become a proper boy / With flesh and blood and meat and bones / And with a stomach, too, / And so I pledge myself to try / To be a son to you.[25]

As Wunderlich notes of Frank's Pinocchio, "Pinocchio, as a child, is lovable and vulnerable, precious and to be protected. The child never gives his parent, or anyone else, grounds for provocation."[26] Pinocchio's determination is to gratify his father's paternal desires, and by this determination signals his fundamental goodness.

But Pinocchio's behavior falls far short of his intentions. When he fails to give money to those in need, the Blue-Haired Fairy Queen must come to emphasize the plenitude in the raw material of boyhood and to warn against abusing its potential. She tells Pinocchio:

> When a puppet first is made, / He is brave and unafraid / He is kind and good. / He's so obedient and sweet; / He is gentle, clean and neat, / But he's made of wood / If he is never mean or mad, / If he is never bold or bad, / If he's never wild, / If he maintains a perfect score / For the whole year and one day more / He then becomes a child. / But if he commits one human sin / Then his troubles will begin; / He will have no rest. / He is tempted twice again, / And if he fails three times—why then / He has failed the test.[27]

Because Pinocchio has withheld his money, she says, "And you have sinned a sin indeed. / You stand condemned of HUMAN GREED!" The Fairy warns that she can triumph over "his evil spirits" two more times:

> Let me once more sum up your case / This is the problem that you face / You will see me twice again / Remember! Only twice! And then / If you have not, by word or deed / Conquered all trace of Human Greed / You'll never, never know the joy / Of being a living, breathing boy / A wooden puppet's all you'll be / From then throughout eternity.[28]

The FTP's Pinocchio certainly hasn't conquered anything the moment he is thrown from a cliff into the sea and the whale's belly. Gepetto saves the two when he lulls the whale asleep to the lullaby he sings to Pinocchio. But when Gepetto gives the puppet four pennies, Pinocchio gives them to a beggar, thus fulfilling the Blue-Haired Fairy's promise. She appears to tell him: "Before night ends, / I shall have gathered all your friends / Who helped you to become a boy. / They'll come to share your father's joy."[29] And on the next day, Pinocchio becomes a boy to the Fairy's words "You've learned the lesson of the penny; / Some have too few—and some too many / But give to those who haven't any, / So let the bells proclaim our joy / While you become a human boy."[30] The play ends with a birthday celebration that integrates father and son into the community. Everyone comes together to celebrate the puppet and he is rewarded by becoming a real boy. If Gepetto's kindliness provides a model for Pinocchio, the feminized community, personified by the Blue-Haired Fairy who orchestrates his lessons and presides over its gathering, is his teacher and the beneficiary of his transformation.

The Disney version keeps the kindly Gepetto figure and the cat, adds a goldfish, and reserves the rhymed speech for a glamorous Blue Fairy. It further brings back the cricket Pinocchio kills in the Collodi story as the winsome, hapless conscience Jiminy Cricket. Jiminy's failures are steadfastly impressive. From the moment the Blue Fairy dubs him "Lord High Keeper of the Knowledge of Right and Wrong, Counsellor in Moments of Temptation, and Guide Along the Straight and Narrow" and changes his rags into spiffy new clothes, Jiminy lets Pinocchio down. He begins a lecture on temptations and becomes mixed up in his own complications. He oversleeps, and Pinocchio falls into the hands of the Fox and Cat. Seeing Pinocchio's successful performance at the puppet show, he leaves in a daze of self-pity. He ducks away from the Blue Fairy, answering Pinocchio's frantic question about what to do with an ambiguous "You might try telling the truth." Pinocchio lies and his nose grows, but Jiminy tells him to lie about the cricket's involvement in the Cat and Fox episode. Jiminy is a spectacular failure as guide, counselor, or in loco parentis role of any kind.

When the Fairy says, "A boy that won't be good / might just as well be made of wood," both cricket and boy promise to be better. As both narrator and authoritative—if ineffective—moral guide, Jiminy individualizes a communal role and allows Gepetto to remain free of responsibilities—for writing his son's tale and supervising his moral development. The fact that Jiminy continually fails in discharging these responsibilities emphasizes Pinocchio's innate goodness and the power of that goodness to transform experience. Gepetto exists within the Disney story to go out in the night, get lost, get swallowed by a whale, and saved by his son. Thus Gepetto is absolved from parental responsibility even as he is the primary beneficiary of Pinocchio's ultimate success. As the story's figurative creator, Jiminy is the one who has his faith tested and who ultimately affirms the movie's message, that "when you wish upon a star, your dreams come true." He is the itinerant witness of Pinocchio's self-sacrificing rescue of his father.

If the FTP's Pinocchio promises to be both food and stomach, consumed and consumer, Disney's becomes Christ and mankind, redeemed by his own act of self-sacrifice. If communal harmony results from the puppet's successful transition in the FTP play, a spectacular reinscription of the male-centered family results from Pinocchio's transformation in the Disney version. The movie ends with Gepetto and Pinocchio dancing to the discordant tunes of the puppet-maker's many clocks, while outside the window and excluded from the celebration Jiminy Cricket receives his badge of good conscience. While the FTP's play affirms family as embedded in community, the Disney version commits to a more traditional narration of the individualistic American family. But both base restoration of the ideal on the innocent child who shoulders responsibility for his ethical/moral development. Situated in the thirties rhetoric of child-rearing, both productions ultimately affirm the value of parenthood even as they construct an adult–child relationship that absolves parents of the awesome responsibilities popular discourse insisted were theirs.

CONCLUSION

DEATH OF A DREAM

This book began with my delighted reading of *The Revolt of the Beavers* playscript before any film showcasing roller-skating beavers had been made. Fascinated by the relationship the play presumed between children's theatre, political action, and social change, I turned to other children's plays in the Federal Theatre Project collection. Though few FTP children's plays overtly comment on political issues at all—particularly after *The Revolt of the Beavers*—they are situated in a chaotic cultural era when economic uncertainty, rising fascism, and changing ethnic and racial demographics created the new social and political formations these plays reflect. And so my initial delight became the scholarly inquiry that produced this first substantial critical treatment of these plays, an inquiry that will perhaps open archived materials to further inquiries into federal children's theatre. When I began this project, scripts were largely unavailable outside of major university libraries or the Federal Theatre Project Collection at the Library of Congress in Washington, DC. Now, some major scripts are available online, part of 13,000 images reproduced from the Library of Congress collection.[1] Children's plays are increasingly mentioned in scholarly texts on the Federal Theatre Project, and *The Revolt of the Beavers* has even been staged in the wake of the 1999 film about the Federal Theatre, *Cradle Will Rock*.

Together, the chapters of this book demonstrate how particular children's plays of Federal Theatre participate in the Popular Front politics of pro-labor, antiracism, and antifascism. This study argues that *The Revolt of the Beavers* controversy highlights the manner in which issues of labor justice and antifascism were subsumed by charges of Communism, and thus anti-Americanism. It examines how the changing social value of children made the play's Popular Front motifs particularly explosive. While FTP officials attempted to defuse the negative ramifications of having produced a Marxist children's play by characterizing *Revolt* as a fairy tale, the play's simple politics aimed at children made it very easy for public officials against the project to use childhood innocence and Americanness as qualities that needed to be safeguarded from the play's ideology.

The Story of Little Black Sambo, by Helen Bannerman, provided a template for federal children's productions that both challenged and reaffirmed America's racial politics. If public reactions were the measure of political and social engagement, productions of *Little Black Sambo* would be characterized as resolutely apolitical. Yet my examination of the plays reveals contradictory rhetorics of race that comment on the deeply divided racial culture and politics of the United States that produced the anti-lynching activism of the Popular Front. In an obscure Newark puppet production and in a three-act Chicago version scripted by Charlotte Chorpenning and directed and scored by Shirley Graham, the story of the little black child facing danger in the jungle is transformed from a parable of white-on-black violence to a tale in which narrative empowerment leads to family security. The Chorpenning–Graham production creates a protagonist who learns to channel his love of beauty and song into productive, responsible actions and who learns the value of family economy and social responsibility. The production yoked this narrative to African motifs designed by Graham that visually and aurally emphasize a dual African American heritage and to critique American racial attitudes that foreclosed African American opportunities. The Newark script presents an intriguing and subversive examination of such racial politics, presenting minstrel caricature as an imposed masquerade that obscures a world limited by poverty and marked with physical danger, realities dismissed by a public invested in the racism that created them. Other scripts and productions, meanwhile, deployed minstrel characterizations and forms to construct familial relationships that locate family irresponsibility as the root cause of danger to the young male black body.

Children's plays in large part stayed away from themes connected to rising fascist power in Europe. However, one play developed as a children's pageant in 1938 took looming war as its topic. *A Letter to Santa Claus* articulates deep cultural anxieties about the threat of war in Europe and the breakdown of civic, economic, and political order it portends. This study's examination of the play compares it to fascist imagery of children in *Triumph of the Will* and *The Little Princess* in order to analyze how the American theatre and film present childhood innocence and morality as powerful antidotes to fascist aggression and the forces of war. Though its planned spectacular effects and circus antics visually connoted the lighthearted pageantry associated with Christmas productions for children, *A Letter to Santa Claus* articulates a very adult sense of bewilderment about the threat of fascism to liberal values and ideals.

My study of these children's plays is bookended by chapters examining the culture centered on children's theatre and the changing social value of the child. Chapter 1 begins with a discussion of the structure of federal children's theatre in the context of children's theatre history. The first chapter also traces key moments in labor rhetoric centered on children and childhood to argue that the FTP's emphasis on children's theatre articulates an increased social investment in the child. The final chapter examines the very popular *Pinocchio* as an articulation of children's centrality to Depression-era popular culture. I argue that the puppet boy produced by both Federal Theatre and Walt Disney studios functions as an anodyne to Depression-era child-raising anxieties showcased in parenting magazine discourse.

The plays of this study were produced in an FTP children's theatre that was designed to introduce children to live theatre. It was also designed to reach out to all audiences, and perhaps in this goal was more successful than any other part of the Federal Theatre. Hoping to raise a new generation of theatre-goers and asserting the importance of theatre for children, children's productions went to parks, schools, orphanages, and Broadway. They hosted theatre parties for large groups of children at extraordinarily low prices. They created fabulous spectacle and the occasionally didactic dramatic moment. Never in America had so much attention been paid to artistic production for children. If the broad scope of the project made it difficult for a coherent set of clear goals to be attained, nonetheless the children's units were remarkably successful in pleasing their audiences across the nation.

During the time these plays were produced, children's theatre was a protean venture. It had been primarily in the hands of service organizations and settlement houses and had never received widespread professional theatre attention. Theatre itself was in flux; the nascent "little theatre" movement in the early years of the new century had widened the scope of performances and produced new scripts even as the advent of the Depression and the rise of movie popularity took audiences and closed theatres. The FTP children's plays helped to shape new audiences and focus attention on the educational aspects of popular entertainment.

With the close of the fiscal year on June 30, 1939, America's experiment with national theatre ended. After years of investigation, the U.S. Congress passed a bill signed by Roosevelt that defunded the Federal Theatre Project immediately. In a final performance of *Pinocchio* at the Ritz Theatre in New York, Yasha Frank responded dramatically. Instead of the usual birthday-celebration ending for the transformed Pinocchio, a gunshot suddenly rang out. A voice cried, "Pinocchio is dead!" The curtain rose to reveal a dead puppet lying on the stage. "So let the bells proclaim our grief," chanted the company, "That this small life was all too brief." With the puppet lying sprawled in front of them, the crew dismantled the set in front of the audience. The crew and cast members, followed by members of the audience, formed a funeral procession and carried Pinocchio's body in a coffin bearing the epitaph "Born December 23, 1938; Killed by an Act of Congress June 30, 1939" up the aisle of the Ritz Theatre and out into the streets of New York.[2] As *Life magazine* recounted for a national audience, "After a hysterical ovation the audience poured into Times Square chanting 'Save the Federal Theatre.'"[3] According to the *New York Times*, the funeral march was led by a member of the Living Newspaper staff and chairman of the Workers Alliance dismissals committee. The *Times* reported that the march picked up about six hundred people on its way to Times Square, where "speakers were permitted to make pleas in behalf of continuing the Federal Theatre."[4] No political transformation resulted from this demonstration, but it must have been fine theatre.

The cinematic story of the Federal Theatre, *Cradle Will Rock*, transforms this finale so that Pinocchio becomes the puppet of an aging, drunken vaudevillian. This shift gives the movie narrative coherence and historical resonance. The Federal Theatre provided new audiences for old artists of a dying form. Without the FTP, vaudevillians could not fill theatres, and without filling theatres, no vaudevillian would be hired by a for-profit theatre system. Bill Murray's Tommy Crickshaw demonstrated that aside from federally funded stages, there was no place in American theatre for the has-been, the old, the sick, the sad. As there is no place in capitalism. Or so the story goes in the agitprop political message of a thirties-styled film created from a cultural panoply as large and all-encompassing and political as the Diego Rivera mural blasted off the walls of Rockefeller's new center.

As the shuffling men and women following the empty-eyed ventriloquist's dummy round the corner into today, moviegoers are asked to imagine what has been sacrificed to capitalism. In the blank neon parade of contemporary Broadway's Disneyfied landscape, artistry has been co-opted and theatre commodified. With the death of the Federal Theatre Project and the triumph of the united business and political culture that killed it, died the joyous, open-ended theatrical possibilities of a *Cradle Will Rock* and the opportunities for regret and reflection inspired by a sparsely attended vaudeville performance. With its death died an alternative possibility to the empty spectacle of Broadway, symbolic of American art in late capitalism.

When the funding expired that June night in 1939, the FTP materials became, instead of the foundation for a national theatre, the detritus of a huge bureaucracy. Some materials went home with participants. Some were lost. But most were quickly packed up, donated to the Library of Congress, and hastily stored away. Years passed and they lay forgotten. It was not until 1974 that Federal Theatre materials were rediscovered in an old, abandoned airplane hangar outside of Washington, DC, by George Mason University scholars Lorraine Brown and John O'Connor. Brown and O'Connor instigated the initial research and cataloguing work that has so indebted subsequent researchers into the Federal Theatre Project. The materials were housed in a new wing of George Mason University's Fenwick Library that held the entire collection until the Library of Congress took it back in 1994. Researchers at George Mason not only spearheaded research into the collected materials, but tracked down old employees of the project and conducted oral interviews with more than two hundred of them. They put out a newsletter, Federal One. They held Federal Theatre Project festivals that brought researchers and project personnel together in 1993, 1994, and 1995. Researchers slowly pieced together a forgotten history. The removal of these materials from their home at GMU's library and from its research program is a second tale of missed opportunities and foreclosed possibilities for Federal Theatre, a story outside the scope of this project, but one worthy of reflection.

Research work at GMU, combined with the initial federal effort to analyze, catalog, and prepare for distribution a vast compilation of children's plays, left a wealth of materials for analysis. There are many plays lying forgotten in the FTP archives that may be studied to discover more about the FTP, children's theatre, and the cultural conditions of America during the Great Depression and the New Deal.

The story of the Federal Theatre Project was not so brave and apolitical as *Cradle Will Rock* would have it. But it would have been beautiful to think so. And in truth, what is so moving about it is the degree to which Federal Theatre really must have been an extraordinary, idealistic vision, one which, fully articulated, might have shaped new possibilities for a vital American theatre. Three words recirculate as description of the Federal Theatre Project's intent: "free, adult, and uncensored."[5] The words with which the Project was introduced were those picked by scholars Lorraine Brown and John O'Connor to title their 1978 book reintroducing the FTP to a community that had forgotten it. With their stirring syllabic progression, Harry Hopkins's adjectives describe a theatre committed to an "adult" population, the nebulous qualities of the adjective both opened and contained by its position between "free" and "uncensored." This descriptor has been widely recirculated as academic works draw on the pioneering scholarship of Brown and O'Conner, and narratives about the FTP's history and the significance of its productions have wrestled with whether the description is accurate or not. It was a theatre born of the need for jobs during the Great Depression, dreamed into being by people who believed that an American national theatre could function as a gadfly to the government that signed its paychecks, and killed by a congressional investigation that slandered it as a hotbed of communism. It was a theatre that was never free and certainly never uncensored. Yet in the grandeur of its vision, the largeness of its struggles, and the irony of its eventual defeat, it has certainly seemed an apt metaphor for all that is hoped may be imagined by "adult."

And yet its symbol at the end was a child. The sigh of what might have been infuses the symbolic connection between the murder of *Pinocchio* and the death of federal theatre. When *Pinocchio* played at the Ritz Theatre on Broadway under the auspices of the FTP, standing room only signs were posted for six months.[6] Hallie Flanagan invited the members of the Dies Committee to see the production, writing:

> I feel that you might be especially interested in this production, not only because it represents one of our major efforts in the field of children's theatre, but because it is a visualization of what we have been able to do by way of rehabilitating professional theatre people and retraining them in new techniques.
>
> In *Pinocchio* we use 50 vaudeville people who were at one time headliners in their profession and who, due to no fault of their own, suddenly found themselves without a market. Now they are artists in a great new field and I feel certain you will find that this creation of fine new theatre personalities is no less exciting than the presentation of the play itself.[7]

Pinocchio was already being used as a symbol of the FTP before Frank staged his dramatic coda to its demise. If *Pinocchio*'s end provides an intriguing glimpse of the high-drama politics and federal art provided in 1939, it also shows how representations of the child demonstrate complex adult political and social realities in simple dramatic configurations and how the child, located in relationships of identification and otherness, serves as metaphor and didactic model. *Pinocchio*'s violent superimposition of adult allegorical fantasies upon the fairy-tale ending of a children's play throws into relief the manner in which adult anxieties shaded the narratives and characterizations of children in FTP plays written and adapted for children. Theatre written for children by adults is always a product of adult visions projected toward the figure of the child. The form of these visions, their texture, their color, their narrative coding, takes shape from their particular historical location—and dream a history yet to come.

Postscript

A Letter to Santa Claus is a mostly forgotten play, but its sentiments are firmly located in the Popular Front despair at the militarization of Germany, the outrages of Stalinism, and domestic impulses toward authoritarianism and racism. It is on the same spectrum of Popular Front feeling as Philip Rahv's well-known essay on the Moscow show trials of the Bolsheviks, which first appeared in the *Partisan Review*. Written in the same year that *A Letter to Santa Claus* was produced, "Trials of the Mind" catalogues the psychological effect of cataclysmic world events. Rahv writes:

> Our days are ceasing to be. We are beginning to live from hour to hour, awaiting the change of headlines. History has seized time in a brutal embrace. We dread the Apocalypse.
> The newspapers recite their tidings: AUSTRALIANS KNEEL BEFORE HITLER; NAZIS FLOG LABORERS INTO LINE. And in Moscow, the State continues to massacre the firstborn of October. What an inexhaustible repertoire of shame and catastrophe! . . .
> We were not prepared for defeat. The future had our confidence, which we granted freely, sustained by Marxism. In that tradition, we saw the marriage of science and humanism. But now, amidst all these ferocious surprises, who has the strength to reaffirm his beliefs, to transcend the feeling that he had been duped. One is afraid of one's fear. Will it soon become so precise as to exclude hope?[8]

A pessimistic reading of *A Letter to Santa Claus* suggests that individually held liberal values construct the only defense against the greed and hatred that precipitates a social strife that culminates in war, and that those values are as ephemeral and naïve as a belief in Santa Claus. As the myth by which the world is made kind for children, Santa Claus offers little realistic hope to the adults who collude to perpetuate his fiction. As an indication of the helplessness of liberalism against fascist power, Santa's role in the play questions the belief in a cosmopolitan rationality. And as a metaphor for the manner in which the world is made bright and shiny by deception, Santa Claus is savage mockery of the very innocence privileged in the play.

But this is pessimism. If Chorpenning was afraid of her fears, her fear had not become so precise as to exclude hope. Her story ends not with Santa Claus but with children and adults together reciting the words that banish the shadows of their fears. If J. M. Barrie's Peter Pan asks his audience to clap together if they believe in fairies so that Tinkerbell might live, the FTP children ask the audience to learn together that which will banish shadows from the world of the stage.[9] Jack Zipes writes in his discussion of Walter Benjamin's storyteller, "There are storytellers who are first and foremost listeners, who listen to the crises and struggles in our societies and try through listening to the temper of our times to extrapolate wisdom and hope in creative ways."[10] In her federal departure from the wildly popular fairy-tale adaptations, Chorpenning brought the temper of her times to children's theatre in order to turn her audience into listeners as well. "Now I have made you wise," chant the children.

A Letter to Santa Claus was a story told for only two weeks in late 1938. There are no funny flickering images of its existence, no scenes that we can watch over and over, as we can watch Shirley Temple's Sara Crewe coming into her transformed attic to marvel at her lovely new things ("It's true! I've touched them all and they're as real as we are") and kiss her father out of his amnesia. *A Letter to Santa Claus* exists as web traces pointing to an absent production, one of six playscripts in Lowell Swortzell's *Six Plays for Young People from the Federal Theatre Project,* and as a manuscript in a box in the Library of Congress. And yet the story speaks to our times. If Rahv catalogued his fears by reciting the headlines of the day, in our time the shadows have sometimes seemed to lie in the absence of images: American soldiers coming home at night in flag-shrouded coffins; empty factories in the upper Midwest; horrors in the villages of Darfur and in the cities of Syria; torture in secret prisons. Images we do see strike us as the shadows of broad narratives whose logic eludes us: bodies floating in New Orleans; beheadings in featureless rooms; starvation in Zimbabwe; a hooded prisoner with arms outstretched in aching, awful mimicry of the Christ pose.

Meanwhile, elections are waged by spectacle and sound bite as the news loops endless stories of celebrity trials (and tribulations) and private agonies writ large. Todd Gitlin writes that media culture saturates our lives because it answers our need to feel, and that while various media experiences may generate different kinds of feelings,

> Deep emotion would incapacitate you for feeling the next frisson. . . . The kinds of feelings and sensations we have from television, popular music, video games, the Internet . . . these feelings are transitory and they are in a sense each a preparation for the next. If we were deeply satisfied, we wouldn't need the next. But we do need the next—or we feel we do.[11]

This is the series of sensations Benjamin ascribed to watching film, and that were harnessed by fascist Germany to connect the individual to the state. It is the feeling evoked by the innocent child whose presence still consoles us in the loss of our own innocence and reassures us of the innocence of our nation. It is, ultimately, a preparation for feeling that can never be—the constant tease of desire. Unabashedly unironic, *A Letter to Santa Claus,* like other plays in this study, speaks to our times with an earnestness our media culture ascribes to the realm of childhood.

What will make us wise, indeed?

NOTES

Introduction

1. *Arena*, 23.
2. *Federal Theatre* 1.6.
3. Paul Sporn remembers attending a production of *A Midsummer Night's Dream* in the Bronx's Crotona Park. "I recall that a huge audience, sitting on newspapers, blankets, handkerchiefs, paper bags, or simply on the grass itself, covered every square foot of the hillside. . . . The drone of sound that issued from it died away shortly after the curtain parted, and this audience of Bronx eastsiders sat as still as it could on a crowded, bumpy hillside that became more and more dampish as the night advanced. When the play was over, it came back to noisy life: cheering, whistling, applauding, and waving handkerchiefs in grateful appreciation of the work the actors had performed" (*Against Itself: The Federal Theatre and Writers' Projects in the Midwest*, 14–15).
4. *The Federal Theatre Project: A Catalogue-Calendar of Productions*, xv.
5. *The Cultural Front*, 50.
6. "Children's Theatre—New York," *Federal Theatre* 2.3.
7. See Roland Marchand's *Advertising the American Dream* (296–99) for a discussion of Depression anxieties focused on children. For discussions of representations of the child and American identity, see Carol Levander's *Cradle of Liberty* and Levander and Carol Singley's *The American Child: A Cultural Studies Reader*. See also Karen Sánchez-Eppler's *Dependent States: The Child's Part in Nineteenth-Century American Culture*.
8. I am indebted to Sánchez-Eppler's "Raising Empires Like Children: Race, Nation, and Religious Education" for the elegantly phrased analogy.
9. In his 1945 study of the Dies Committee, August Raymond Ogden writes that "The *St. Louis Post Dispatch* of 20 October 1938 carried an article in which it was stated that, for the first time, Dies revealed that two of the outstanding results of his inquiry had been to paralyze the left-wing element in the Administration and to discredit John L. Lewis and the

CIO" (*The Dies Committee: A Study of the Special House Committee for the Investigation of Un-American Activities, 1938–1944*, 152).

10. By then Oscar Saul, co-author of *The Revolt of the Beavers*, was a Hollywood screenwriter with one film to his credit; Jules Dassin, the dashing Oakleaf, was directing films noirs; and Elia Kazan was making his name as a director.

11. *Naming Names*, xiii.

12. *Radical Visions and American Dreams*, 98.

13. Ibid. See chapter III, "The Search for Community."

14. Ibid., 97.

15. *The Cultural Front*, xvii.

16. Ibid., xxvii.

17. Ibid., xviii.

18. Ibid.

19. *Reading American Photographs*, 247.

20. For a comprehensive look at certain government investigations into the New York units of the Federal Theatre Project, see *Government Investigations of Federal Theatre Project Personnel in the Works Progress Administration, 1935–1939 (The show must NOT go on!)*, by Judith Brussell. As she writes, "By fall, 1936, the Department of Justice had directed the DOI [Division of Investigation] to investigate all supervisors of all Arts Projects and find models for criminal prosecution" (iv). The DOI began as an agency to investigate economic fraud but reported all manner of accusations to the WPA Division of Investigation, the Dies Committee, and the FBI. These investigations, which preceded the Dies Committee hearings, are not well known. Brussell writes that even people in the Federal Theatre Project were not aware of them, though Brussell's investigation makes clear that people were fired on account of them.

21. For information about the economic, social, and political upheavals caused by the Depression, see Robert McElvaine's *The Great Depression*. For an account of the Roosevelt presidency and the programs it instituted, see William Leuchtenberg's *Franklin D. Roosevelt and the New Deal: 1932–1949*.

22. Her travel to the Soviet Union would later be seized upon by the Dies Committee as proof of her radical leftism, and she would be questioned about it in hearings.

23. The Federal Theatre Project's Living Newspapers were staged productions of current events, drawing on epic theatre staging techniques developed by Bertolt Brecht and Erwin Piscator. FTP Living Newspapers included *Triple A Plowed Under*, about the crisis of agriculture and practices that were exacerbating it; *Power*, about the relation of consumers and the electrical industries; *Spirochete*, about syphilis; and *Injunction Granted*, about labor. For extensive treatment of the Living Newspapers, see Laura Browder's *Rousing the Nation: Radical Culture in Depression America*.

24. Quoted in Mathews, *The Federal Theatre, 1935–1939*, 21.

25. Flanagan, "The People's Theatre Grows Stronger," *Federal Theatre* 1.6, p. 6. *Federal Theatre* was distributed free within the FTP and sold for fifteen cents a copy on newsstands and in bookshops. It was shut down in 1937. Tony Buttitta discusses his employment with *Federal Theatre* in *Uncle Sam Presents*.

26. Mathews, 22–23.

27. *Federal Theatre* 2.4, p. 28.

28. *Federal Theatre* 1.4.

29. See "Censorship in the Federal Theatre" (*Theatre History Studies*), by Barry With-

am, for an excellent discussion of the administrative organization of the FTP with regard to WPA state directors that created so many censorship problems for the project.

30. See *Arena*, 55. See also Mathews, 52–53. For a description of strikes from an actor's perspective, see John Randolph's oral interview with Diane Bowers.

31. Quoted in Goldstein, *The Political Stage*, 250.

32. All were directors of particularly vibrant regional theatres: Gilmor Brown came from the Pasadena Playhouse, Frederick McConnell from the Cleveland Playhouse, Thomas Wood Stevens from the Goodman Memorial Theatre in Chicago, and Jaspar Deeter from the Hedgerow Theatre outside of Philadelphia (Mathews, 26).

33. Fraden writes that *Hymn to the Rising Sun* was also not supported by the cast. She quotes Richard Wright, who was working as publicity director for the unit and who had helped decide what plays would be produced for that particular series. In his autobiography, he writes that after he passed out copies of *Hymn to the Rising Sun* and cast members looked at it, " . . . something went wrong. The Negroes stammered and faltered in their lines. Finally they stopped reading all together." Wright remembers that one of the cast told the director they thought the play was indecent. "We don't want to act in a play like this before the American public. I don't think any such conditions exist in the South. I lived in the South and I never saw any chain gangs . . . we want a play that will make the public love us" (Fraden, 114).

34. *Government Investigations of Federal Theatre Project Personnel in the Works Progress Administration 1935–1939 (The Show Must NOT Go On!)*.

35. Ibid., v.

36. Ibid., vii.

37. The figure for productions comes from Goldstein, 250. Although the FTP was in existence for four years, and although CCC touring companies that had been inherited from a small Federal Emergency Relief Agency theatrical project performed, only the Los Angeles project opened a play in 1935, according to Goldstein.

38. "Nothing to Write About," *Federal Theatre* 2.1, p. 1.

39. *The Federal Theatre Project: A Catalog-Calendar of Productions*, xiii–xiv. The figure is echoed in Buttitta and Witham, *Uncle Sam Presents*, 231.

40. For a description of the project's activities in Oklahoma, see Flanagan, *Arena*, 97–101.

41. New York Children's Unit Director Jack Rennick, quoted in *Stage Left*, a reminiscence written on leftist theatre in the thirties by Jay Williams.

42. Saul would co-write one more play for Federal Theatre, a critique of the American medical system, *Medicine*, with H. R. Hays. The play was produced on Broadway in 1940. Both Lantz and Saul became screenwriters. Saul, who died in 1994, received screenwriting credit for *Once Upon a Time* (1944), *Strange Affair* (1944), *The Dark Past* (1948), *Roadhouse* (1948), *The Lady Gambles* (1949), *Once More, My Darling* (1949), *Woman in Hiding* (1949), *The Secret of Convict Lake* (1951), *Thunder on the Hill* (1951), *Affair in Trinidad* (1952), *The Joker Is Wild* (1957), *The Helen Morgan Story* (1957), *The Naked Maja* (1959), *The Second Time Around* (1961), *Major Dundee* (1965), *The Silencers* (1966), and *Man and Boy* (1972). He received screenwriting credit for the film version of *Streetcar Named Desire*, directed by Elia Kazan, and adapted the play for television in 1984. He published one novel, *The Dark Side of Love*, in 1974. Saul also lectured on screenwriting at the University of California at Los Angeles and the Writers Guild Open Door School.

43. *New York Herald Tribune,* June 2, 1937, p. 21, mimeograph, National Archives Box 154 (Vassar Collection).

44. When *The Revolt of the Beavers* opened, a number of pro-labor New York FTP plays were either in rehearsal or had been produced. These include, notably one of the first Living Newspapers, *Injunction Granted,* on labor unions, and Frank Wilson's *Walk Together Chillun* and J. A. Smith's *Turpentine for the Negro Unit* at the Lafayette Theatre. Pro-Communist sympathies took the FTP stage, notably in *Professor Mamlock,* by Friedrich Wolf, and *Battle Hymn,* by Michael Gold. And anticapitalist sentiments infused productions from the Living Newspaper *Triple A Plowed Under* to W. H. Auden's expressionistic *Dance of Death.* The very structure of the FTP recognized America's ethnic diversity and reached out to different audiences in Yiddish, German, Russian, and Spanish, particularly through its active Yiddish Theatre.

45. Even the three playreader reports located in the FTP Collection at the Library of Congress fail to anticipate the political controversy the play would generate. The play was recommended by all three reviewers. And though one, Robert Ewing, recommended with reservations (of the categories "reject," "reject with reservations," "recommend with reservations," and "recommend"), he wrote, "This play is well written and the authors understand child psychology. The lines and action are kept on a child's level. There is a good villain. The animals add much to the general interest. The individual moral needs clarifying. It is questionable if the implications and talk about <u>adult</u> industrial injustice should be thrust upon children (or animals)" [underline his]. A second reviewer wrote enthusiastically that the play is "a charming tale originally intended for children, but having enough up-to-date material and moral to be of interest to adults. A play any amateur group, especially Junior League dramatic clubs, would enjoy presenting for children's entertainment." In her dissertation, *A Production History of the New York City Children's Theatre Unit of the Federal Theatre Project,* Doreen Heard notes that "Dorothy Hailparn, the author of *Horse Play,* was the first person to recommend the script" (166).

46. The extant photo of the Newark production is at the Special Collections Department at George Mason University.

47. Denning, *The Cultural Front,* xvi.

48. McClendon, who was ill with a fatal cancer, would take little role in shaping the Harlem unit. She argued for white co-directors because she believed the African American theatre workers, shut out from the commercial theatre, needed training from established professionals to develop a strong and skilled community. Furthermore, individual productions often integrated cast and crew members in slight but unprecedented ways; for example, the wise Hoot Owl in *The Revolt of the Beavers* was played by an African American actor.

49. Audiences were integrated except by the division created by the largely racially separated productions. The Federal Theatre Project houses were open to all and did not separate black and white audience members.

50. Swortzell, "Introduction," *Six Plays for Young People from the Federal Theatre Project (1936–1939),* 22–23.

Chapter 1

1. Jack Rennick, "Children's Theatre—New York," *Federal Theatre* 2.3 (1936).

2. Cleveland may seem an unlikely city to form a triad with New York and Los Angeles, but the lively children's theatre developed by the directors of the settlement house the Karamu House had created an existing theatre community that the FTP recognized. See Noerena Abookire and Jennifer Scott McNair, "Children's Theatre Activities at Karamu House, 1915–1975," in *Spotlight on the Child*, 69-84.

3. An exception is *A Letter to Santa Claus*. According to its production book, children Joe and Mary were played by children.

4. *Six Plays for Young People from the Federal Theatre Project*, 10.

5. Rennick, "Children's Theatre—New York," *Federal Theatre* 2.3

6. Rennick, Report, August 28, 1936, Box 495, National Archives.

7. Ibid.

8. Letters of sponsorship acceptance in the National Archives records include Dorothy McFadden, executive director of Junior Programs; Lewis Chisholm, Acting Lieutenant of the Juvenile Aid Bureau of the New York City Police Department; Goodman Theatre Children's Director Charlotte Chorpenning; and numerous university professionals in child development and theatre. See also Heard, *A Production History of the New York City Children's Theatre Unit*.

9. Letter from George Kondolf, New York City project director, to Richard Whorf, Schubert Theatre. In the letter, Kondolf was soliciting sponsorship for the "Children's Holiday Festival" to be held December 27 through January 1. Kondolf writes that "$1.25 will provide 25 children with balcony seats, and $3.75 with orchestra seats."

10. Heard, *A Production History of the New York City Children's Theatre Unit*, 263.

11. *Free, Adult, and Uncensored* notes that during the 1937 Federal Theatre Project's run of *Pinocchio*, advertisements notified the public that adults could attend the production only if accompanied by a child.

12. National Archives Box 496. Although the motion picture traveling road shows never happened, Frank did produce his *Pinocchio* for television in 1957, with Mickey Rooney in the title role.

13. *Spotlight on the Child*, 1.

14. McCaslin, *Theatre for Children in the United States: A History*, 15.

15. Ibid., 16.

16. Quoted in "Junior League Children's Theatre," in *Spotlight on the Child*. See also Janet Gordon and Diana Reische, *The Volunteer Powerhouse*.

17. McCaslin, *Theatre for Children in the United States: A History*, 78.

18. See "The King-Coit School and Children's Theatre," in *Spotlight on the Child*, 51–67.

19. Ward would write four books in all: *Creative Dramatics*, *Theatre for Children*, *Playmaking with Children*, and *Stories to Dramatize*.

20. Lewis Wickes Hine, National Child Labor Committee Collection. Titles of photographs taken from National Child Labor Committee caption cards.

21. *Pricing the Priceless Child*, 21.

22. *The Cultural Front*, 7.

23. Ibid., 9.

24. Samuel Gompers at the Chicago International Labor Conference, quoted in Kent, *Culture, Gender, Race, and U.S. Labor History*, 21.

25. Lewis Wickes Hine, National Child Labor Committee Collection.

26. *The Cry of the Children*, xv.

27. The similarity of titles recalls Elizabeth Barrett Browning's poem "The Cry of the

Children," decrying the wasted lives of English working children. The poem was published in 1844.

28. *The Bitter Cry of the Children,* 216.

29. *Shifting Gears: Technology, Literature, Culture in Modernist America.* See chapters 1 and 2.

30. Conceptually, this spatial relationship might have been at work in stage designing the wheel for *Revolt of the Beavers.*

31. "Child Labor in the Southern Cotton Mills," 11.

32. Lewis Wickes Hine, National Child Labor Committee Collection.

33. Margaret Larkin, *The Nation.* Larkin's "The Story of Ella May" was also published in *New Masses* in November, and her "We'll Never Let Our Union Die" was published nearly ten years later, in the *Daily Worker* (September 14, 1938). I would like to thank Dr. Patrick Huber, Missouri University of Science and Technology, for sharing his then unpublished manuscript about the songs of Ella May Wiggins and for drawing my attention to this article.

34. Quoted in Salmond, *Gastonia, 1929: The Story of the Loray Mill Strike,* 129–30. In the Lawrence strike of 1912 against a number of mills, children played an important representational role in focusing attention on the plight of the striking textile workers, most of whom were immigrants. As Elizabeth Gurley Flynn, an International Workers of the World (IWW) organizer, remembered, children were sent out of the city. "On February 17, 1912, the first group of 150 people were taken to New York City. . . . Five thousand people met them at Grand Central Station. People wept when they saw the poor clothes and thin shoes of these wide-eyed little children" (*Talkin Union,* 44).

35. Salmond, *Gastonia,* 127.

36. Ibid., 131.

37. *American Labor on Stage,* 25.

38. Pittenger, Mark. "A World of Difference: Constructing the 'Underclass in Progressive America," *American Quarterly* 49.1 (March 1997): 26–65.

39. Ibid., 48–49.

40. See Margaret Mead's *Coming of Age in Somoa* and Franz Boas's *The Mind of Primitive Man.* In 1934, *Race and Culture,* by Ruth Benedict, a student of Boas, became a staple in college classrooms and greatly helped popularize anthropological theories of difference based on culture, not essentialized race.

Chapter 2

1. All of the press releases cited are archived in the Federal Theatre Project Collection of the National Archives, Box 531, Children's Theatre Folder.

2. All of these plays were extremely successful productions that generated positive theatre reviews and support for the Federal Theatre Project. *The Emperor's New Clothes* was a colorful retelling of the classic story. A May 12, 1937, press release sent to the *Bronx Home News* says that in the play, "Children shouted directions to the characters and all but rushed on the stage in certain scenes" (Box 531, Children's Theatre Folder). *Flight* took its newsreel form from the Living Newspapers and employed a cast of 144 to tell the history of flight from historic times to the present in 28 quickly moving scenes that employed spotlights, a loudspeaker narrator, and blackouts.

3. Lantz and Saul copyrighted the play in 1936; in the fall of 1936 continuing through the spring of 1937, the Congress of Industrial Organization union members won victories in Akron, Ohio, and Flint, Michigan. As Denning notes, "it was the year of 'sit-down fever'" (23). A release for *Revolt* exclusive to the *Herald Tribune* describes potsie as a kind of hopscotch. "Finally, actors and directors visited the lower East Side to get the authentic New York version and took notes as the street urchins showed them how 'potsie' is really played—with a banana peel."

4. New York publicity had reason to be concerned about potential problems for plays that dealt with contemporary topics. The New York Project's first Living Newspaper, *Ethiopia*, was censored because Washington officials decreed that no heads of foreign governments could be depicted in a Living Newspaper.

5. The accumulated audience for the performances was 8,395, with gross receipts of $1,076.76. This compares to an accumulated audience of 129,029 after 97 performances for the New York run of *The Emperor's New Clothes*, which grossed $2,596.85 ("New York Children's Unit Monthly Progress Report for June, 1937").

6. Atkinson had generally supported the Federal Theatre Project; on May 2, 1937, the *New York Times* published a lengthy article of his in which he called Flanagan a "person of considerable vision" who had not only expanded the American theatre audience by producing affordable theatre but also set up an infrastructure that would benefit community productions for years ("Federal Theatre: Something of What It Has Been doing under Mrs. Flanagan's Leadership," *New York Times*, May 2, 1937).

7. Ibid.

8. *Six Plays for Young People*, 14.

9. *The Revolt of the Beavers* was the only children's play to succumb to this kind of censorship, although a number of FTP plays were successfully shut down, including the Chicago project's production of Theodore Brown's *Stevedore* and the Seattle Negro Unit's production of Aristophanes' *Lysistrata*. In New York, in addition to *Ethiopia*, Marc Blitzstein's contemporary labor opera *The Cradle Will Rock*, produced by John Houseman and Orson Welles, was censored. Blitzstein's musical, which had won the leftist New Theatre League's major prize in 1937, was a labor play dealing with union organizing in the steel industry. It was censored indirectly by a Washington edict several days before opening. The order said that no new play, musical, or art gallery could be opened before July 1 because of recent budget cuts. While Washington officials insisted the memorandum was an attempt not to stop *The Cradle Will Rock* but only to postpone it, Houseman and Welles said if the government wouldn't let them open it in June, they would do so privately. Fourteen thousand tickets had already been sold. The story of the play's impromptu performance is one of the great dramas of the FTP. After Welles and Houseman invited an audience to a run-through—technically not violating the ban—the WPA authorities locked the Maxine Elliot theatre where *Cradle* had been scheduled to open June 16. Houseman and Welles notified ticket holders that the performance would take place even as they were told by the musicians' union that they had to pay for new rehearsal sessions at Broadway salaries and by the Actors Equity Union that any of the union actors (not the principals, but most of the rest of the cast) who performed on stage would have to obtain Federal Theatre permission. As crowds of ticket holders began to mass outside the Maxine Elliott, Will Geer and Howard Da Silva entertained them until, at the last minute, Houseman and Welles discovered that the Venice Theatre, twenty blocks to the north, was available. Producers, actors, lighting director Abe Feder, Blitzstein, and a crowd of ticket holders walked uptown. As Flanagan's

biographer Joanne Bentley writes: "No one, least of all Houseman and Welles, knew what sort of performance the audience would see—perhaps only Blitzstein singing at the piano and three or four actors singing from their seats in the auditorium.... By nine o'clock every seat in the Venice Theatre was filled, every inch of standing room taken. Blitzstein, in shirtsleeves and suspenders, had taken his place stage center at the untuned upright piano behind the curtain. After some preliminary remarks by Welles and Houseman, the curtain rose and the composer, looking pale and tense in the glare of a spotlight, announced, 'A street corner—Steeltown, USA.' He then began to play and sing. 'It was a few seconds,' Houseman later recalled, 'before we realized that another voice, a faint, wavering soprano,' had been added to Blitzstein's. All heads in the audience turned as the spotlight moved offstage and onto the lower left box, where Olive Stanton, dressed in green and with hair dyed red, was standing. At first her voice was barely audible but she gradually gained courage. After she had finished, a second actor, also on relief, stood up. From the front row of the orchestra, he made his rejoinder. The first scene took place with the actors positioned thirty feet apart" (*Hallie Flanagan: A Life*, 262, 263). See also Goldstein, *The Political Stage*, 263, 264. The story of the event forms the basis for the 1999 film *Cradle Will Rock*, written, directed, and produced by Tim Robbins.

10. Flanagan writes in *Arena* that in the middle of May, "after a performance of *Candide* and *How Long Brethren*, audience and cast joined in an all-night sit-down demonstration against cuts, while 44th Street was filled with marchers" and on May 27 various FTP and WPA unions called a one-day work stoppage. "Seven thousand out of 9,000 relief employees in all the art fields joined the stoppage; all of our theatres were dark, with box-office men on hand to refund money or exchange tickets" (201).

11. According to Judith Brussell's research into government investigations of FTP personnel, Rennick led and participated in Workers Alliance demonstrations. A look at the overall structure of the New York Children's Unit showcases leftist theatre credentials in Jay Williams as Assistant to Managing Project Supervisor (Rennick) and former Theatre of Action member (and co-director of *The Revolt of the Beavers*) Peter Hyun as Assistant Play Director (*A Production History of the New York City Children's Theatre Unit of the Federal Theatre Project, 1935–1939*, 27).

12. Dies Committee 1, page 58, Box 496, National Archives collection. See also *Hallie Flanagan: A Life in the American Theatre*, 318 and *The Political Stage*, 258. Writing that the number of FTP plays that took "serious issue with traditional social and political issues" was very small, Malcolm Goldstein notes that even those that engaged seriously with social and political issues would be later considered moderate, "with the exception of those in Oscar Saul and Lou Lantz's *Revolt of the Beavers*, a children's play; Michael Gold and Michael Blankfort's *Battle Hymn*; and the productions of the Living Newspaper Unit."

13. And, as Kazan notes in his autobiography, a very tightknit world in the early to mid-thirties. He writes of how members of the Group Theatre worked with the "newborn 'workers' theatres" downtown. "Many of us, while living on weekly salaries from Broadway, did our 'real work' south of Fourteenth Street—the accepted dividing line between the bourgeoisie and the radicalized masses" (*Elia Kazan: A Life*, 105).

14. According to an article from the *New York Post*, June 2, 1937, reprinted in the FTP brief prepared for the Dies Committee, Oscar Saul and Lou Lantz were noms de plumes for Oscar Alpern, 242 Eighth Ave., and Louis Rosenthal, 1970 85th St. (Dies Committee Folder, p. 64, Box 496, National Archives Collection). Oscar Saul continued to use this name professionally. According to *Stage Left*'s Jay Williams, Saul and Lantz were playwrights for the Workers Laboratory Theatre, whose *Jews at the Crossroads* was performed in 1934.

"Dealing with Jews under the Nazi regime (the play) was criticized for its draggy opening in which everyone talked like mad for several minutes to establish situation and character. Ben Berenberg, taking some time off from Red Vaudeville, played the boss of the factory, a part which whetted his taste again for acting. Although both plays had weaknesses (*Jews at the Crossroads* played in repertory with *Daughter*, a Peter Martin adaptation of an Erskine Caldwell short story), they also had tensely dramatic moments, and both were competently done and were given regular performances, although neither had anything like *Newsboy*'s success," Williams writes (152–53). Saul also had at this time a commedia dell'arte piece, *Hot Pastrami*, in repertory for the WLT. In *Stage Left*, Saul is given credit for helping write the lyrics to the popular labor song "Flying Squadron" for new member Earl Robinson. Lantz and Saul had *A Day at Bord Motors* for the New Theatre League listed in the FTP's collection of labor plays. The synopsis reads, "A Satirical sketch giving a picture of what the boss would like the public to believe about his treatment of workers." For an excellent discussion of the leftist theatre in New York during the late 1920s and 1930s, see *Stage Left*. See also Morgan Himelstein's *Drama Was a Weapon* and Harold Clurman's *The Fervent Years*.

15. In *Stage Left* Williams downplays the connection between former Theatre of Action members and *The Revolt of the Beavers*. Furthermore, though Williams actually did the makeup for the play, he neglects to mention this. All Williams says about the play is, "But when it (the FTP) presented a fantasy called *The Revolt of the Beavers*, by Oscar Saul and Lou Lantz, in which the inhabitants of Beaverland kick out their wicked king in the best approved fairy-tale style so that they can play games, eat ice cream, and stay nine years old, a perfect scream of wrath went up that it was a Communist allegory" (228). This, even though Saul and Lantz had both been mentioned in connection with the Communist WLT.

16. Artef, which is a Yiddish abbreviation for Workers Theatrical Alliance, performed from a small theatre on Broadway. Founded in 1927, the company sponsored acting studios that resulted in a permanent company of 29 people. The company performed in Yiddish. Its director Benno Schneider studied with Stanislavsky in Russia; the company was known for a distinctive collective acting style. See Karen Malpede Taylor's *People's Theatre in Amerika*, 139–44. Elia Kazan had worked with the Theatre of Action, whom he describes in *Elia Kazan: A Life* as "a group of fifteen actors and actresses . . . Jewish street-smart, many of them brought up by left-wing parents. A true collective, they lived in a Lower East Side five-story walk-up, took turns cooking, slept three or four to a room" (107). Kazan writes well of the company, but then disparages it for two reasons: he is personally not attuned to collective life, and the company performed a play first supporting then attacking New York Mayor Fiorello LaGuardia; the change in politics, he notes, came not from collective decision making but reflected the Communist Party's rejection of LaGuardia (108). Perry Bruskin, who played a skating beaver, recalls the Theatre of Action life in his oral interview archived at George Mason University.

17. Lewis Leverett had taught acting at the Theatre Collective's school, where FTP New York director Philip Barbour had taught playwriting with Walter Hart and George Sklar, and where Lee Strasberg taught directing. He had also taught classes to Workers Laboratory Theatre members on the Group Theatre's acting technique formulated by Strasberg and following the Stanislavsky method (see Constantin Stanislavsky, *An Actor Prepares*, trans. Elizabeth R. Hapgood [New York: Theatre Arts Books, Robert M. MacGregor, 1955]). For the transcript of Kazan's testimony, see Bentley, *Thirty Years of Treason: Excerpts from Hearings before the House Committee on Un-American Activities, 1938–1968*. Jules Dassin (*Never on Sunday, Topkapi, Night and the City*) was blacklisted and left the United States in 1953.

18. The play's colorful costumes were reproduced in *Cradle Will Rock*. Robbins plays with the facts about *Revolt*, though the film notes the controversy its production would bring. The film shows its writers as a young couple who are outside the FTP and who pitch their idea by going to Flanagan's office on roller skates and dressed in beaver costumes.

19. Transcript of oral interview by Diane Bowers, 28 archived at George Mason University.

20. The music is preserved in a 1936 copyrighted play that was distributed by the Dramatists Play Service, Inc., of New York after the FTP production.

21. *The Revolt of the Beavers* opened one year after the release of Charlie Chaplin's *Modern Times*, with its enormous wheels symbolizing the mechanism of industrialized America and its elegant roller-skating on the edge of a precipice.

22. Bedard and Tolch, *Spotlight on the Child*.

23. Dies Committee Testimony, National Archives administrative records collection. As Hallie Flanagan recounts in her autobiography, when she was asked by HUAC about the play, she replied that "an audience survey by trained psychologists brought only favorable reactions from children such as 'teaches us never to be selfish'—'it is better to be good than bad'—'how the children would want the whole world to be nine years old and happy'" (*Arena*, 342, 343). See also *Six Plays for Young People*, introduction, and Heard's production history of the New York children's theatre. Heard details the survey alluded to in the testimony. She writes that the survey was conducted by Dr. Frances Holden of the department of psychology at New York University, "with the aid of four students trained in analyzing the reactions of children" in an interviewing process in which hundreds of children were asked questions designed to discover if they had understood a "class angle" to the play (111, 112). Swortzell writes that the survey "revealed that audiences found no similarity to present-day conditions, did not come away with a unified idea of the action, nor discover social implications beyond 'Don't be selfish'" (14).

24. The play, indeed, is central to FTP histories because it was the children's play that Flanagan spent thirteen pages defending in a brief she prepared for testimony before the House Committee on Un-American Activities in August 1938, and she was again asked about the play's politics when she appeared before the Committee in December 1938. Although Flanagan insisted to the Dies Committee that the play was a modern-day fairy tale, as Jane DeHart Mathews has noted, she told her husband and wrote to Philip Davis that she thought it was "class conscious." Mathews writes of Flanagan's decision to produce the play:

> Her failure to anticipate the reaction to *The Revolt of the Beavers* is even more surprising in light of her recent fight with the Living Newspaper staff over *Injunction Granted* and the still more recent furor over *It Can't Happen Here*. Perhaps she expected Marxian overtones to go unnoticed. The play, she may have reasoned, was, after all, for the Children's Theatre, not the much praised, much damned, and very much publicized Living Newspaper. Whatever her reasons, the choice was a highly inappropriate one—particularly since the play opened at a time when the future of the entire WPA was once again up for debate. In short, *The Revolt of the Beavers* was a blot on the Federal Theatre's record, but in the context of two seasons of productions it seemed a rather small one. (117–118)

25. *The Revolt of the Beavers*, act 1, scene 2, line 19.

26. Department of Information Folder, Box 525, National Archives Collection.

27. The playscript is available in PDF form online in George Mason University's Federal Theatre Project Materials Collection (http://digilib.gmu.edu:8080/jspui/handle/1920/3594). A 1936 playscript is similar to one reproduced in Lowell Swortzell's *Six Plays for Young People*. It is an earlier version of the script that begins "The curtain rises on a meadow. It is on the outskirts of an industrial city and in the distance we can see the jagged outlines of skyscrapers and factories" (127). The staged version, on the other hand, introduces the children in a vacant lot with an old automobile top and seat. In addition to dialogue differences, the *Six Plays* script also has the children enter carrying schoolbooks in shoulder bags, whereas the staged version has them enter with Paul kicking a box into which they are putting firewood.

28. *The Revolt of the Beavers*, act 1, scene 1, line 1

29. Ibid., act 1, scene 1, line 3.

30. When Windy agrees to take them away to have a good time, Mary asks him, "How are y'gonna take us? On a magic carpet?" Windy answers, "What kind of a magic carpet? I'm gonna blow up a big hurricane—and blow you there" (Ibid., act 1, scene 1, line 16).

31. *From the Beast to the Blonde*, xx.

32. Dies Committee Brief 64–65, Dies Committee Folder One, Box 496, National Archives.

33. *Arena*, 200.

34. According to theorist Jack Zipes, the relegating of fairy tales to childhood and the commodification of fairy tales was a nineteenth-century phenomenon that produced a split in the genre correspondent to the Industrial Revolution's idealization of childhood and its imagination. If the Industrial Revolution's work conditions radically regularized and mechanized lives, childhood and the imagination were privileged as an ideal that made this bearable. As economic changes produced an institutionalization of life, the stock of childhood imagination rose. See "The Flowering of the Fairy Tale in Victorian England," in *When Dreams Came True: Classical Fairy Tales and Their Tradition*.

35. *Six Plays for Young People*, 128.

36. However, the socialist utopian fantasies of L. Frank Baum's fairy-tale series *The Wizard of Oz* also drew criticism for their alleged communism in the late 1930s and 1940s. While Baum may have used the fairy tale to critique American social and political structures, it is hardly an overt plea for communism. See Zipes in chapters "Inverting and Subverting the World with Hope," in *Fairy Tales and the Art of Subversion* and "L. Frank Baum and the Utopian Spirit of Oz," in *When Dreams Came True: Classical Fairy Tales and Their Tradition*.

37. In 1923 Marxist Edwin Hoernle argued, in "Work in the Communist Children's Groups," that "The proletariat will create the new fairy tales in which the workers' struggles, their lives, and their ideas are reflected and correspond to the degree to which they demonstrate how they can become human time and again, and how they can build up new educational societies in place of the decrepid [sic] old ones. It makes no sense to complain that we do not have suitable fairy tales for our children. Professional writers will not create them. Fairy tales do not originate from the desk. The real fairy tale originates unconsciously, collectively in the course of longer time-spans, and the work of the writer consist mainly in refining and rounding out the material at hand. The new proletarian and industrial fairy tale will come as soon as the proletariat has created a place in which the fairy tales will be told, not read aloud, and will be composed orally, not repeated. Then machines, tools, boilers, trains, ships, telegraphs and telephones, mine shafts and chemical tubes will become

alive and begin to speak just as previously the wolf or the water kettle in the folk tales of the peasantry and petit bourgeois spoke" (Quoted in Zipes, *Fairy Tales and Fables from Weimer Days*, 13). For information on leftist German emigrés in New York, see Williams, *Stage Left*.

38. *Fairy Tales and Fables of the Weimer Republic*. Zipes notes five major tendencies of the Weimer Republic proletarian fairy tales, all of which are displayed in *The Revolt of the Beavers*. They "(1) project an ideal societal organization that would bring an end to all suffering, (2) portray children whose honesty and clairvoyance endowed them with the ability to expose hypocrisy and made them into harbingers of a bright future, (3) develop exemplary heroes who bring about solidarity and collaboration in a struggle against exploitation, (4) reveal how social class exploitation worked and how it could be stopped, and (5) show the brutality of war and competition and underline the need for peace and coexistence" (20).

39. The positions each take in their argument recall Michael Gold's memory of his relationship to his sister in *Jews Without Money*. While his adaptation to life in the streets suggests the young Gold's ability to survive, the fragile purity of a sister too good for her harsh world is suggested by her reading of fairy tales:

> Once my little sister sat on the tenement stoop, reading the Blue Fairy Tale Book. This book was her treasure. It was a big beautiful edition with colored pictures that Harry had given her. She had copied many of those pictures with her crayons, and knew every story in the book by heart. But she loved to read them again and again, her lips moving dreamily, as if she were singing to herself. She was reading now on the stoop, while the New York sun burned out above the tenements in glorious purple, amber, and rose.
>
> Esther was in her own world. The street whirled and clashed around her, the gray old solemn Jews went by, and gabbling mommas, and pimps, pushcarts and rattling wagons. A scabby dog rummaged with its front paws in a garbage can. Three tough guys lounged nearby, and quarreled, and spat tobacco juice. The saloon was busy, the prostitutes were busy, the slum wretchedness was huge and triumphant. But Esther had escaped from it all. She was reading her book. The twilight fell on the white pages and illuminated her face. (275–76)

The memory of Esther's love of fairy tales creates a fragile moment of beauty in Gold's squalid tenement day; her surrender to their language, art, and narrative inspires Esther's brother to remember the tenements as a chiaroscuro of squalor and splendor in a passage that suggests the two might coexist. But each of the above paragraphs ends in light imagery that self-consciously draws attention to the darkness near. And two pages later, Esther is dead, run over while gathering wood on a snowy night, and the fairy child reading on the stoop has been literally crushed by a tenement life too harsh for dreamers. The bond of child and fantasy is remembered as beautiful, like the sunset above the restless systole and diastole of tenement life. But as with the colors of the sunset, Esther's dreamworld of the porch is incidental. The reality is that the sun has set and a tenement girl who dreams of magic and what might be cannot survive the reality what is.

40. Quoted in Denning, *The Cultural Front*, 230.

41. Ibid., 231.

42. Michael Gold further wrote in the *Liberator* that "Art is the tenement pouring out its soul through us, its most sensitive and articulate sons and daughters." His own recounting of a tenement childhood attests to the power of the sons and daughters of the ghetto to

artistically imagine an urban, working-class ethnicity that is intrinsically American and not exotically other. Denning argues: "The plebian writers were united by a common historical situation that was not a common ethnicity but a common ethnic formation: the restructuring of the American peoples by the labor migrations of the early twentieth century from Southern and Eastern Europe and the sharecropping South. These peoples were ethnicized and racialized by that social formation.... The invention of ethnicity was a central form of class consciousness in the United States" (*The Cultural Front*, 42). Thus the tenement evokes an ethnicity that, in the case of *The Revolt of the Beavers*, is not made explicit by rituals or behaviors located within a particular ethnic group. Gold's novel, published in 1930, went through eleven printings by the fall of that year.

43. The film version of the play, directed by William Wyler and starring Humphrey Bogart and Joel McCrea, was in production during the run of *The Revolt of the Beavers* and would be released August 24, 1937.

44. Quoted in *From Class to Caste in American Drama*, 24.

45. Whether the scene with these children was staged or not remains a question. In the final script at the Federal Theatre Project Collection in the Library of Congress, the scene is marked out. However, in the program, located in the National Archives, the characters are listed.

46. Sigmund Freud, *The Interpretation of Dreams*. See chapter 3, "The Dream as Wish Fulfilment."

47. See John Howard Lawson's *Theory and Technique of Playwriting*.

48. *The Revolt of the Beavers*, act 1, scene 1, line 9.

49. Ibid., act 1, scene 2, line 5.

50. Ibid., act 1, scene 2, line 6.

51. Ibid., act 1, scene 2, line 9.

52. Ibid., act 1, scene 2, line 10.

53. Ibid., act 1, scene 2, line 18.

54. Ibid., act 1, scene 2, line 22.

55. Ibid., act 1, scene 3, line 10.

56. Ibid., act 1, scene 3, lines 9–12.

57. Ibid., act 1, scene 3, lines 14, 15.

58. Ibid., act 2, scene 3, line 21.

59. Ibid., act 2, scene 1, line 8.

60. Ibid., act 2, scene 1, line 10.

61. Ibid., act 2, scene 1, line 17.

62. Ibid., act 3, scene 1, lines 9–13.

63. Page 63, Box 496, National Archives.

64. "Once Upon a Time," *Saturday Evening Post*, June 26, 1937, p. 22.

65. *Radical Visions*, 99.

66. *Blackface, White Noise: Jewish Immigrants in the Hollywood Melting Pot*, 45–46.

67. See "Nationalism, Blackface, and the Jewish Question," in *Blackface, White Noise*, 45–47.

Chapter 3

1. The units were administered by the FTP, though they were often formed through

the sponsorship of community groups. Thus the Harlem Negro Unit was sponsored by the New York Urban League; the Seattle Unit was sponsored initially by Florence and Burton James of the Seattle Repertory Playhouse and the Unit's core formed by the cast of their production of Paul Green's *In Abraham's Bosom*. For a comprehensive examination of the administrative setup of units in Harlem, Birmingham, and Seattle, see Tina Redd's 1996 dissertation, *The Struggle for Administrative and Artistic Control of the Federal Theatre Negro Units*.

2. The phrasing is Rena Fraden's from *Blueprints for a Black Federal Theatre, 1935–1939* to describe an idea developed not only by Alain Locke and W. E. B. Du Bois, but also Sterling Brown and Anne Cooke, the director of dramatics at Spelman College (61–62). The Federal Theatre was only the most funded and publicized attempt at African American theatre in Harlem. Du Bois organized the Krigwa Players Little Negro Theatre. McClendon founded the Negro People's Theatre in 1935, which presented Clifford Odet's *Waiting for Lefty* (and had *The Revolt of the Beavers* director Lewis Leverett on its board of directors). In 1938, Langston Hughes was a founding member of the Harlem Suitcase Theatre; the group disbanded in 1939. And in 1939 founding People's Theatre member Dick Campbell, with his wife, singer Muriel Rahn, organized the Rose McClendon Players; the company disbanded at the start of World War II. In addition, plays were published in *Crisis* and *Opportunity*. See Du Bois, "Krigwa Players Little Negro Theatre." See also White, "The Negro on the American Stage"; Locke, "The Negro's Contribution to American Art and Literature"; and Ross, "The Role of Blacks in the Federal Theatre, 1935–1939."

3. The editorial was published December 21, 1935. Folder Six, Box 142, National Archives.

4. 1935 Photo donated by Esther Porter Lane to the GMU collection.

5. These figures come from Fraden, *Blueprints for a Black Federal Theatre*. Units were established in Birmingham, Durham, Okmulgee, Oklahoma, Chicago, Peoria, New York City, Boston, Newark, Hartford, Oakland, Los Angeles, and Seattle. Some cities, such as New York and Chicago, had more than one unit; for example, New York had a black dance unit, youth unit, and vaudeville unit, and Chicago had an "all-colored" minstrel revue. Cities with those existing in 1939 were Hartford, Boston, Raleigh, Los Angeles, Seattle, New York, San Francisco, Newark, and Philadelphia.

6. See chapters 5 and 7 in Witham, *The Federal Theatre Project: A Case Study*.

7. Fraden, *Blueprints for a Black Federal Theatre*, 59.

8. The prolific Reich also wrote a *Beauty and the Beast, Baba Yaga, Cinderella, Death Takes the Wheel, Dutch Romance, Hansel and Gretel, Jack and the Beanstalk, Little Red Riding Hood, Mother Goose Review, Snow White, The Three Bears, The Three Wishes,* and *Uncle Sam's Hope* for the federal children's stages. Chorpenning is listed as author of the puppet play that opened March 14, 1936, in Philadelphia and is co-author with Reich on the Miami production's listing, according to the George Mason University catalog, although the extant Molka Reich script is credited only to her and bears no similarity besides title to the Chorpenning play.

9. The photo, which is reproduced at the beginning of this chapter, was given to George Mason University by Esther Porter Lane, who worked briefly in Washington and was then transferred by Hallie Flanagan to Seattle, where she would direct, among other projects, *Brer Rabbit and the Tar Baby*. The only indications that there was a puppet version of *Little Black Sambo* in Washington, DC, besides the photo, are a ticket stub for a marionette show and brief references in her oral interview archived at George Mason to having

produced puppet shows in the parks, none of which are named. Prior to my research, the photo was assumed to have been of puppets used for the Newark production.

Although there was no Washington unit, the catalogue of FTP productions compiled by George Mason University shows that five puppet shows were performed on December 5, 1936: *Birthday of the Infanta, Hansel and Gretel, Health Skit, Hirschvogel of Nurnburg,* and *Sambo.* All the productions are listed as "puppet theatre," except *Sambo* (the title under which George Mason University researchers originally classifed the Washington production), which is listed under "black theatre." Thanks to Jennifer Bradshaw, GMU Special Collections, for pointing this out.

10. Because the photos are not close-ups, the actor's faces are not clear; however, there is a clear ring of white around their mouths. Director's notes for the Cincinnati production state, "The actors experimented a number of days (on their own time) on the make-up. The first results with the animals resembled masks worn on the face, but eventually the right shade and correct line gave the desired effect." While this would suggest that the actors chose to produce a blackface effect, as the director had been discussing animal costumes prior to the cited paragraph, it's unclear whether he means that all actors created their makeup or just the tigers and monkeys. Production Book, Federal Theatre Project Collection, Library of Congress.

11. A visitor to a *Little Black Sambo* rehearsal in Philadelphia (which used the Chorpenning script) "remarked . . . that it was not the Sambo with which she was familiar. 'Of course not,' she was assured, 'It is a new Sambo, re-written with a keen eye out for its modern social implications'" (Jarvis, *Cultural Nationalism in an Urban Setting,* 67).

12. In the files are three Charlotte Chorpenning scripts. The script that I will discuss later has no date or place description, though it does have penciled changes marking it as a probable script used in production. None of the penciled changes were marked in a copy evidently typed in 1939. The introductory notes that refer to the Goodman Theatre production, where Chorpenning directed children's plays from 1932 to 1952, aren't attributed. The Chorpenning-attributed Seattle version was the first *Little Black Sambo* to open. Although the *Catalog-Calendar of Productions* lists an extant playscript, it is not in the Library of Congress; however, the catalogue of FTP materials housed at the University of Southern California collection, where some of the Los Angeles units' materials are archived, indicates that the Seattle unit staged a Chorpenning version of the play. (Seattle was under the Los Angeles bureau.)

13. Jodi Van Der Horn-Gibson makes a compelling argument for the Africanness of the production in "Dismantling Americana: Sambo, Shirley Graham, and African Nationalism." Graham's work with the Federal Theatre is discussed in Gerald Horne's *Race Woman: The Lives of Shirley Graham du Bois.* See 75–76 for a discussion of *Little Black Sambo.*

14. Chicago Production Book, Federal Theatre Project Archives, Library of Congress.

15. For an extensive bibliography on the Scottsboro trial compiled by Douglass O. Linder, University of Missouri–Kansas City School of Law, see http://law2.umkc.edu/faculty/projects/FTrials/scottsboro/SB_bibl.html.

16. Eric Lott, *Love and Theft: Blackface Minstrelsy and the American Working Class.* Michael Rogin, *Blackface, White Noise: Jewish Immigrants in the Hollywood Melting Pot.* See also Robert C. Toll, *Blacking Up: The Minstrel Show in Nineteenth-Century America.*

17. Lott, *Love and Theft,* 5, 6. See also Boskin, *Sambo: The Rise and Demise of an American Jester,* for descriptions of blackface shows.

18. FTP playreader reports on minstrel shows archived at the Library of Congress demonstrate familiarity with the minstrel form. Writing in 1937, reader Gus Weinburg rejects "Alabama" by Aurthur Leroy Kaser with, "The minstrel first part has long outlived its usefulness. It was written long ago. The material is so out of date and oldfashioned that a presentation of it now would be a waste of time and money. It belongs in the dim corridors of the past." Yet his further comments show that while he insists on the dated quality of the material, he is quite familiar with it. "We have the customary minstrel first part routine. A medley of songs by the company opens the show. Then the usual wrangle and arguments between the interlocutor and end man follow" (Box 137).

19. *Love and Theft*, 6.

20. *Blackface, White Noise*, 14.

21. White producer John Houseman was chosen by Rose McClendon to co-direct the Harlem unit with her. Yet, a year earlier, ill with terminal cancer, McClendon had been unable to perform the lead role written for her in Countee Cullen's *Medea*, directed by Houseman, and in July 1936, she died. Houseman continued to direct the unit through *Turpentine*, after which he left, and the project was led for the next three years by African American directors J. Augustus (Gus) Smith and Carlton Moss.

22. Folder One, Box 142, National Archives.

23. Folder Two, Box 142, National Archives. *Macbeth*'s opening drew a crowd of 10,000 people and all the major reviewers came, one "having requested in advance that he and his wife be given seats 'not next to Negroes' if possible" (Goldstein, *The Political Stage*, 260). Many reviewers echoed the condescending tone of Pollack's review. See Fraden, *Blueprints for a Black Federal Theatre*, 153–54. The production was set in nineteenth-century Haiti. Welles and Houseman gave the production colorful costumes and jungle settings. The production was paced by a troupe of African drummers, and the witches were a trio of voodoo practitioners. Welles and Houseman rearranged and somewhat altered the text, but kept the Shakespearean prose.

24. *New Theatre* 3.5, p. 24.

25. *Vaudeville*, narr. Ben Vareen, American Masters series, Winstar TV & Video, 1999.

26. *The Daily Worker* also praised *Macbeth*, with its reviewer writing that "For the first time, in a generally recognized sense, the Negro actor was permitted to drop his inane and innocuous 'blackface' role and emerge in a piece that truly revealed his many talents held in abeyance because of unjustified prejudices harbored by Broadway producers" (May 10, 1936, Folder One, Box 142, National Archives).

27. *New Theatre* 3.5, p. 24.

28. Playreader reports for Paul Green, perhaps the most widely respected white playwright writing about race in the 1920s and 1930s, demonstrate the problems of a white-imposed (no matter how sympathetically meant) black subjectivity. Reader Harold Berman writes that the play "compresses within a few pages rich characterization and background, and a frustration and exaltation that seems to come from the very core of the Negro people." An unnamed reader writes that the play is "ringing with the accents of the naïve, superstitious, spiritual-singing Negro folk of North Carolina." Pragmatic reader Katharine Roberts writes that the play's sexual scene might inflame anti-FTP passions, while the presentation of volatile race relations might provoke a too credulous racially mixed audience. She writes that it is "definitely not a play for the project. Among other things, the scene in which Goldie and Abraham go off to lie in the bushes and the other negroes discuss their being 'like hawgs' and get so sensuous a thrill out of it vicariously that they

break into a primitive dance, punctuated by odd giggles—well it might be interesting to a different audience, but it might be censored by those ready enough at best to criticize the project. Moreover, the conditions of negro education which existed in 1885, the time of the play, have been largely overcome and the prejudice on which the play is based is certainly mostly dissipated. Even ten years ago when the play was written, the subject matter was frankly dated though the treatment was modern, and the only audience interested was that which enjoyed the technical power of the author, or that which enjoyed the emotional orgy. Granted this, why bring up to a mixed audience, not always composed of the most controlled elements, the bitterness and vicious enmity between the blacks and whites which exited fifty years ago and why deliberately do a play which works so powerfully on the emotions of race antagonism? . . . If there are any reactionary sparks, they should not be lit in the mass mind." (*In Abraham's Bosom*, Playreader Reports File, 1935–39. Box 137)

29. Box 142, Negro Theatre, Folder 1, National Archives. *Women's Wear,* June 24, 1936. *New York News,* June 24, 1936. *Bronx Home News,* June 25, 1936.

30. See "The South and the Politics of Anti-Lynching Legislation," by George C. Rable. Of particular interest, Rable discusses the New Deal–era political complexities of successful Southern legislative opposition to the Costigan-Wagner anti-lynching bill of 1935 and the Wagner–Van Nuys bill of 1937.

31. The horrifying conditions of the Florida turpentine camps are mentioned in Happy James Lawrence's dissertation, *The Statewide Tours of the Florida Federal Theatre Project.* The camps had no schools, churches, or hospital, and the only store was the company store. Workers lived in two-room cabins with no indoor plumbing and worked under the supervision of a "white, whip-wielding 'woodsrider' [who] would move through the pine forest on horseback making sure the black 'chippers' and 'dippers' did their jobs" (10). According to Lawrence, the camp overseer would arbitrarily marry two people and give them one shack to cut down on housing needs (10). The turpentine camps supplied the raw materials for the naval stores industry.

32. Mosely's character Colonel Dutton is, as E. Quita Craig has written, a mediator. He owns the camp commissary and is a white man; on the other hand, he has had a black mistress for years with whom he has had three unacknowledged children. Attempting to mediate a strike and worker rage over a young man who has been shot, Dutton is first betrayed by the camp owner and then is shot by the white sheriff at the end.

33. Fraden, *Blueprints for a Black Federal Theatre,* 151, 156–57.

34. *Representations* 24:132.

35. Ibid. See *Blueprints for a Black Federal Theatre* for a discussion of African American intellectual interest in the folk play. Fraden writes, "In 1927 [Alain] Locke had contrasted the 'drama of discussion and social analysis and the drama of expression and artistic interpretation,' and had chosen the 'folk play' as the form from which will grow 'the real future of Negro drama'" (88–89). One year earlier, Langston Hughes had argued for much the same emphasis on black expressive culture in "The Negro Artist and the Racial Mountain."

36. Van Der Horn-Gibson's "Dismantling Americana" argues the significance of Graham's contributions.

37. Chinitz, "Rejuvenation through Joy," 67.

38. "The Conservation of Races," quoted in Appiah's "The Uncompleted Argument: du Bois and the Illusion of Race" (24).

39. There has been a backlash against removing *The Story of Little Black Sambo* from circulation; for a fairly recent Internet debate on the issue, see http://www.fairrosa.info/

disc/lbs.html. The discussion, which occurred at the time of the new retelling of the story, *Sam and the Tigers*, had participants ranged on either side of the question of whether the original book was racist or not. A beautifully illustrated version by Christopher Bing, with Bannerman text, was published in 2003.

40. It appeared on the American Library Association list of recommended books from 1912 to 1936, when the publication was suspended. In that year, Bannerman published a new book, *Sambo and the Twins*, and in the book review section of the November 1936 *Horn Book*, Anne Carol Moore of the New York Public Library included the new Bannerman offering with nine other books in a list of the year's outstanding children's stories. Some librarians and educators had begun to protest the treatment of African Americans in books for children in the 1930s. *We Build Together: A Reader's Guide to Negro Life and Literature for Elementary and High School Use* would be published by the National Council of Teachers of English in 1941. See also "The 'Real' Doctor Doolittle" for a discussion of the character of Bumpo, in MacCann and Woodard, *Readings in Racism*, 151–61, and the following essay, "The Persistence of Uncle Tom: An Examination of the Image of the Negro in Children's Fiction Series" (162–68), for a discussion of the portrayal of African Americans in early-twentieth-century children's book series such as the Bobbsey Twins and the Hardy Boys.

41. According to Yuill: "from the beginning well known librarians were actively involved in promoting its use. . . . In 1927, a comparative study of 'several of the best book lists prepared by both librarians and teachers for use in elementary schools' was compiled by a class in children's literature at Johns Hopkins. The report included data showing that *Little Black Sambo* was recommended on five out of seven lists. No statement was made as to why the remaining two lists excluded the book" (*Little Black Sambo: A Closer Look*, 5).

42. Whether or not Bannerman had ever attended a minstrel show, England had hosted American minstrels as early as the Virginia Minstrels' 1843 tour. And whether she was familiar with the American cultural implications of the name (or perhaps the Spanish "zambo," which means "bowlegged"), Boskin writes that "the 1873 [Scottish published] *Encyclopaedia Britannica* listed 'Zambo' as 'Any *half-breed*, but mostly the issue of Negro and Indian parents. . . . " *Sambo: The Rise and Demise of an American Jester*, 39.

43. One debt seems clear; what her Sambo walking away from the whirling tigers with his umbrella strongly resembles is Heinrich Hoffman's drawing of a "Black-a-moor" in "The Inky Boys," a story in his odd and enormously popular German *Der Struwwelpeter*, published first in England in 1848. (The connection was made by Yuill.) Hoffman's sly delight in dreadful punishments to the bad child finds splendid analogue in his crude drawings and shocking disproportions. In "The Inky Boys,"

> As he had often done before,
> The woolly-headed Black-a-moor
> One nice fine summer's day went out
> To see the shops and walk about
> And as he found it hot, poor fellow
> He took with him his green umbrella

The story describes three boys whose teasing of the black man enrages "tall Agrippa," who "had a mighty inkstand too, / In which a great goose-feather grew." When the boys refuse to stop laughing at the black man, Agrippa dips them in ink. The story ends,

> They have been made as black as crows
> Quite black all over, eyes and nose,

And legs, and arms, and heads, and toes,
And trousers, pinafores, and toys—The silly little inky boys
Because they set up such a roar,
And teased the harmless Black-a-moor

44. Joseph Boskin and Joseph Dorinson, "Ethnic Humor: Subversion and Survival," 92.

45. *Sambo: The Rise and Demise of an American Jester*, 4. The image was used in children's toys. For example, "Sambo Five Pins" enabled turn-of-the-century children to knock down wooden Sambo pins with a bowling ball," notes Gary Cross in *Kids' Stuff: Toys and the Changing World of American Childhood*.

46. "The Trope of a New Negro and the Reconstruction of the Image of the Black," 150.

47. The illustrations are reproduced in Phyllis Yuill's *Little Black Sambo: A Closer Look*.

48. Chicago Production Book, Federal Theatre Project, Library of Congress.

49. The reviewer of the play for the *Chicago Daily News* thought it did not extend far enough in its treatment of the symbolism of the jungle as well as an attempt to universalize the story (Ibid.).

50. *A History of the Chicago Federal Theatre Project Negro Unit: 1935–1939*, 148. According to Fraden, Graham wrote a master's thesis at Oberlin College titled "The Survival of Africanism in Modern Music." See also Van Der Horn-Gibson's "Dismantling Americana: Sambo, Shirley Graham, and African Nationalism" for a discussion of Graham's reappropriation of the story in her use of African motifs. After years of correspondence, the director of the Chicago Unit's *Little Black Sambo* married W. E. B. Du Bois in 1951.

51. Chicago Production Book, Federal Theatre Project, Library of Congress. Graham's further notes on the production make clear her particular emphasis on music and percussion as a motif for the production's "primitive" qualities.

52. Chorpenning script, act 1, scene 1, line 2.

53. Ibid., act 2, scene 1, line 10.

54. Ibid., act 2, scene 1, line 16.

55. Ibid., act 3, scene 1, line 13.

56. *Sambo: The Rise and Demise of an American Jester*, 88. Boskin also notes that federal marionette vaudeville shows in the Northern cities "had stringed dolls jumping to minstrel tunes and skits" (88). Ralph Ellison, who worked briefly for federal art, may have remembered these skits when writing of Tod Clifton's Sambo puppets.

57. Reich script, act 1, scene 1, line 1.

58. Ibid., act 1, scene 1, line 2.

59. Ibid., act 1, scene 2, line 1.

60. Ibid., act 1, scene 2, line 3.

61. There is no record at the Library of Congress about the playwright, Robert Warfield, and the play is listed as having been performed by the puppet theatre and not a Negro Unit in the standard production list compiled while the materials were housed at George Mason University.

62. Warfield script 1, act 1, scene 1, line 1.

63. Ibid., act 1, scene 1, line 2.

64. Ibid., act 1, scene 2, line 5.

65. Ibid., act 1, scene 4, lines 9–10.

66. "Black Nationalism and the Italo-Ethiopian Conflict 1934–1936," 130.

67. Following Schmeling's 1935 victory over Louis, a German article linked Louis's defeat with Ethiopia's: "Schmeling . . . checked the arrogance of the Negro race and clearly

demonstrated to them the superiority of white intelligence. He restored the prestige of the white race and in doing so accomplished a cultural achievement.... The victory of Italy in Abyssinia must be regarded in the same light.... After the war started there was only one thing left, the fight of a white against a black nation.... The same question must be asked: What would have happened if Abbysinia had won? The same answer applies: the whole black world would have risen up against the white race in arrogance and bestial cruelty" (*Spandau, 1936*, 301; quoted in Evans, "Joe Louis as a Key Functionary," 105).

68. Ibid., 119. As Scott details, African American support for Ethiopia ranged from attempts to volunteer in the Ethiopian army to financial support. Scott writes that although support was highest in the urban northeast, columnist George Schuyler wrote "that he had not met one black person in his travels across the country who did not wish to do something to aid the Ethiopians. He pointed out that even in the most rural and remote parts of Mississippi 'the colored people [were] intensely interested in the ... struggle and burning to do their little bit to aid the largest independent colored nation in the world'"(123).

69. Typed in larger size, the second script is two pages shorter.

70. It is unclear which script was used, although the second script seems to reference the first at the end with a parenthetic note paraphrasing dialogue from the first one. It is not clear that Warfield made the changes, which include Jumbo saying to Sambo that he can help his father but that "you yo'll [sic] bettah put yo' new clothes away first. You know all good chil'ren keeps dere clothes neat." The second script contains a number of spelling errors that indicate it was typed very quickly, for example, "Dambo" for Sambo and "Hoe" Louis for Joe Louis.

71. Warfield script 1, act 1, scene 4, line 13.

72. Ruth Comfort Mitchell was a successful author who lived in Los Gatos, California. Her papers are archived at the University of California at Santa Cruz. *Brer Rabbit and the Tar Baby* is not included on her list of publications with the collection. Married to state senator Sanborn Young, she was a staunch member of the Republican Party, though her interest in African American literature might be inferred from a letter from her to William Stanley Beaumont Braithwaite, African American poet and editor of the annual *Anthology of Magazine Verse* and the *Year Book of American Poetry* (1913–29). There are two letters from Mitchell in the Braithwaite archives at the University of Virginia. One, signed "Ruth Comfort Mitchell (Mrs. Sanborn Young)," asks Braithwaite to sign an enclosed book for her. Then she continues " ... Last year I gave a program of negro poetry for the Browning Society in San Francisco.... All the long years since the first two years of my marriage when we were in New York I have been so very grateful and thankful for the tremendous help you gave me thro' your Boston Transcript page. I have been very fortunate in my work—thirteen novels and four novelettes of OLD SAN FRANCISCO (no unsold manuscripts) and over a hundred published short stories and two books of verse many many poems in anthologies...." Two months later she wrote again to thank him for the autograph and mentioned how she much she would like to be "sporting up Fifth Avenue as we did thirty years ago" and says she has not been East since 1940. One of Mitchell's best-known works was a novel written as a rebuttal to John Steinbeck's *Grapes of Wrath* that tells the story of migrant workers from the ranchers' perspective.

73. Redd, *The Struggle for Administrative and Artistic Control of the Federal Theatre Negro Units*, 97. The Negro Unit was ordered to close its production of *Lysistrata* the day after its sold-out opening and in spite of the remainder of its scheduled performances being sold out as well. See Redd's chapter "Seattle: Labor, Race, and the Politics of Production" for a

detailed description of the conflict; see also Fraden, *Blueprints for a Black Federal Theatre;* Witham, *The Federal Theatre Project: A Case Study;* and "Others, Adults, Censored: The Federal Theatre Project's Black *Lysistrata* Cancellation" by Ron West.

74. Redd, 103. The couple had been active in producing theatre within and for a number of Seattle's ethnic communities, according to Redd. See also *Left Out: The Seattle Repertory Playhouse, Audience Inscription and the Problem of Leftist Theatre During the Depression Era.* They first produced an African American production of Paul Green's *In Abraham's Bosom* in 1933 and found their cast members at the African Methodist Church. Because of this contact, many of those who found employment in the Negro Unit had been able to cite "actor" as occupation on their relief applications (Redd, 105). *Stevedore* was the unit's second production, following *Noah,* a musical version of the Biblical story.

75. Interestingly, however, *Stevedore* was not the James's first choice; they wanted to produce Dubose Heywood's *Porgy.* But, as Redd notes, the actors' discomfort with the production caused "a committee consisting of African Americans from the Citizen's Committee and King County Colored Progressive Democratic Club" to visit the WPA state director. Quoting from the log of the Seattle Repertory Playhouse (of which the Burtons were directors), Redd notes the committee said, "[*Porgy*] is too degrading to be put on at this time.... Any play that is elevating to the race, we have no objections to, but any play that is not elevating.... There is nothing to be gained from it." The committee's first choice was *Stevedore,* which tells the story of black and white dockworkers uniting to protect a group of blacks from a white lynch mob in recognition that their class position makes it necessary for them to support each other. The story had particular resonance in Seattle because many members of the African American community came to the city during a 1916 longshoreman strike as strikebreakers and conflicted labor relations between black and white remained, although in the wake of the strike, blacks were admitted into the International Longshoremen's Association. See Redd, 103, 115–117.

76. *Brer Rabbit and the Tar Baby,* act 1, scene 1, lines 1–2.

77. Esther Porter Lane, oral interview with John O'Connor and Karen Wickre, 23, George Mason University.

78. Box 946, Play Lists File, 1934–39, Library of Congress Federal Theatre Project Collection. The National Service Bureau was designed as a central organizing division that would facilitate the movement of personnel, materials, and services across the project and make available its library to community theatres and its technological developments to professional theatres. Mathews, *The Federal Theatre, 1935-1939: Plays, Relief, and Politics.* See pp. 148–49.

79. According to theatre historian Paul Nadler, Silvera was also a Republican who later worked for Nelson Rockefeller. He was, Nadler writes, "made a play reader by the Federal Theatre's National Service Bureau, which charged him 'to weed out anything that was unjust or unproduceable [sic] or too militant'" ("Liberty Censored: Black Living Newspapers of the Federal Theatre Project," 618). Co-writer of *Liberty Deferred* Abram Hill later helped found and direct the American Negro Theatre.

80. Silvera's was one of at least three plays written by FTP playwrights that attempted to dramatize the history of racism in America. *Liberty Deferred* has two young couples, one white and one black, who, "While touring Manhattan island, [. . .] learn and argue about the history and current status of African Americans, while observing almost 40 scenes" ("Liberty Censored," 619). The scenes cover the historical period from the early slave trade to the presence of African Americans in World War II. Another FTP playreader, Paul Lip-

schutz, composed his *Negro Symphony* (an unproduced play the entire script of which is in the Library of Congress archives), which used the Christ figure of "the Negus" to tell the history of African Americans in America. And finally, Hughes Allison's FTP-produced *The Trial of Dr. Beck* is a three-act play that goes forward from 1800 to his contemporary time.

81. "A List of Negro Plays," Box 937, Play Lists File, 1934–39, Library of Congress Federal Theatre Project Collection.

82. See *The Federal Theatre Project: A Catalog-Calendar of Productions*.

83. The playreader reports in general provide a fascinating, complex look at the manner in which people thought about race and representation during the Federal Theatre Project. Plays were reviewed not only for production but also for distribution, and so there are a great number of opinions by people in the division in the archive. While the playreaders were located in New York City and so reflect a geographical uniformity, the opinions reflect a wide variety of views. A number of readers seem to be budding writers and so bring a sense of style to their critical endeavors.

84. Chicago Production Book, Federal Theatre Project Archives, Library of Congress.

85. Playreader Reports File, 1935–39. Box 137.

Chapter 4

1. The *Washington Post* itself miscalculated the committee's historical reach, however, in initial reporting on the witness testimony: "The old saying that 'the truth can never catch up with a lie' will probably cause the House committee investigation of un-American activities to go down in history as the probe that sought to make Shirley Temple out a communist" (Jack Beall, September 3, 1938).

2. "Shirley's Feat," November 2, 1938.

3. *Child Star: An Autobiography*, 60.

4. *Baby, Take a Bow* was released in 1934 and *Triumph of the Will* was technically released in 1935.

5. See "Winning Over the Young" (261–90) in Richard Evans's *The Third Reich in Power* for a discussion of the Nazi regime's focus on the young, including through pedagogic directives to schools and the takeover of youth groups and activities. See also his chapter "Prosperity and Plunder," particularly the section "The Battle for Work" (322–50), for a discussion of the German economy in the prewar years of Nazi power.

6. The play opened about one month after Kristallnacht, which occurred on November 9, 1938.

7. The story began its life as a serialized narrative in *St. Nicholas*, the magazine for children, in 1885. In 1902 it was produced as a play, *The Little Princess*, in London's Avenue Theatre. For a description of the various versions of the story, see Janice Kirkland's "Frances Hodgson Burnett's Sara Crewe through 110 Years." See the introduction of Paula Krebs's *Gender, Race, and the Writing of Empire* for a discussion of the role of Mafeking Night in the manufacture of British patriotic support for the Boer War. See Jyotsna Kapur's *Coining for Capital: Movies, Marketing, and the Transformation of Childhood* for a discussion of the three film versions of *A Little Princess*.

8. A 1995 remake of *A Little Princess* follows the narrative of the Temple film rather than the Burnett book; in the film Sara's father takes her to a boarding school in New York as he goes to fight in World War I. In the 1990s Hollywood was reluctant to make Sara even

look for her father, much less suffer his loss; he is brought all the way from the trenches to right next door to her to convalesce.

9. Quoted in Hamida Bosmajian, *Sparing the Child: Grief and the Unspeakable in Youth Literature about Nazism and the Holocaust*, 7.

10. For a discussion of fascism, see Mosse's *The Fascist Revolution: Toward a General Theory of Fascism*. See also Evans's chapter "Blood and Soil" (414–34) in *The Third Reich in Power*. William Dudley Pelley's life was the subject of Scott Beekman's 2005 *William Dudley Pelley: A Life in Right-Wing Extremism and the Occult*.

11. Thus, Nazi Germany prized fairy tales as Aryan relics.

12. Sontag's "Fascinating Fascism" and Benjamin's "The Work of Art in the Age of Mechanical Reproduction" offer foundational analyses of Riefenstahl's film and fascist aesthetics.

13. The other studios were MGM and Paramount. See Colgan's *Warner Brothers Crusade against the Third Reich: A Study of the Anti-Nazi Activism and Film Production, 1933-1941*.

14. John Diggins, "Flirtation with Fascism: American Pragmatic Liberals and Mussolini's Italy," 494.

15. Hence the popularity of Sinclair Lewis's novel *It Can't Happen Here*, which depicted the rise of a homegrown fascist government in the United States. Lewis donated a script to the FTP, and the play opened in seventeen cities across the United States in October 1936, two weeks before the presidential election. And, while proposing a fundamentally liberal New Deal, Roosevelt kindled people's need to be assured. In his call for the nation to act as a "trained and loyal army willing to sacrifice for the good of a common discipline" and his insistence that if his plan to combat the economic crisis were not approved he would ask for broad executive powers, he responded to the American impulse for an authoritative figure at the head of state (Quoted in Leuchtenburg, 41).

16. Quoted in Albert E. Stone, Jr., "Seward Collins and the *American Review*: Experiment in Pro-Fascism 1933-37," 6.

17. Production Book, *A Letter to Santa Claus*, Box 1031.

18. According to the production book, each unit that was involved rehearsed separately for two weeks and the whole production came together only just before the opening. Unfortunately, there seems to be no review available for the production; a notice of an upcoming performance in the *Chicago Tribune* is all the record I have been able to find.

19. Charlotte Chorpenning, who studied under George Pierce Baker at Harvard's 47 Workshop, was the most prolific and influential children's playwright through the midcentury, although she did not become active in children's theatre until she was sixty years old. She wrote more than fifty plays, doubling midcentury theatre for children, and taught classes in children's playwriting at the Goodman Theatre, where she was director of children's theatre from 1932 to 1951. See her autobiography *Twenty-One Years with Children's Theatre*. See also Roger Bedard's "Charlotte B. Chorpenning: Playwright and Teacher," in *Spotlight on the Child* (85–98).

20. *Six Plays for Young People*, 22–23.

21. It could be argued that federal theatre's most famous play, *The Revolt of the Beavers*, was antifascist, but its antifascism is usually overlooked in the face of its overt Marxism and Soviet theatre aesthetics. Nonetheless, the argument can be made that the villainous Chief with his brutal thugs offers as many satirical points of comparison to Benito Mussolini as to a fat-cat industrialist. The FTP collected and released a list of antiwar plays. "These lists

were created at the request of religious, recreational, and educational groups connected with over 100 peace organizations," the introduction states. Box 496, National Archives.

22. Mickenberg's *Learning from the Left* offers a groundbreaking examination of the connection between modernist and Popular Front works for children (89).

23. Ibid., 93.

24. For a discussion of the fairy tale in the Weimer Republic, see Zipes's *Fairy Tales and Fables from the Weimer Days*.

25. *Six Plays for Young People*, 11.

26. Although the New York Children's Unit communicated with Soviet children's theatre directors and archived materials sent from them, only a handful of children's plays evinced either the overtly political rhetoric or the staging associated with leftist theatre. The first production of the New York Unit was Chorpenning's immensely popular adaptation of *The Emperor's New Clothes*. In Los Angeles audiences flocked to Yasha Frank's adaptations of *Hansel and Gretel* and *Aladdin*. Nine versions of Cinderella were produced from Florida to Louisiana to Oklahoma to Colorado. Chorpenning adapted not only *The Emperor's New Clothes* but also successful versions of *Rip Van Winkle* and *Jack in the Beanstalk*.

27. *Six Plays for Young People*, 179.

28. Ibid., 180.

29. Ibid., 182.

30. Ibid., 183.

31. Interestingly, in light of *The Wizard of Oz*'s effects one year later, "the CHILDREN are whirled around and disappear to reappear on the screen, being whirled madly through space. Snow grows thicker and thicker, the stage lights dance and then dim, and when the lights come up again, the snowy scene at the North Pole is revealed" (185–86). It is unclear whether this conceptualized flight was actually staged. Pictures from the production in the production book show very conventional and static moments in the play with polar bears and the snow ballet. The production book notes that the snow ballet appeared three times as a transition vehicle between scenes. The curtain never goes down, and it would be consistent with the play that the snow ballet appear as the children are whirling through the air.

32. *Six Plays for Young People*, 196.

33. Their innocence creates a profound opposition to the intense emotional strife of the shadows and their accompanying voices. The play's emphasis on the values of tolerance, sharing, and cooperation is amplified by a setting and staging that opposes darkness to light and fearful images with the children's dialogue, which centers on understanding how social interactions can function appropriately. It drew from expressionistic staging of psychological forces and leftist techniques (such as were also used in Federal Theatre's Living Newspapers) that visually invoke the energy and mass of the crowd.

34. See Debra Werrlein's "Not So Fast, Dick and Jane: Reimagining Childhood and Nation in *The Bluest Eye*."

35. *The Intellectuals and the Flag*, 103.

36. *Six Plays for Young People*, 177.

37. Ibid., 193–94. The director's notes turn the Aurora Australis into a giant Christmas decoration. The notes indicate colors by quoting the diaries of the Byrd expedition: "every shade of red, from palest pink to crimson, from brilliant orange to primrose, every shade of green from softest apple to shining emerald with shadows purple, and in the crevices cones of purest blue all against the celestial blue of the sky."

38. Ibid., 202.
39. Ibid., 204.
40. Ibid., 205. Chorpenning had employed audience participation to great effect in her adaptation of *The Emperor's New Clothes*. A May 12, 1937, press release sent to the *Bronx Home News* says that in the play, "Children shouted directions to the characters and all but rushed on the stage in certain scenes" (Box 531, "Children's Theatre," National Archives).
41. *Six Plays for Young People*, 205.
42. *A Little Princess*, 193 (emphasis in original).
43. See McGillis, *A Little Princess: Gender and Empire*.
44. While Burnett's popularity today is assured, as Beverly Lyons Clark notes in *Kiddie Lit: The Cultural Construction of Children's Literature in America*, Burnett had fallen out of favor as a children's author by the 1920s, perhaps as part of a backlash against the Fauntleroy fashion fad of the turn of the century (27, 28).
45. Burnett was born in England but moved to America as a girl. As the *New York Times* review of the film notes, and perhaps not affectionately, "Mrs. Burnett, as you possibly recall, was a lady who had coronets on the brain" ("At the Roxy," *New York Times*, March 11, 1939, http://www.nytimes.com [accessed July 7, 2006]).
46. Warner Brothers also used historical England as the setting for an antifascist *The Adventures of Robin Hood* in 1938.
47. "At the Roxy," *New York Times*, March 11, 1939.
48. See Karen Sánchez-Eppler's "Temperance in the Bed of a Child: Incest and Social Order in Nineteenth-Century America" for an excellent discussion of the sentimentalized child of reform fiction.
49. I am indebted again to Sánchez-Eppler's "Raising Empires like Children: Race, Nation, and Religious Education," which points out the connection between the domestic and imperial projects of nation-building in its study of nineteenth-century Sunday school missionary tracts.
50. The *New York Times* review indulges in a snarky aside about the penultimate hospital scene: "Until you see that dramatic sequence in which Shirley Temple meets Queen Victoria, her best friends, Richard Greene and Anita Louise, the ex-music hall pal, Mr. Treacher, and her long-lost father, Ian Hunter, all in the space of a few minutes prowling about a hospital corridor, you haven't really lived, in the cinematic sense" ("At the Roxy").
51. "Group Plans Films to Aid Democracy," *New York Times*, November 15, 1938. Other archived materials include articles in the *New Republic* and *the World-Telegram*, as well as an undated telegram accepting an Advisory Board position from Thomas Mann and a November 18, 1938 telegraph of support from Fritz Lang. Mann wrote "Throughout the world it has become precarious to take democracy for granted—even in America." Archived materials also include Organization Committee and Advisory Board members and the organization's mission statement. National Archives, Box 566.
52. Ibid.

Chapter 5

1. "The Yasha Frank Version," Boston Production Book.
2. Carlo Collodi, *Pinocchio*. For criticism of Pinocchio's representational shift, see *Pinocchio Goes Postmodern*.

3. Yasha Frank Adap., *Pinocchio*, Box 739, Library of Congress Federal Theatre Project Collection.

4. This letter is cited in Jane DeHart Mathews's seminal *The Federal Theatre, 1935-1939*. The letter is in WPA record group 69, FTP Records, National Office Testimonial Letters.

5. "The Tribulations of Pinocchio: How Social Change Can Wreck a Good Story," 211.

6. "The Yasha Frank Version," Boston Production Book.

7. Press release, December 22, 1938, Box 531, National Archives.

8. Ibid.

9. Martin Star, drama critic, Radio Station WMCS, Box 531, National Archives.

10. "Federal Theatre in Los Angeles," 132. Published in 1962, Holcomb's *California Historical Society Quarterly* study is a very early historical account.

11. Ibid.

12. Ibid., 136, 145.

13. While Frank was the producer for the 1957 live televised version, American composer Alec Wilder was hired to compose the music. Wilder's music for the production is available on podcast through the Wilderwood PodOmatic, http://wilderworld.podomatic.com/rss2.xml. A transcribed 2007 interview with lyricist William Engvick suggests the frustrations Frank experienced after the end of the FTP (interview reproduced in its entirety).

> On October 13, 1957—50 years ago today—NBC aired a live, nationally-televised) production of Pinocchio featuring music composed by Alec Wilder. It is widely considered one of the classics from "the Golden Age of Television." Wilderworld recently asked Pinocchio lyricist William Engvick to share his recollections of the production. Here is some of what he related:
>
> I thought it was pretty good. The night of the broadcast I was in the studio. I watched it from a room—I wasn't with the players. Mickey Rooney was friendly and nice. I can't remember if Alec was there. Even if he was, he always pretended he wasn't. They had never done it live before, and it had to be perfect because you couldn't edit like you can today. There were a number of rehearsals of which I attended a few.
>
> It might have been a more pleasant experience were it not for the "producer" [and scriptwriter], a terrible guy named Yasha Frank who resented us because he wanted to do it all himself. He'd been successful with Pinocchio in WPA days. The real producer was David Susskind of Talent Associates. He was a nice guy. He liked us. He also hired us for Hansel and Gretel [broadcast in April of 1958].
>
> I worked on Pinocchio from July to September. The Lullaby was something Alec and I had written a while before called Simple As ABC. I thought it would work in the show, suggested it and changed the words. Alec wrote all the music very quickly. It takes me longer to write, so Alec took off for Rochester—or wherever—and left me alone with these monsters! I felt like I was doing all the work. Sometimes he'd never say where he was. I think it was a real weakness of his: he simply couldn't be tied down to anything, or own anything. Except for books. Bookstore owners loved Alec. He bought loads of books and gave most of them away.

After Hansel and Gretel, Alec and I decided not to do anymore. We were offered a third program [Hiawatha] but turned it down. The drug company [Rexall] that sponsored them pulled out. Yasha Frank killed himself shortly after that. Several years later his son called me for permission to produce Pinocchio again. I said that would be fine, but nothing came of it.

That was a long time ago. It's all part of a dream.

14. "Federal Theatre Does Itself Proud with Presentation of *Pinocchio*," p. 2, cols. 1–2.

15. There have been several recent productions of the FTP *Pinocchio*, including one by Pennsylvania Youth Theatre in May 2010.

16. "The Making of Children's Culture," 108.

17. Pinocchio's early publication history in the United States is described in Wunderlich, "The Tribulations of Pinocchio: How Social Change Can Wreck a Good Story," 197–98.

18. Harvey J. Graff, *Conflicting Paths: Growing Up in America*, 303.

19. Numerous critical works have charted nineteenth-century representations of the child. See U. C. Knoepflmacher's *Ventures into Childhood: Victorians, Fairy Tales, and Femininity*; see also Carol Mavor's *Stolen Pleasures* and Jack Zipes's work on fairy tales. With her examination of American temperance fiction, Karen Sanchez-Eppler traces the manner in which many a sentimentalized daughter reformed many a hardened drunk with her sweet patience and innocent caresses.

20. *Behaviorism*, 104. Watson wrote for popular magazines and newspapers, including *Harpers, Colliers*, the *New York Times*, and *The Nation*.

21. *Parents Magazine*, June 1930, p. 65.

22. Dorothy Canfield Fisher, "Getting Acquainted with His World," *National Parent Teacher*, 6.

23. *Pinocchio*, act 1, scene 1, p. 8.

24. Ibid., act 1, scene 1, p. 10.

25. Ibid., act 1, scene 1, pp. 19–20.

26. "The Tribulations of Pinocchio: How Social Change Can Wreck a Good Story," 210.

27. *Pinocchio*, act 2, scene 1, p. 5.

28. Ibid., act 2, scene 1, pp. 5–6.

29. Ibid., act 3, scene 3, p. 6.

30. Ibid., act 3, scene 3, p. 9.

Conclusion

1. *The New Deal Stage: Selections from the Federal Theatre Project 1935–1939*, Federal Theatre Project Collection: A Registry of the Library of Congress Collection of the Works Projects Administration Records.

2. Richard Wunderlich and Thomas Morrissey, *Pinocchio Goes Postmodern*, 88. See also Lowell Swortzell's *Six Plays for Young People from the Federal Theatre Project*.

3. "Pinocchio Dies in New York as Federal Theatre Drops Curtain," *Life Magazine*, July 17, 1939, p. 20.

4. "3 WPA Shows Close Amid Hot Protests," *New York Times*, July 1, 1939, sec. 1, p. 2, col. 8.

5. Quoted in *Arena*. Flanagan writes that Harry Hopkins concluded his speech announcing the birth of the Federal Theatre Project at the National Theatre Conference at Iowa University with the declaration "I am asked whether a theatre subsidized by the government can be kept free from censorship and I say, yes, it is going to be kept free from censorship. What we want is a free, adult, uncensored theatre" (28).

6. Lowell Swortzell writes that attempts were made to revive the show under private management when the FTP ended, but the cost of its huge cast was too much for private management to bear.

7. Press release, Box 531, National Archives. Robbins consulted with members of the George Mason University Federal Theatre Collection staff, who perhaps pointed him to the link between vaudevillians and *Pinocchio*.

8. "Trials of the Mind," 3.

9. Many of the federal plays encouraged audience engagement with onstage action. Chorpenning's adaptations for federal theatre also made use of the breakdown of the fourth wall. In *The Emperor's New Clothes* tailors Zar and Zan rely on audience suggestions in order to determine which direction to go. However, the direct plea of *A Letter to Santa Claus* was unusual.

10. *Happily Ever After: Fairy Tales, Children, and the Culture Industry*, 142.

11. *The Intellectuals and the Flag*, 106.

WORKS CITED

Books, Articles and Periodicals, Dissertations, and Web Publications

"111—Pinocchio (1957)." *Wilderwood: 100 Records to Celebrate 100 Years of Alec Wilder . . . And More.* Podcast. October 13, 2007. http://wilderworld.podomatic.com/rss2.xml (accessed May 16, 2011).

"3 WPA Shows Close Amid Hot Protests." *New York Times.* July 1, 1939, sec. 1, p. 2, col. 8

Abookire, Noerena, and Jennifer Scott McNair. "Children's Theatre Activities at Karamu House, 1915-1975." In *Spotlight on the Child: Studies in the History of American Children's Theatre,* ed. Roger L. Bedard and John C. Tolch. Contributions in Drama and Theatre Studies. New York: Greenwood, 1989. 69-84.

American Authors and Books. 3rd rev. ed. New York: Crown, 1972.

Anderson, John. "Pinocchio at the Ritz Has Real Charm." *New York Journal and American,* January 3, 1939.

Appiah, Anthony. "The Uncompleted Argument: Du Bois and the Illusion of Race." *Critical Inquiry* 12.1 (1985): 21-37.

"At the Roxy." *New York Times.* March 11, 1939. 24.

Atkinson, Brooks. "Federal Theatre: Something of What It Has Been Doing Under Mrs. Flanagan's Leadership." *New York Times,* May 2, 1937.

———. "*The Revolt of the Beavers,* or Mother Goose Marx, Under WPA Auspices." *New York Times,* February 20, 1937, sec. 11, p. 1, cols. 1-3.

Bannerman, Helen. *The Story of Little Black Sambo.* London: Grant Richards, 1899.

Beall, Jack. "Dies Body May Be Remembered for Its Attack on Shirley." Washington Post. September 4, 1938: B5. ProQuest Historical Newspapers: University of North Carolina at Chapel Hill Lib, Chapel Hill, NC.

Bedard, Roger L. "Junior League Children's Theatre: Debutantes Take the Stage." In *Spotlight on the Child: Studies in the History of American Children's Theatre,* ed. Roger L. Bedard, and John C. Tolch. Contributions in Drama and Theatre Studies. New York: Greenwood, 1989. 35-50.

Bedard, Roger L., and C. John Tolch, eds. *Spotlight on the Child: Studies in the History of American Children's Theatre*. New York: Greenwood, 1989.
Benjamin, Walter. *Illuminations*. Ed. and intro. Hannah Arendt. New York: Schocken, 1973 (1955).
Bentley, Eric, ed. *Thirty Years of Treason: Excerpts from Hearings before the House Committee on Un-American Activities, 1938-1968*. New York: Viking, 1971.
Bentley, Joanne. *Hallie Flanagan: A Life in the American Theatre*. New York: Knopf, 1988.
Black, Shirley Temple. *Child Star: An Autobiography*. New York: McGraw-Hill, 1988.
Boas, Franz. *The Mind of Primitive Man*. New York: Macmillan, 1938.
"Boro Girl's Play Makes Hit." *Times Union* (Brooklyn), September 6, 1936, sec. A, p. 7a, cols. 1-3.
Boskin, Joseph. *Sambo: The Rise and Demise of an American Jester*. New York: Oxford University Press, 1986.
Boskin, Joseph, and Joseph Dorinson. "Ethnic Humor: Subversion and Survival." *American Quarterly* 37.1 (Spring 1985): 81-97.
Bosmajian, Hamida. *Sparing the Child: Grief and the Unspeakable in Youth Literature about Nazism and the Holocaust*. New York: Routledge, 2002.
Browder, Laura. *Rousing the Nation: Radical Culture in Depression America*. Amherst: University of Massachusetts Press, 1998.
Brown, Lorraine, and John O'Connor. *Free, Adult, and Uncensored: The Living History of the Federal Theatre Project*. Washington, DC: New Republic Books, 1978.
de Brunhoff, Laurent, ed. *Fifty Years of Babar: Watercolors by Jean and Laurent de Brunhoff*. Intro. Maurice Sendak. New York: The Arts Publisher, 1983.
Brussell, Judith Ellen. *Government Investigations of Federal Theatre Project Personnel in the Works Progress Administration (The show must NOT go on!)*. PhD diss., City University of New York, 1993.
Burnett, Frances Hodgson. *A Little Princess*. Philadelphia: Lippincott, 1963 (1905).
Buttitta, Tony, and Barry Witham. *Uncle Sam Presents: A Memoir of the Federal Theatre 1935-1939*. Philadelphia: University of Pennsylvania Press, 1982.
Chambers, Jonathan. "How Hollywood Led John Howard Lawson to Embrace Communism and How He Turned Hollywood Red." *Theatre History Studies* 17 (1997): 15-32.
Chinitz, David. "Rejuvenation through Joy: Langston Hughes, Primitivism, and Jazz." *American Literary History* 9.1 (Spring 1997): 60-78.
Chorpenning, Charlotte. *Twenty-One Years with Children's Theatre*. Anchorage, KY: Anchorage Press, 1974.
Clark, Beverly Lyons. *Kiddie Lit: The Cultural Construction of Children's Literature in America*. Baltimore: Johns Hopkins University Press, 2003.
Clurman, Harold. *The Fervent Years*. New York: Da Capo, 1983. Orig. publ. by Harcourt, Brace, Jovanovich, 1975.
Contemporary Authors. Detroit, MI: Gale Research, 1981.
Cooney, Terry. "Cosmopolitan Values and the Identification of Reaction: *Partisan Review* in the 1930s." *Journal of American History* 68.3 (1981): 580-98.
Craig, E. Quita. *Black Drama of the Federal Theatre Era: Beyond the Formal Horizons*. Amherst: University of Massachusetts Press, 1980.
Cross, Gary. *Kids' Stuff: Toys and the Changing World of American Childhood*. Cambridge, MA: Harvard University Press, 1997.
Curtis, Verna Posever, and Stanley Mallach, eds. *Photography and Reform: Lewis Hine and the National Child Labor Committee*. Milwaukee, WI: Milwaukee Art Museum, 1984.

Denning, Michael. *The Cultural Front: The Laboring of American Culture in the Twentieth Century.* The Haymarket Series, ed. Mike Davis and Michael Sprinker. London: Verso, 1998 (1997).
Diggins, John P. "Flirtation with Fascism: American Pragmatic Liberals and Mussolini's Italy." *The American Historical Review* 71.2 (1966): 487–506.
———. "The Italo-American Anti-Fascist Opposition." *The Journal of American History* 54.3 (December 1967): 579–98.
Du Bois. W. E. B. "Krigwa Players Little Negro Theatre." *Crisis* 32 (July 1926): 134–36.
Duffy, Susan. *American Labor on Stage: Dramatic Interpretations of the Steel and Textile Industries in the 1930s.* Westport, CT: Greenwood, 1996.
Evans, Art. "Joe Louis as a Key Functionary: White Reactions toward a Black Champion." *Journal of Black Studies* 16.1 (September 1985): 95–111.
Evans, Richard J. *The Third Reich in Power: 1933–1939.* New York: Penguin, 2005.
The Federal Theatre Project: A Catalog-Calendar of Productions. Compiled by staff of Fenwick Library, George Mason University. Bibliographies and Indexes in the Performing Arts, Number 3. New York: Greenwood, 1986.
Fisher, Dorothy Canfield. "Getting Acquainted with His World." *National Parent Teacher* 32.1 (September 1937): 6–7.
Flanagan, Hallie. *Arena: The History of the Federal Theatre.* New York: Benjamin Blom, 1965 (1940).
———. "First Federal Summer Theatre: A Report." *Federal Theatre* 1.4 (1935).
———. "The People's Theatre Grows Stronger." *Federal Theatre* 1.6 (1936).
Fraden, Rena. *Blueprints for a Black Federal Theatre, 1935–1939.* New York: Cambridge University Press, 1994.
Freud, Sigmund. *The Interpretation of Dreams.* Trans. A. A. Brill. New York: Macmillan, 1945.
Garnett, Michael. "Nothing to Write About." *Federal Theatre* 2.1 (1936).
Gassner, John. *Dramatic Soundings.* New York: Crown, 1968.
Gates, Henry Louis, Jr. "The Trope of a New Negro and the Reconstruction of the Image of the Black." *Representations* 24 (Fall 1988): 129–55.
Gilbert, Douglas. "Four Weekly Matinees of 'Beavers' Revolt.'" *World Telegram,* May 21, 1937, sec. 1, p. 20, cols 1–2.
Gill, Glenda. *White Greasepaint on Black Performers: A Study of the Federal Theatre, 1935–1939.* New York: P. Lang, 1988.
Gitlin, Todd. *The Intellectuals and the Flag.* New York: Columbia University Press, 2006.
Gold, Michael. *Jews without Money.* 1930. New York : Carroll & Graf, 1996.
Goldstein, Malcolm. *The Political Stage: American Drama and Theater of the Great Depression.* New York: Oxford University Press, 1974.
Gompers, Samuel. "An Analysis of Fascism." *American Federationist* 30 (November 1923): 927–33.
Gordon, Janet, and Diana Reische. *The Volunteer Powerhouse.* New York: Rutledge, 1982.
Graff, Harvey J. *Conflicting Paths: Growing Up in America.* Cambridge, MA: Harvard University Press, 1995.
Harkins, John. "'Beaver's Revolt' Pleasing Fantasy for the Children." *New York American,* May 21, 1937, sec. 1, p. 11, col. 1.
Heard, Doreen B. "Children's Theatre in the Federal Theatre Project." In *Spotlight on the Child: Studies in the History of American Children's Theatre,* ed. Roger L. Bedard and John C. Tolch. Contributions in Drama and Theatre Studies. New York: Greenwood, 1989. 99–118.

———. "A Production History of the New York City Children's Theatre Unit of the Federal Theatre Project, 1935–1939." PhD diss., Florida State University, 1986.
Himelstein, Morgan Y. *Drama Was a Weapon: The Left-Wing Theatre in New York 1929–1941*. New Brunswick, NJ: Rutgers University Press, 1963.
Holcomb, Robert. "The Federal Theatre in Los Angeles." *California Historical Society Quarterly* 42.2 (June 1962): 131–47.
Horne, Gerald. *Race Woman: The Lives of Shirley Graham du Bois*. New York: New York University Press, 2000.
Hughes, Langston. "The Negro Artist and the Racial Mountain." *The Nation* (23 June 1926): 692–94.
Jarvis, Arthur R., Jr. "Cultural Nationalism in an Urban Setting: The Philadelphia Experience with Federal Project Number One of the Works Progress Administration." PhD diss., Pennsylvania State University, 1995.
Kapur, Jyotsna. *Coining for Capital: Movies, Marketing, and the Transformation of Childhood*. New Brunswick, NJ: Rutgers University Press, 2005.
Kazacoff, George. *Dangerous Theatre: The Federal Theatre Project as a Forum for New Plays*. New York: P. Lang, 1989.
Kazan, Elia. *A Life*. New York: Knopf, 1988.
Kent, Ronald C., ed. *Culture, Gender, Race, and U.S. Labor History*. Westport, CT: Greenwood, 1993.
Kirkland, Janice. "Frances Hodgson Burnett's Sara Crewe through 110 Years." *Children's Literature in Education* 28.4 (December 1997): 191–203.
King, Wilma. *Stolen Childhood: Slave Youth in Nineteenth-Century America*. Bloomington and Indianapolis: Indiana University Press, 1995.
Kingsley, Sidney. *Dead End: A Play in Three Acts*. New York: Random House, 1936.
Kline, Herbert. *New Theatre and Film, 1934–1937*. New York: Harcourt, Brace, Jovanovich, 1985.
Kline, Stephen. "The Making of Children's Culture." In *The Children's Culture Reader*, ed. Henry Jenkins. New York: New York University Press, 1998. 95–109.
Krebs, Paula. *Gender, Race, and the Writing of Empire: Public Discourse and the Boer War*. New York: Cambridge University Press, 2004.
Larkin, Margaret. "Ella May's Songs." *The Nation* 129.3353 (October 1929): 382–83.
———. "The Story of Ella May." *New Masses* 5.6 (November 1929): 3–4.
———. "We'll Never Let Our Union Die." *Daily Worker*, September 14, 1938, p. 7, cols. 2–4.
Lantz, Lou, and Oscar Saul. *The Revolt of the Beavers*. New York: Dramatists Play Service, 1936.
Lawrence, Happy James. "The Statewide Tours of the Florida Federal Theatre Project, October 1937–June 1939: A Description and Evaluation of Two Seasons on the Road for the 'People's Popular Theatre.'" PhD diss., Florida State University, 1988.
Lawson, John. *Theory and Technique of Playwriting*. New York: G. P. Putnam's Sons, 1936.
Leuchtenburg, William E. *Franklin D. Roosevelt and the New Deal: 1932–1949*. New York: Harper and Row, 1963.
Levander, Caroline. *Cradle of Liberty: Race, the Child, and National Belonging from Thomas Jefferson to W. E. B. Du Bois*. Durham, NC: Duke University Press, 2006.
Levi, Primo. *If Not Now, When?* New York: Summit Books, 1982.
Levine, Ira A. *Left-Wing Dramatic Theory in the American Theatre*. Ann Arbor, MI: UMI Research Press, 1985 (1980).

Levine, Lawrence. "Hollywood's Washington: Film Images of National Politics during the Great Depression." In *Prospects: An Annual of American Cultural Studies* 10 (Essays). New York: Cambridge University Press, 1985. 169-95.
Linder, Douglass O. *Famous Trials: The "Scottsboro Boys" Trial 1931-1937. Famous Trials.* University of Missouri–Kansas City School of Law. 2012. February 2, 2012. http://law2.umkc.edu/faculty/projects/FTrials/scottsboro/SB_bibl.html.
Locke, Alain. "The Negro's Contribution to American Art and Literature." *The ANNALS of the American Academy of Political and Social Science.* 140 (November 1928): 234-47.
Lott, Eric. *Love and Theft: Blackface Minstrelsy and the American Working Class.* New York: Oxford University Press, 1995.
MacCann, Donnarae, and Gloria Woodard, eds. *The Black American in Books for Children: Readings in Racism.* Metuchen, NJ: Scarecrow, 1985 (1972).
Macleod, Anne S. "The Child in American Literature for Children: The 1930's and Now." In *The Portrayal of the Child in Children's Literature: Proceedings of the 6th Conference of the International Research Society on Children's Literature,* ed. Denise Escarpit. New York: K. G. Saur, 1985. 79-85.
Marchand, Roland. *Advertising the American Dream: Making Way for Modernity, 1920-1940.* Berkeley: University of California Press, 1985.
Mathews, Jane DeHart. *The Federal Theatre, 1935-1939: Plays, Relief, and Politics.* Princeton, NJ: Princeton University Press, 1967.
McCaslin, Nellie. *Theatre for Children in the United States: A History.* Norman: University of Oklahoma Press, 1971.
McGillis, Roderick. *A Little Princess: Gender and Empire.* New York: Twayne, 1996.
McKelway, A. J. "Child Labor in the Southern Cotton Mills." *Annals of the American Academy of Political and Social Science* 27, Child Labor (March 1906): 1-11.
McElvaine, Robert S. *The Great Depression, 1929-1941.* New York: Times Books, 1984.
Melosh, Barbara. *Engendering Culture: Manhood and Womanhood in New Deal Art and Theater.* Washington, DC: Smithsonian Institution Press, 1991.
Mickenberg, Julia. *Learning from the Left: Children's Literature, the Cold War, and Radical Politics in the United States.* London: Oxford University Press, 2005.
Moffard, Juliet Haines, ed. *Talkin' Union: The American Labor Movement.* Carlisle, MA: Discovery Enterprises, 1997.
Mosse, George L. *The Fascist Revolution: Toward a General Theory of Fascism.* New York: Howard Fertig, 1999.
Motion Picture Almanac. New York: Quigley, 1998.
Nadler, Paul. "Liberty Censored: Black Living Newspapers of the Federal Theatre Project." *African-American Review* 29.4 (Winter 1995): 615-22.
Navasky, Victor S. *Naming Names.* New York: Viking, 1980.
Ogden, August Raymond. *The Dies Committee: A Study of the Special House Committee for the Investigation of Un-American Activities, 1938-1944.* Washington, DC: Catholic University of America Press, 1945.
"Once Upon a Time." *Saturday Evening Post,* June 26, 1937, p. 22.
Ottley, Roi. "The Negro Theatre *Macbeth.*" *New Theatre* 3.5 (May 1936): 24.
Pells, Richard H. *Radical Visions and American Dreams: Culture and Social Thought in the Depression Years.* New York: Harper and Row, 1973.
"Pinocchio Dies in New York as Federal Theatre Drops Curtain." *Life,* July 17, 1939, p. 20.
Pittenger, Mark. "A World of Difference: Constructing the 'Underclass in Progressive America." *American Quarterly* 49.1 (March 1997): 26-65

Plum, Jay. "Rose McClendon and the Black Units of the Federal Theatre Project: A Lost Contribution." *Theatre Survey* 33 (November 1992): 144–53.
Political Plays for Children: The Grips Theatre of Berlin. Trans. Jack Zipes. St. Louis, MO: Telos, 1976.
Quinn, Susan. *Furious Improvisation: How the WPA and a Cast of Thousands Made High Art out of Desperate Times*. New York: Walker, 2008.
Rable, George C. "The South and the Politics of Anti-Lynching Legislation." *The Journal of Southern History* 51.2 (May 1985): 201–20.
Rahv, Philip. "Trials of the Mind." *Partisan Review* 4 (April 1938): 3–4, 8–9.
Redd, Tina. "The Struggle for Administrative and Artistic Control of the Federal Theatre Negro Units." PhD diss., University of Washington, 1996.
Rennick, Jack. "Children's Theatre—New York." *Federal Theatre* 2.3 (1936).
Rice, Robert. "Federal Theatre Does Itself Proud with Presentation of *Pinocchio*." *New York Morning Telegraph*, January 4, 1939, p. 2, cols. 1–2.
Rodman, Ellen. "Edith King and Dorothy Coit and the King-Coit School and Children's Theatre." *Spotlight on the Child: Studies in the History of American Children's Theatre*. New York: Greenwood, 1989. 51–68.
Rogin, Michael. *Blackface, White Noise: Jewish Immigrants in the Hollywood Melting Pot*. Berkeley: University of California Press, 1996.
Ross, Ronald. "The Role of Blacks in the Federal Theatre, 1935–1939." *The Journal of Negro History* 59.1 (January 1974): 38–50.
Salmond, John A. *Gastonia, 1929: The Story of the Loray Mill Strike*. Chapel Hill: University of North Carolina Press, 1995.
Sánchez-Eppler, Karen. *Dependent States: The Child's Part in Nineteenth-Century American Culture*. Chicago: University of Chicago Press, 2005.
———. "Raising Empires Like Children: Race, Nation, and Religious Education." *American Literary History* 8.3 (Fall 1996): 399–425.
———. "Temperance in the Bed of a Child: Incest and Social Order in Nineteenth-Century America." *American Quarterly* 47.1 (March 1995): 1–33.
Scharne, Richard G. *From Class to Caste in American Drama: Political and Social Themes since the 1930s*. New York: Greenwood, 1991.
Scott, William R. "Black Nationalism and the Italo-Ethiopian Conflict 1934–1936." *Journal of Negro History* 63.2 (April 1978): 118–34.
"Shirley's Feat." *Washington Post*, November 2, 1938, p. X8. ProQuest Historical Newspapers: University of North Carolina at Chapel Hill Lib, Chapel Hill, NC.
Silone, Ignazio. "Two Syllables." *Partisan Review* 3.6 (October 1936): 3–5.
Six Plays for Young People from the Federal Theatre Project (1936–1939). Ed. Lowell Swortzell. New York: Greenwood, 1986.
Spargo, John. *The Bitter Cry of the Children*. New York: Macmillan, 1909.
Sporn, Paul. *Against Itself: The Federal Theater and Writers' Projects in the Midwest*. Detroit, MI: Wayne State University Press, 1995.
Stanislavsky, Constantin. *An Actor Prepares*. Trans. Elizabeth R. Hapgood. New York: Theatre Arts Books, Robert M. MacGregor, 1955.
Stone, Albert E., Jr. "Seward Collins and the *American Review*: Experiment in Pro-Fascism 1933–37." *American Quarterly* 12.1 (Spring 1960): 3–19.
Taylor, Karen M. *People's Theatre in Amerika*. New York: Drama Book Specialists, 1972.
"Three WPA Shows Close Amid Hot Protests." *New York Times*, July 1, 1939, sec. 1, p. 2, col. 8.

Tichi, Cecilia. *Shifting Gears: Technology, Literature, Culture in Modernist America.* Chapel Hill: University of North Carolina Press, 1987.

Toll, Robert C. *Blacking Up: The Minstrel Show in Nineteenth-Century America.* New York: Oxford University Press, 1974.

Trachtenberg, Alan. *Reading American Photographs: Images as History, Mathew Brady to Walker Evans.* New York: Noonday, 1989, 1990.

Vactor, Vanita Marion. "A History of the Chicago Federal Theatre Project Negro Unit: 1935–1939." PhD diss., New York University, 1998.

Van Der Horn-Gibson, Jodi. "Dismantling Americana: Sambo, Shirley Graham, and African Nationalism." *Americana: The Journal of American Popular Culture* 7.1 (Spring 2008). 8 Jan. 2011. http://www.americanpopularculture.com/journal/articles/spring_2008/van_der_horn_gibson.htm. Online.

Van Vorst, Mrs. John. *The Cry of the Children: A Study of Child Labor.* New York: Moffat, 1908.

Ward, Winifred. *Creative Dramatics for the Upper Grades and Junior High School.* New York: Appleton, 1930.

Warner, Marina. *From the Beast to the Blonde: On Fairy Tales and Their Tellers.* New York: Farrar, Straus and Giroux, 1995.

Watson, John B. *Behaviorism.* Chicago: University of Chicago Press, 1930.

Werrlein, Debra T. "Not So Fast, Dick and Jane: Reimagining Childhood and Nation in *The Bluest Eye.*" MELUS 30.4. (Winter 2005): 53–72.

West, Ron. "Left Out: The Seattle Repertory Playhouse, Audience Inscription and the Problem of Leftist Theatre During the Depression Era." PhD diss., University of Washington, 1993.

———. "Others, Adults, Censored: The Federal Theatre Project's Black *Lysistrata* Cancellation." *Theatre Survey* 37.2 (November 1996): 93–113.

White, Walter. "The Negro on the American Stage." *The English Journal* 24.3 (March 1935): 179–88.

Whitman, Willson. *Bread and Circuses; a Study of Federal Theatre.* New York: Oxford University Press, 1937.

Williams. Jay. *Stage Left.* New York: Charles Scribner's Sons, 1974.

Wilson, Earl. "Beavers' Fairy-Tale C.I.O. Too Tough for City's Finest." *New York Post,* June 2, 1937, p. 9, cols. 2–7.

Witham, Barry. "Censorship in the Federal Theatre." *Theatre History Studies* 17 (1997): 3–14.

Witham, Barry B. *The Federal Theatre Project: A Case Study.* Cambridge: Cambridge University Press, 2003.

Wunderlich, Richard, and Thomas J. Morrissey. *Pinocchio Goes Postmodern: Perils of a Puppet in the United States.* New York: Routledge, 2002

Wunderlich, Richard. "The Tribulations of *Pinocchio*: How Social Change Can Wreck a Good Story." *Poetics Today* 13.1 (Spring 1992): 197–219.

Yuill, Phyllis J. *Little Black Sambo: A Closer Look.* New York: The Racism and Sexism Resource Center for Educators, a division of the Council on Interracial Books for Children, 1976.

Zelizer, Viviana. *Pricing the Priceless Child: The Changing Social Value of the Children.* Princeton, NJ: Princeton University Press, 1994.

Zipes, Jack, ed. and trans. *Fairy Tales and Fables from the Weimer Days.* Hanover, NH: University Press of New England, 1989.

———. *Happily Ever After: Fairy Tales, Children, and the Culture Industry*. New York: Routledge, 1997.
———. *When Dreams Came True: Classical Fairy Tales and Their Tradition*. New York: Routledge, 1999.
———. *Fairy Tales and the Art of Subversion : The Classical Genre for Children and the Process of Civilization*. New York: Routledge, 2006.

Films

Chaplin, Charles, dir. *Modern Times*. United Artists, 1936.
Lang, Walter, dir. *The Little Princess*. Based on the novel by Frances Hodgson Burnett. Twentieth Century-Fox, 1939.
Riefenstahl, Leni, dir. *Triumph of the Will*. Festival Films, 1935.
Robbins, Tim, dir. *Cradle Will Rock*. Touchstone Pictures, 1999.
Wyler, William, dir. *Dead End*. Based on the play by Sidney Kingsley. Samuel Goldwyn Co., 1937.

Archival Sources

RECORDS OF THE FEDERAL THEATRE PROJECT

Records of the Works Progress Administration
Record Group 69, National Archives, Washington, DC

Afro-American. December 21, 1935. Negro Unit Folder Six. Box 142.
Boehnel, William. "Film Group Organized to Defend Democracy." *New York World Telegram*. November 26. 1938. Box 566.
Children's Autumn Festival. Children's Autumn Festival Folder. Box 495.
"Dies Committee Invited to Premiere of WPA's *Pinocchio*." Press Release. December 22, 1938. Box 531.
"Federal Theatre Support." Federal Theatre Project—WPA Folder. Box 496.
"Films for Democracy." *The New Republic*. November 30, 1938. Box 566.
Flanagan, Hallie. Brief to the Dies Committee, 1938. Dies Committee Folder. Box 496,.
Frank, Yasha. "A Survey for a Proposed National Plan for Children's Theatre: Prepared at the Direction of Mrs. Hallie Flanagan." October 6, 1938. Box 495.
"Group Plans Films to Aid Democracy." *New York Times*. November 15, 1938. 25. Box 566.
Hill, Lawrence. "The Children's Theatre." Prospectus. August 28, 1936. Box 495.
Kondolf, George. Letter to Richard Whorf. Children's Autumn Festival Folder. Box 495.
"A List of Anti-War Plays." Community Service Report of Activism Folder. Box 496.
"New York Children's Unit Monthly Progress Report for June, 1937." Box 531.
"Police Gnaw at WPA over Beavers' Play." *New York Herald Tribune*, June 2, 1937, p. 21, cols. 1–2. Mimeograph. Box 154 (Vassar Collection).
Press release announcement of WPA Children's Theatre Club. Department of Information Folder. Box 525.
Press Release. *The Emperor's New Clothes* to the *Bronx Home News*. May 12, 1937. Children's Theatre—1937 Folder. Box 531.

Press Release. *The Revolt of the Beavers* to the *Daily Worker.* May 12, 1937. Children's Theatre—1937 Folder. Box 531.
Press Release. *The Revolt of the Beavers* to the *Daily Worker.* April 23, 1937. Children's Theatre—1937 Folder. Box 531.
Press Release. *The Revolt of the Beavers* to the *Herald Tribune.* Children's Theatre—1937 Folder. Box 531.
Press Release. *The Revolt of the Beavers* to the *World Telegram.* May 18, 1937. Children's Theatre—1937 Folder. Box 531.
Program. *The Revolt of the Beavers.* Vassar Collection Box 154.
Rennick, Jack. Report on "The Children's Theatre. August 28, 1936. Box 495.
Review of *Turpentine. Women's Wear.* June 24, 1936. Negro Theatre Folder One. Box 142.
Review of *Turpentine. New York News.* June 24, 1936. Negro Theatre Folder One. Box 142.
Review of *Turpentine. Bronx Home News.* June 25, 1936. Negro Theatre Folder One. Box 142.
Teegen, Dorothy, and Helenka Adamowska. "Tentative Outline for Children's Entertainment Project." Box 495.
"Testimony to Hazel Huffman." Dies Committee Folder One. Box 496.
"That 'MacBeth Troupe." *The Daily Worker,* May 10, 1936. Mimeograph. Negro Theatre Folder. Box 142.
WPA Children's Theatre Club. Announcement. May 26, 1937. Department of Information Folder, Box 525

LIBRARY OF CONGRESS

Music Division

Federal Theatre Project Collection

Allen, Alfred and Ruth Comfort Mitchell. *Brer Rabbit and the Tar Baby.* Library Records 1932–40. Playscripts File 1936–39. Box 601.
Amberg, Louis. Playreader Report "Alabama Minstrels." Play Service and Research Records, 1933–40. Playreader Reports File, 1935–39. Box 137.
———. Playreader Report "Alabama Attaboy Minstrels." Play Service and Research Records, 1933–40. Playreader Reports File, 1935–39. Box 137
Bannerman, Helen. *Little Black Sambo.* Adapt. Charlotte Chorpenning. S1147, Copy 8. Library Records, 1932–40. Playscripts File. Box 696.
———. *Little Black Sambo.* Adapt. Edwine Noye Mitchell. Typed manuscript. Library Records, 1932–40. Playscripts File. Box 696.
———. *Little Black Sambo.* Adapt. Molka Reich. S1117b, Copy 4. Library Records, 1932–40. Playscripts File. Box 696.
———. *Little Black Sambo.* Adapt. Robert Warfield. S1117c Copies 1, 3. Library Records, 1932–40. Playscripts File. Box 696.
Berman, Harold. Playreader Report *In Abraham's Bosom.* Play Service and Research Records, 1933–40. Playreader Reports File, 1935–39. Box 225.
Chorpenning, Charlotte. *A Letter to Santa Claus.* Typed manuscript. Library Records, 1932–40. Playscripts File. Box 694.
Collodi, Carlo. *Pinocchio.* Adap. Yasha Frank. S1157b, Copy 4. Library Records, 1932–40. Playscripts File. Box 739.

Ewing, Robert. Playreader Report *The Revolt of the Beavers.* Play Service and Research Records, 1933–40. Playreader Reports File, 1935–39. Box 295.

"56 Minstrels Compiled by Music Vaudeville Service Department." Playlist. Box 946.

Fishel, H. L. Playreader Report *In Abraham's Bosom.* Play Service and Research Records, 1933–40. Playreader Reports File, 1935–39. Box 225.

Hall, Walter. Playreader Report "Nigger Baby." Play Service and Research Records, 1933–40. Playreader Reports File, 1935–39. Box 266.

Lake, Paul. Playreader Report "Nigger Baby." Play Service and Research Records, 1933–40. Playreader Reports File, 1935–39. Box 266.

Lantz, Lou and Oscar Saul. *The Revolt of the Beavers.* Library Records, 1932–40. Playscripts File. S1681, Copy 1. Box 753.

"A List of Negro Plays." Library Records 1932–40. Play Lists File, 1934–39. Box 937.

The New Deal Stage: Selections from the Federal Theatre Project 1935-1939. Federal Theatre Project Collection: A Registry of the Library of Congress Collection of the Works Projects Administration Records. September 23, 1999. http://www.loc.gov/teachers/classroommaterials/connections/new-deal-stage/ (accessed May 17, 2011).

Osgood, Helen. Playreader Report *The Revolt of the Beavers.* Play Service and Research Records, 1933–40. Playreader Reports File, 1935–39. Box 295.

Photograph. *The Revolt of the Beavers.* Photographic Prints File 1934–39. Box 1183.

Production Book. *Little Black Sambo.* Boston Negro Unit Production. Production Records, 1934–43. Production Title File, 1934–39. Box 1054.

Production Book (2). *Little Black Sambo.* Chicago Negro Unit Production. Production Records, 1934–43. Production Title File, 1934–39. Box 1032.

Production Book (2). *Little Black Sambo.* Cincinnati Negro Unit Production. Production Records, 1934–43. Production Title File, 1934–39. Box 1032.

Production Book (2). *Little Black Sambo.* Philadelphia Marionette Theatre Production. Production Records, 1934–43. Production Title File, 1934–39. Box 1032.

Production Book (2). *A Letter to Santa Claus.* Chicago Production. Production Records, 1934–43. Production Title File, 1934–39. Box 1031.

Roberts, Katherine. Playreader Report *In Abraham's Bosom.* Play Service and Research Records, 1933–40. Playreader Reports File, 1935–39. Box 225.

Sharkey, Gertrude M., and Edward Cramer. *Bunk, Bullets, and Babies.* Library Records, 1932–40. Playscripts File. Box 604.

Silver, J. Edward. Playreader Report *The Revolt of the Beavers.* Play Service and Research Records, 1933–40. Playreader Reports File, 1935–39. Box 295.

Unsigned. Playreader Report *In Abraham's Bosom.* Play Service and Research Records, 1933–40. Playreader Reports File, 1935–39. Box 225.

Weinburg, Gus. Playreader Report "Alabama." Play Service and Research Records, 1933–40. Playreader Reports File, 1935–39. Box 137.

National Child Labor Committee Collection

Photographs

Hine, Lewis Wickes. *Boy Sweeper, Lincoln Cotton Mills, Evansville, Ind. Carding Machines: Floor Slippery. (See report for conditions.) Location: Evansville, Indiana.* 1908 October.

National Child Labor Committee Collection. Library of Congress. February 28, 2012. http://www.loc.gov/pictures/resource/cph.3b37794/.

Hine, Lewis Wickes. *Gastonia, N.C. Boy from the Loray Mill. "Been at it right smart two years."Location: Gastonia, North Carolina*. 1908 October. National Child Labor Committee Collection. Library of Congress. February 28, 2012. http://hdl.loc.gov/loc.pnp/nclc.01344.

Hine, Lewis. *A typical spinner. Mamie—Lancaster Cotton Mills, S.C. Location: Lancaster, South Carolina*. 1908 December. National Child Labor Committee Collection. Library of Congress. February 28, 2012. http://hdl.loc.gov/loc.pnp/nclc.01448/.

GEORGE MASON UNIVERSITY

Fenwick Library

Special Collections and Archives: Federal Theatre Project

Bruskin, Perry. Oral interview conducted by John O'Connor. October 22, 1976, Box 2, Folder 9.

Lane, Esther Porter. Oral interview conducted by Mae Mallory Krulak. September 7, 1976, Box 6, Folder 16.

———. Oral interview conducted by John O'Connor and Karen Wickre. July 11, 1977, Box 6, Folder 16.

Lantz, Lou and Oscar Saul. *The Revolt of the Beavers*. Mason Archival Repository Service. http://digilib.gmu.edu:8080/jspui/handle/1920/3594

Randolph, John. Oral interview conducted by Diane Bowers. May 20, 1976. Box 8, Folder 20.

Photographs

Little Black Sambo (Chicago Illinois). Box 42, Folder 5.

Little Black Sambo (Newark, New Jersey). Box 42, Folder 8.

Little Black Sambo (Washington, DC). Donated by Esther Porter Lane. Box 42, Folder 4.

Pinocchio (New York City, New York). Box 57, Folder 12.

Revolt of the Beavers (New York City, New York). Paul, Mary, and Windy. Box 64, Folder 27.

Revolt of the Beavers (New York City, New York). Paul, Professor Beaver, and Mary lean their heads together. Box 64, Folder 27.

Revolt of the Beavers (New York City, New York). Professor Beaver tells a story. Box 64, Folder 26.

INDEX

advertising, 22, 132–35
Advertising the American Dream (Marchand), 134
African American actors, 72, 73–74; *Macbeth*, 77, 164nn23, 26; racist reviews of, 77–78; roles available to, 106–7; whiteness, presentation of, 79–80. *See also* Negro Units
African Americans, 6; barred from education, 95, 99–100; black bodies, portrayal of, 75–79; black mammy stereotype, 18–19, 84; children, portrayal of, 74–75, 83, 101–2; complementary racial contributions, 81–82; denied Americanness, 77, 91; minstrelsy negates fear of, 76–77, 91; New Negro philosophy, 80; otherness and, 76–77; portrayed in plays, 18–20; surplus symbolic value, 77. *See also* minstrelsy; Negro Units
Afro American, 71
"All-American Minstrels," 25
allegory, 1, 54, 57–59, 58–59, 66, 69–70
Allen, Alfred, 102
amateur groups, 14, 23
American Communist Party, 6, 9–10; National Textile Workers' Union, 38–41. *See also* communism
American Dream, 30
American Federation of Labor, 31
American Review, 113
Americanism, 6, 30–31, 113–14
Americanness, as innocent, 118–19
anti-fascism, 4, 6, 20–21, 108–10, 124–25, 140–42
anti-lynching movement, 19, 75, 141
Appiah, Anthony, 81
Arent, Arthur, 56
Aries, Philippe, 29
Artef Theatre (Arbeiter Teater Verband), 47, 157n16
Association of Junior Leagues of America, 27, 101
Atkinson, Brooks, 17, 45–46, 55, 66, 68, 70; *Macbeth,* review of, 77; support of Federal Theatre Project, 155n6
audience, 4, 9, 23, 129, 155n5; adult/child perceptual binary, 48; adults, 26, 129; African American, 80; age groups, 24–25; education of children, 5, 16, 25–28, 142; free admission, 25, 114, 142; for *Pinnocchio,* 129; segregated, 19–20;

surveys of, 25, 48, 158n23; venues, 18, 26. *See also* children's theatre

Babar books, 85
Baby, Take a Bow, 109
Bannerman, Helen, 18–20, 81, 83, 166n40
Baum, L. Frank, 159n36
Beard, Charles, 113
Bedard, Roger L., 27
behaviorism, 133–34
Benjamin, Walter, 147–48
Bentley, Joanne, 155–56n9
Beveridge, Albert J., 32–34
Big White Fog (Ward), 73
Biggs, Howard, 73
The Bitter Cry of the Children (Spargo), 34
Black Legion, 113
Black Nationalism, 99
Blackface, White Noise (Rogin), 68–69
Blackstone Theatre, 114
Blitzstein, Marc, 1, 155–56n9
Blueprints for a Black Federal Theatre (Fraden), 73, 165n35
Boas, Franz, 42
body, social, 32
Boskin, Joseph, 84, 91
Brer Rabbit and the Tar Baby, 18–19, 24, 73–74, 102–4
Brooklyn Eagle, 77
Browder, Earl, 6
Brown, Lorraine, 48, 144
Brown, Theodore, 73
Bruskin, Perry, 47
Brussell, Judith, 150n20, 156n11
Bufano, Remo, 25
Bunk, Bullets, and Babies, 21
Burke, Kenneth, 2, 30
Burnett, Frances Hodgson, 110, 173nn44, 45

Call It Sleep (Roth), 56
capitalism, 1, 5–6, 37, 40, 143–44; in *Revolt of the Beavers*, 55, 60, 64, 66, 68–70

Carnera, Primo, 98–99
Carolina Spinner, A (Hines), 33, 37
casting, 23–24
Catholic Right, 113
censorship, 1, 3, 14, 145; *The Cradle Will Rock*, 16–17; *The Revolt of the Beavers*, 16–17, 45–46
Centuries of Childhood (Aries), 29
Chicago Federal Theatre Project, 114
Chicago Negro Unit, 74–75, 81–91
"Chief Aderholt" (Wiggins), 40
child: body of, 135–36; changing social value of, 28–42, 49, 66, 128, 141–42; class issues and, 28–32; cultural power of figure of, 50; economic hardship and rhetoric of, 110–11; goodness of, 118, 131; ideal citizen, 111–12, 115, 121; as innocent, 28, 54, 70, 117–19, 121, 125, 128, 171n33; morality, sense of, 21, 48, 54, 118; as morally unfixed, 133; parent–child relations, role in, 131–32; sacralization of, 30, 34; in sentimental and reform fiction, 122–23; as site of hope, 5, 55, 115, 133, 146–47; tenement world, 56–57, 160–61n42, 160n39; universalization of, 30, 34, 37, 41, 49–50, 102, 109; as victimized, 28, 37, 40
child actors, 24, 114
child laborers: machine ideology and, 34–36; songs about, 38–40; visual representations of, 29, 33, 34–37, 39, 41. *See also* working class
child psychology, 133–34, 136
children: active choices of, 50; African American, 74–75, 83, 101–2; civic responsibility toward, 31–32; effect of hard labor on, 29, 31–34, 33; experiential nature of learning, 28; immigrant, 30–31; Nazi portrayal of, 109–11, 114; as peace-seeking, 114–15; political consciousness, 54–55; representations of, 5, 30; state, relation to, 110–12, 114, 124, 127; storytelling equated with, 50–52
Children's Autumn Festival, 25

Children's Educational Theatre, 27
children's theatre, 4–5; age groups, 24–25; apparatus of, 16; consultants, 24; early initiatives, 27–28; types of plays, 25–26
Children's Theatre Club (WPA), 49
"The Children's Theatre" (Rennick), 25
Chinitz, David, 81
Chorpenning, Charlotte, 18, 43, 147, 171n19; *The Emperor's New Clothes*, 18, 25. See also *Letter to Santa Claus, A*; *Little Black Sambo*
Christian didacticism, 53
Cincinnati Children's Theatre, 74
citizenship: children as ideal, 111–12, 115; family responsibilities and, 31–32, 125, 131; as submission to state, 111–12, 124, 127
civic responsibility, 31–32, 125, 131
Civilian Conservation Corps, 3
class issues: childhood and, 28–32; in *A Little Princess*, 121–22, 125; race subsumed under, 79–80; social journalists, 41
collective bargaining, 6
collective consciousness, 68–69
Collodi, Carlo, 128, 131
colorblind tenets, 79
communism, 4–9, 38, 40, 46–48, 53–54, 59, 68. See also American Communist Party; House Committee on Un-American Activities (Dies Committee)
Communist International Legal Defense, 75
Congress of Industrial Organizations, 6, 9, 155n3; affiliations and loyalties, 30; *The Revolt of the Beavers* controversy, 16–17, 43
"The Conservation of Races" (du Bois), 81
Cotton, Joseph, 3
Cowley, Malcolm, 8
Cradle Will Rock (Robbins), 1, 16, 22, 140, 143, 158n18
Cradle Will Rock, The (Blitzstein), 1, 155–56n9

Cradle Will Rock, The (Welles-Houseman), 16–17, 155–56n9
Crane, Stephen, 41
creative dramatics, 28
Creative Dramatics: For the Upper Grades and Junior High School (Ward), 28
Crewe, Sara (*A Little Princess*), 110–11, 121–25, 147, 170–71n8, 170n7
The Cry of the Children (Van Vorst), 34
cultural apparatus, 3–4, 9
Cultural Front, The (Denning), 7–9, 7–10, 19, 30–31, 56, 153n3, 161n42
culture of affiliations and loyalties, 9–10

Daily Worker, 40, 43–45, 54, 164n26
Dassin, Jules, 3, 47, 150n10, 157n17
Dead End (Kingsley), 17, 55, 56–57
democracy, 5–6, 9–10, 30–32, 67–68; ethnic tolerance and, 41–42; individualism and, 124–25; values, 6, 28
Denning, Michael, 7–10, 19, 56, 155n3; on ethnicity, 161n42; on immigrants, 30–31
Depression, 68–69; Federal Theatre Project and, 11–16; parenting concerns, 131–33; Popular Front and, 5–10
Dewey, John, 28
Dies, Martin, Jr., 2, 149–50n9
Dies Committee. See House Committee on Un-American Activities
Disney, Walt, 129
Disney's *Pinocchio*, 22, 128–29, 131, 138–39
dreaming, 52, 54, 58–59
Du Bois, W. E. B., 81, 162n3
Duffy, Susan, 41

education: African Americans barred from, 95, 99–100; bourgeois, 136; of children as audience, 5, 16, 25–28, 142; early-twentieth-century theory, 16, 28, 36, 133–34; script must provide, 25
Educational Alliance, 27
émigrés, 6, 112

The Emperor's New Clothes (Chorpenning), 18, 25, 43, 154n2
Enlightenment values, 119
Ethiopia, 99, 168n67
ethnicity, 5, 41–42, 56, 160–61n42; ethnic Americanism, 6, 30–31; subsumed by child, 28–30, 34. *See also* working class
European theatre, 23
Evening Troupe (WLT), 47
Evening with Dunbar, An, 73

fairy stories, 48–55, 115–16; alleged communism of, 159–60n37, 159nn24, 26; as appropriate genre, 53–54; blurred lines with reality, 54–55; gendered female, 50–52; Weimar Republic, 55, 59, 68–69, 115, 160n38
family: civic responsibilities and, 31–32, 125, 131; parenting concerns, 22, 131–33, 136; relations outside of work, 37–38; as separate from larger community, 22
fascism: American attraction to, 112–14; anti-fascism, 4, 6, 108–10, 124–25, 140–42; Joe Louis fight and, 98–99, 167–68n67; *Triumph of the Will,* 109–12, 114, 127, 141
Federal Art Project, 10
Federal Music Project, 10, 25, 114
Federal One, 2, 10, 23, 46, 144
Federal Theatre newsletter, 2
Federal Theatre Project (FTP), 1–2; "56 Minstrels," 104–6; administrators, 46–47; black bodies, portrayal of, 75–79; Boston Production Book, 129; children's units, 23–24; defunded, 7, 143–44; Depression and, 11–16; employees, 3, 24, 47, 129–31, 169n74; extravaganzas, 74, 114; funding, 46–47; "A List of Negro Plays," 104–5; Los Angeles Unit, 24, 128–29, 131; Music Vaudeville Service Department, 106; naïveté of, 49–50; National Service Bureau, 104–5; as One-Act Experimental Theatre, 47; as people's theatre, 1–4; *Pinocchio* and, 21–22; race, positions on, 19–20; as Theatre of Action, 47, 157n16. *See also* audience; Negro Units (Federal Theatre Project)
Federal Theatre Project Collection, 43, 140
Federal Theatre Project festivals, 144
Federal Theatre report, 24
Federal Writers Project, 10
fellow traveler, image of, 8–9
Fenwick Library, 144
Films for Democracy, 126
Fishel, H. L., 79
Flanagan, Hallie, 2, 4, 23, 26, 46, 155n6, 156n10; on *Pinocchio,* 145; on *Revolt of the Beavers,* 53–54; testimony before HUAC, 67–68, 158nn23, 24
Flight (Saul and Lantz), 18, 43, 154n2
folk plays, 74, 80–81, 165n35
Fraden, Rena, 73, 151n33, 165n35
Frank, Yasha, 21–22, 26, 116; *Pinocchio,* 129–31, *130*
Free, Adult, and Uncensored: The Living History of the Federal Theatre Project, 144–45
From the Beast to the Blonde (Warner), 52

gangster figure, 57–58
Garvey, Marcus, 99
Gary, Indiana, children's unit, 24
Gates, Henry Louis, 80, 84
George Mason University, 144
German American Bund, 113
Germany: Nazi, 41–42, 55, 97, 98, 109–12, 126; Weimar Republic, 55, 59, 68–69, 115, 160n38
Gitlin, Todd, 118–19, 147–48
Gold, Michael, 17, 56, 160–61n42, 160n39
Goldstein, Malcolm, 156n12
Gompers, Samuel, 31–32, 37
Gordon, Janet, 27
Graff, Harvey, 133
Graham, Frank Porter, 40
Graham, Shirley, 18, 74, 81
Great Northern Theatre (Chicago), 74

Green, Paul, 79, 164–65n28, 164n28

Hailparn, Dorothy, 18, 25, 43
Hansel and Gretel (Frank), 21
Harlem Negro Unit, 19, 71, 77–80
Harris, Joel Chandler, 102
Hays Office, 112
Herald and Examiner, 75
Herts, Alice Minnie, 27
Hine, Lewis, 34–37
Hitler, Adolf, 99, 100, 108, 110, 111–12, 113, 114, 146
Hoernle, Edwin, 159–60n37
Hoffman, Ross J. S., 113
Holcomb, Robert, 129–31
Hollywood, 2–3, 21, 77, 108, 112
Hopkins, Harry, 67, 176n5
Horse Play (Hailparn), 18, 25, 43
House Committee on Un-American Activities (Dies Committee), 2, 6–7, 108, 142–43; *Pinocchio* and, 145; *The Revolt of the Beavers* hearings, 17, 47, 53, 66–68, 70, 155n9
Houseman, John, 3, 16–17, 71–72, 164n21
Hyun, Peter, 17, 47

idealism, intellectual, 7–8
immigrants, 4, 27, 30–31, 37, 50, 56, 133
In Abraham's Bosom (Green), 79, 164–65n28
individualism, 58, 124–25
International Labor Congress, 31
It Can't Happen Here (Lewis), 4, 20, 21, 171n15
Italian Americans, 98–99

James, Burton, 102
James, Flora, 102
Jersey City race riots, 98–99
Jews at the Crossroads, 156–57n14
Jews Without Money (Gold), 17, 56, 57, 160n39
John Henry folk tale, 73
Journal of Negro History, 99

Junior League, 73, 91, 101
Junior League for the Promotion of the Settlement Movements, 27

Kaser, Arthur Leroy, 107, 164n18
Kazan, Elia, 3, 17, 47, 156n13, 157n16
King-Coit School and Children's Theatre, 28
Kingsley, Sidney, 17, 56, 57
Kline, Stephen, 132
Krigwa Players Little Negro Theatre, 162n3

laboring of American culture, 4, 8–10
Lafayette Theatre, 74
LaFollette, Robert, 47
Lane, Esther Porter, 102–3, 162n9
Lantz, Lou, 17, 43, 47, 55
Larkin, Margaret, 38
Lawson, John Howard, 47
Learning on the Left (Mickenberg), 115, 172n22
leftism, 5–9, 115; in fairy stories, 55, 59; fascism, attraction to, 112–13; in Negro Unit plays, 73
Letter to Santa Claus, A (Chorpenning), 20–21, 27, 146–47; as anti-fascist play, 109–10, 141–42; departure of Santa Claus, 110, 116–17; innocence of child, 117–19, 121, 125; Joe and Mary (characters), 116–21; light and dark imagery, 119–20; moral binary, 120–21; Santa Claus as moral leader, 117–20; "shadows," 110, 115–19; war, portrayal of, 110, 114–15, 119
Leve, Samuel, 47
Leverett, Lewis, 17, 47, 157n17
Lewis, Sinclair, 4, 20, 21, 171n15
Liberty Deferred (Silvera), 105, 169–70n80
Life Magazine, 143
Little Black Sambo (Chorpenning-Graham), 74–75, 81, 163n12; costuming, 86; monkeys, 82, 85, 89–90; plot, 83–91; Sambo as poet, 87–90; skin color as theme, 88–89. See also *Story*

of *Little Black Sambo, The* (Bannerman)
Little Princess, A (Burnett), 110–11, 121–22
Little Princess, The, 21, 108–9, 121–27, 141, 170–71n8, 170n7; code of the little soldier, 121, 123–24; redemption theme, 123–24, 133; war, portrayal of, 110, 112
Living Newspaper, 18, 43, 105, 143, 150n23, 155n4
London, Jack, 41
Loray Mill (Gastonia, NC), 31, 37–41, *39*, 154n34
Los Angeles Federal Theatre Unit, 24, 128–29, 131
Lott, Eric, 75–76
Louis, Joe, 98–99, 167–68n67
Love and Theft: Blackface Minstrelsy and the American Working Class (Lott), 76
lynching, 19, 75, 141
Lysistrata (Seattle Negro Unit), 14, 102, 155n9, 168–69n73

Macbeth, Negro Unit performance, 77, 164nn23, 26
MacDonald, Byrnes, 17
machine ideology, 34–37, 70
Malden, Karl, 3
Marchand, Roland, 134
marionette shows, 23, 25, *72*, 73, 91, 131, 167n56
Marxism, fears of, 17, 32, 45–46, 48, 54–55, 60
Mathews, Jane DeHart, 49, 158n24
McClendon, Rose, 19, 164n21
McKelway, Alexander J., 37
Mead, Margaret, 12
media, 40–41, 77–78, 133, 147
Mercury Theatre, 47
Metro-Goldwyn-Mayer, 20
Mickenberg, Julia, 115
"Mill Mother's Song" (Wiggins), 38–40
Mills, C. Wright, 3
minstrelsy, 25, 68–69, 164n18; "56 Minstrels" list, 104–6; African American actors, 76; black–white binary in, 75–79, 101; in children's theatre, 73–74; cross-racial desire, 75–76; infantilized characters, 77–78; Jewish performances in Hollywood, 77; malapropisms, 76, 78, 91–95; motherhood distorted in, 84–85, 90–91, 102–4; negates fear of African Americans, 76–77, 91; reverse, 79. *See also* African Americans; Sambo stereotype
Mitchell, Edwine Noye, 73, 74
Mitchell, Ruth Comfort, 102, 168n72
Moffit, John C., 20
Morrell, Peter, 19, 73
Moscow State Central Theatre for Juvenile Audiences, 24
Moseley, Thomas, 79–80, 165n32
Mussolini, Benito, 64, 99, 112–13

Nadler, Paul, 169n79
Naming Names (Navasky), 6–7
National Association for the Advancement of Colored People (NAACP), 75
National Child Labor Committee (NCLC), 34–37
national identity, 5, 10, 68–69
National Parent Teacher, 135
National Socialist Teachers Federation, 111
National Textile Workers' Union, 38–41
national theatre, 1–4, 12–16
National Youth Administration, 26
The Nation, 38
Natural Man, 73
nature, mysticism of, 111
Navasky, Victor S., 6–7
Negro theatre, 162n3
Negro Units (Federal Theatre Project), 4, 19–20, 25; Chicago, 74–75, 81–91; combating racism, 73–74; Harlem, 19, 71, 77–80; *Macbeth,* 77, 164nn23, 26; media reviews, 77–78; Miami, 73, 91–94, 101; Seattle, 14, 73–74, 102–4, 155n9, 168–69n73; social realism in, 104–6; sponsorship of, 71–72, 162n2. *See also* African American actors;

African Americans; Federal Theatre Project (FTP)
New Deal, 3–6, 11, 144
New Generation, The: The Intimate Problems of Modern Parents and Children, 134
New Masses, 38
New Negro, 80
New Republic, 113
New Theatre, 78
New Theatre League, 155n9
New York Children's Unit, 17, 24–25, 43, 47, 115. See also *Revolt of the Beavers, The*
New York Project, 16
New York Times, 143
"Nigger Baby" (Wilson), 106–7
novels, tenement, 56

O'Connor, John, 144
One-Act Experimental Theatre, 17, 47
One-Third of a Nation (Arent), 56
oppression, 62
oral culture, 68–69, 74
otherness, 56, 76–77, 122
Ottley, Roi, 78

parenting concerns, 22, 131–39, 142; in advertising, 22, 132–35; father-son relationship, 136–39
Parents, 134–35
Parks, Larry, 7
Partisan Review, 146
patrician benevolence, 37
patriotism, 109, 121–22; code of the little soldier, 121, 123–24; feminine space and, 123–24
Pelley, William Dudley, 113
Pells, Richard, 7–8, 68
Peter Pan, 147
Peters, Paul, 73, 102
photography of children, 29, 33, 34–37, 39, 41
Pinocchio (Collodi), 128, 131, 132–33, 136

Pinocchio (Disney version), 22, 128–29, 131, 138–39, 142
Pinocchio (Frank, Federal Theater Project version), 21–22, 26, 128–39, *129*, 142, 145–46
Pinocchio (televised version), 131, 174n13
Plantation Days, 106
Plenn, Abel, 114
Police Athletic League, 46
Pollitzer, Alice K., 53
Popular Front, 1–4, 74, 81, 106, 112; antiracism, 74; cultural production, 69–70, 74–75, 115–16; Depression and, 5–10; major planks, 6; modernist aesthetics, 81; "the people," 30, 69; pro-labor stance, 4, 6, 17, 46, 48, 140, 152n44; Spain and, 47
Porgy and Bess, 77
Pricing the Priceless Child: The Changing Social Value of Children (Zelizer), 28–29
primitivist discourse, 41; African stereotypes, 74, 77, 80–81, 84, 86, 90–91
Production Code Administration, 112
progressive rhetoric, 10, 28, 34–35, 45, 115, 126
puppet shows, 71, 73–74, 85, 91, 94, 101–2

race issues: in children's plays, 18–19; democracy equated with ethnic tolerance, 41–42
racism: difference, denial of, 81, 85, 93; in media, 77–78; monkeys as pejorative, 90; segregated theatre units and audiences, 19–20; subsumed under class, 79–80; visual, *72*, 73, *82*, 83–85, 91
Radical Visions and American Dreams (Pells), 7–8
Rahv, Philip, 146
Randolph, John, 3, 47–48
rationality, 119–20
rationalization, 37
realism, 25, 55, 59. See also social realism
Redd, Tina, 102
regional pluralistic voices, 2

Reich, Molka, 73, 74, 91–94, 97
Reische, Diana, 27
Rennick, Jack, 4, 23, 24, 47, 70
Republic Steel, 47
Revolt of the Reapers, The (Artef Theatre), 47
Revolt of the Beavers, The (Saul and Lantz), 17, 25, 44, 61, 140–41, 152n45; allegory in, 1, 54, 57–59, 66, 69–70; anti-capitalism in, 55, 60, 64, 68–70; Barkless Beavers, 60–61, 64–65; capitalism, 55, 60, 64, 66, 68–70; censorship, 16–17, 45–46; Chief, character of, 48, 60–65; children's response to, 47–49; Children's Theatre Club, 49; cleansing by genre, 53–54; double reading of, 59; as fable, 45, 53–54; fairy tale genre, 48–55; FTP response to, 46; gendered desires in, 50–52; German progressive tradition, 55; intellectual class satirized, 60–62, 64; Marxist dynamics in, 17, 46, 54–55, 60, 141; Mary, character of, 44, 49–52, 51, 54–55, 59–60, 65; as "Mother Goose Marxism," 17, 45–46; music, 48; Oakleaf, character of, 49, 62–64; Paul, character of, 44, 46, 49–52, 51, 54, 58–60, 63–65; Pinky, Skeeball, and Sally (characters), 58; plot, 46, 50, 58–66; press releases, 17, 43, 48; Professor Beaver, character of, 51, 60–64; public reading of, 66–67; "sad" as metaphor, 49, 52, 56, 60, 62–64; tenement world in, 56–57, 161n42; Whistling Club, 62–64; Windy, character of, 44, 53, 59–60, 65, 159n30; Working Beavers, 48, 63–64
Rice, Elmer, 56
Rice, Robert, 131
Riefenstahl, Leni, 109–10
Riis, Jacob, 41
Rivera, Diego, 1, 16
Robbins, Tim, 1, 16, 158n18. See also *Cradle Will Rock*
Rockefeller Center, 1
Rogin, Michael, 68–69, 75–76

Rooney, Mickey, 131
Roosevelt, Franklin D., 67, 143, 171n15
Roth, Henry, 56

Sambo (character in plays), 18, 75, 166nn42, 43
Sambo stereotype, 18, 74–75, 166–67n43, 166n42; reversal of, 86–87, 97–101; vanity, focus on, 85, 87–90, 93–95. See also *Little Black Sambo*; minstrelsy; *Story of Little Black Sambo, The*
Saul, Oscar, 17, 43, 47, 55, 150n10, 151n42. See also *Revolt of the Beavers, The*
Schem, Hans, 111
Schmeling, Max, 98, 167–68n67
Schuyler, George, 168n68
scientific engineers, 38
Scott, William R., 99
Scottsboro Boys case, 75, 101
Scottsboro Defense Committee, 75
Seattle Negro Unit, 73–74, 102–4; *Lysistrata*, 14, 73–74, 102–4, 155n9, 168–69n73
Secret Garden, The (Burnett), 121
settlement house activities, 26–27
Seventh World Congress of the Communist International (Comintern), 4, 5
Shifting Gears (Tichi), 35
Shock Troupes (Workers Laboratory Theatre), 47
Silver Legion, 113
Silvera, John, 104–5, 169nn79, 80
sit-down demonstrations, 47, 155n9, 156n10
Six Plays for Young People (Swortzell), 20, 115, 147, 158n23, 159n27
Skinner, B. F., 134
Sklar, George, 73, 102
Smith, J. Augustus, 19, 25, 73
social realism, 41, 73, 104–6; racist stereotypes in, 72, 78–80. See also realism
Soviet Union, 5–6, 24, 45, 68
Spain, war in, 47
Spargo, John, 34
Spotlight on the Child: Studies in the His-

tory of American Children's Theatre (Bedard and Tolch), 27
Stage Left (Williams), 157nn14, 15
Steel Workers Organizing Committee, 47
Stevedore (Sklar and Peters), 73, 102
Story of Little Black Sambo, The (Bannerman), 18, 82, 87, 141, *141*; Chicago production, 74–75, 81–91; drawings, 83–85; education theme, 95, 99–100; family, portrayals of, 74, 85, 87, 90–95, 99–101; feast at end, 83, 85, 91–92, 100–101; as folk play, 80–81; Goodman Theatre production, 81, 85–86; Junior League script, 101–2; liberal self-actualization in, 74–75, 81; libraries and, 83, 165–66n39, 166n40, 41; Miami production, 73, 91–94, 101; Newark production, 74–75, 94–97, *96*, 141; setting, 81–83, *82*; visual racism in, *72*, 73, *82*, 83–85, 91. See also Little Black Sambo
Street Scene (Rice), 56
stretch out, 37–38
strikes: Flint, Michigan, 47; Loray Mill (Gastonia, NC), 37–41, 154n34; narratives of, 49; portrayed in plays, 79; Revolt of the Beavers linked to, 37–41, 47
Susman, Warren, 10
Swortzell, Lowell, 20, 115, 147, 158n23, 159n27

Tamaris, 25
Temple, Shirley, 21, 108–9, 121–25
tenement world, 56–57
textile mills, 35
"The Federal Theatre in Los Angeles" (Holcomb), 129–31
Story of Little Black Sambo, The (Bannerman), 18–20, 81
"The Trope of a New Negro and the Reconstruction of the Image of Black" (Gates), 80, 84
Theatre for Youth proposal, 26
Theatre of Action, 47, 157n16

Tichi, Cecilia, 35
Tolch, C. John, 27
"Towards Proletarian Art" (Gold), 56
Trachtenberg, Alan, 10
"Trials of the Mind" (Rahv), 146
Triumph of the Will, 109–12, 114, 127, 141
Turpentine (Smith and Morrell), 19, 73, 74, 77; African American response to, 80; racially mixed cast, 79
turpentine camps, 79, 165n31
20th Century Fox, 112, 126

Uncle Remus figure, 19
Uncle Tom's Cabin (Stowe), 84, 106
unconscious, 119
United Auto Workers, 113
urban agitprop troupes, 3

Van Vorst, Bessie, 34
vaudeville performers, 3, 25, 129–31, 143, 145

Wagner Act (1937), 6
Waltzer, Oscar, 48
war, as theme in children's theatre, 20, 110, 112, 114–15, 119, 121
Ward, Theodore, 73
Ward, Winifred, 28
Warfield, Robert, 73, 94, 99, 168n70
Warner, Marina, 52
Washington Post, 108
Watson, John B., 133–34
Welles, Orson, 1, 3, 47, 71–72; The Cradle Will Rock, 16–17, 155–56n9
Whiteside, Duncan, 114
Wiggins, Ella May, 31, 38–41
Wiggins, Myrtle, 38, 40
Wilder, Alec, 174–75n13
Willett, Charles, 59–60
Wilson, Bertha M., 106–7
Wilson, Earl, 66–67
Wilson, Edmund, 8
Workers Alliance, 143, 156n11

Workers Laboratory Theatre (WLT), 17, 47, 156–57n14
working class, 9, 41; childhood and, 16, 30; fear of, 37, 57; ungrammatical language as mark of, 49, 58. *See also* child laborers; ethnicity
Works Progress (Projects) Administration, 2, 46
Wright, Richard, 151n33

Wunderlich, Richard, 129, 137

Young, Sanborn, 168n72

Zelizer, Viviana, 28–29
Zip Coon figure, 80
Zipes, Jack, 55, 147, 159n34, 160n38